Seen in Bucharest

As much East as West

Since the fall of the Iron Curtain more than twenty years ago much has happened in the contemporary art scenes in Central and Eastern European capitals, at least in terms of infrastructure and within the context of a globalised standard for the art market including galleries, institutions, and biennials. But only time will tell whether the artistic positions that have developed in the course of the last two decades have written art history, led to social changes, created new styles and schools or merely delivered new global curatorial goods.

The year 1989 did not mark a new start in the art scenes in these countries, despite what many in the West may like to believe, but only a democratisation, a new organisation and, in the best of cases, an internationalisation. Under Communism a number of things did in fact happen on an art level, in the off-scene, in the underground, but of course always against the background of a state censorship that differed in severity from country to country. After the Second World War art was still often collected privately in the East Bloc and in former Yugoslavia, artists were both persecuted by the state and in equal part received massive support. Scenes were informed about current international developments in the art world, but for all

[Mayer, Antje, Vitorelli, Rita (Ed): *Art Guide East. Briefing on contemporary art and culture in Central and Eastern Europe*, Volume 1, *Spike*, Vienna 2009, ISBN 978-3-200-01499-2]

PUBLISHED BY
spike art magazine OG
Lilienbrunngasse 18/2/37
A–1020 Vienna
www.spikeart.at

EDITORS
Antje Mayer, Rita Vitorelli

ADVERTISING & MARKETING
Susanna Hoffmann-Ostenhof

EDITORIAL OFFICE
Redaktionsbuero
Lilienbrunngasse 8/2/4
A–1020 Vienna
www.redaktionsbuero.at

MANAGING EDITOR
Nora Dünser

CONTRIBUTORS
Heinrich Deisl, Silvija Dervišefendić, Matthias Dusini, Maria Farcas, Susanne Firzinger, Visar Geci, Herwig Höller, Manuela Hötzl, József Készman, Asja Mandic, Antje Mayer, Lýdia Pribišová, Marko Rajkovic, Mimi Fronczak Rogers, Katarína Slaninová, Tina Smekar, Maria Vassileva, Rita Vitorelli, Raluca Voinea

TRANSLATER (German – English)
Virginia Dellenbaugh, Julia Goette, Roderick O'Donovan, Nelson Wattie

COPYREADER (English)
Virginia Dellenbaugh

ART DIRECTOR
Christoph Steinegger/Interkool

ASSISTANT
Nina Janßen

CONCEPT
spike art magazine & Redaktionsbuero

PRINTED BY
Holzhausen Druck & Medien GmbH, Vienna, Austria
Printed on G-Print 130 g/m², produced by Grycksbo Paper

ISBN 978-3-200-01499-2

PHOTOGRAPHERS
Daniela Dostálková (Cover); Herwig Höller (pp. 89, 12-16, 19,21-29); Vlad Efimov (p. 10; Arka Barka Hostel (pp. 20, 29); Boris Ondreička (pp. 36-37, 40, 42-43); Andrea Kalinová (pp. 46-49, 53-54, 56-60); Filip Vanco (p. 50); Catalin Olteanu (pp. 6, 68-69, 72-78); Ergo (p. 81); Gábor Benedek (pp. 4, 102-103, 105-108, 131); László Magyar (p. 113); Csaba Nemes (pp. 116-118, 120); Tomaž Tomažin; (pp. 134-135, 137-141, 144-147, 155-157); Dejan Habicht and P.A.R.A.S.I.T.E. Institute (p. 146); Jane Štravs (p. 155); Ondřej Polák (pp. 164-165, 169, 170-171, 173, 195); Jiří David (pp. 169, 179, 181, 185, 188); Daniela Dostálková (pp. 172, 176-180, 183, 190); Slavisa Ivezic (pp. 198-199, 202- 203); Branimir Prijak (pp. 199, 202); Wolfgang Thaler (pp. 203-205, 208, 216); Dzenat Drekovic, (p. 211); Dimitar Solakov (pp. 222-223); Gerhard Flora (pp. 226-228, 247); Georgi Georgiev – Jorrras (pp. 232-242); Redaktionsbuero (pp. 241, 243); rois&stubenrauch (pp. 250, 255); Julia Schulz (pp. 251, 254, 258, 266-268, 271-272, 276-279); Werner Kaligofsky (p. 266); Lisa Rastl (p. 270); Paul Sturm (p. 274); Markus Strasser (p. 275); Victoria Schaffer (p. 281); Petar Glazar (pp. 294-295, 298-300, 304, 307-308, 311, 316, 319-320, 326)

SUPPORTED BY
departure

ERSTE

Kontakt. The Arts and Civil Society Program of Erste Group

SPECIAL THANKS
Anetta Mona Chisa, Nandinjargal Davaadorj, Ruth Goubran, Christian Kobald, Philip List, Mathilda Mayer, Oskar Mayer, Michael Salvi, Matthias Schnell, Petra Zechmeister

All facts (including names, telephone numbers, internet addresses and links, prices and other numerical values) are, to the best of our knowledge and research, correct as of 04/2009. Changes in exchange rates, address and prices are, of course, possible. We apologise in advance for any possible mistake. If you find any errors, please email us to let us know.

The source for average national income is the Vienna Institute for International Economic Studies.

ADVERTISERS
We would like to stress that no shop, restaurant, gallery or other establishment has been included in this book because it has advertised in it. No payment of any kind has had any influence on the reviews. The opinions/selections in this book are solely those of spike Art Guide East contributors and entirely independent.

intents and purposes the West took no notice of art scenes in the East, and this is essentially still the case today. Collectors from these countries are regarded with suspicion, the artists are seen as exotic creatures, and hardly anyone knows these places, their histories or the active protagonists in their art scenes.

We thought it was high time to address this gap, to travel to these cities and form our own impressions. Based on the experience of the successful city portraits that have been published regularly since 2004 in the art magazine *spike art quarterly* we asked our local authors to bring their material up-to-date for this guide and to provide us with an even more comprehensive list of insider tips for short city visits, of the kind not to be found in standard tourist guides. We interviewed protagonists locally and put together short art histories, which do not claim to be exhaustive or objective. We would like to thank all of those involved in the project for their enthusiasm and their immense patience.

For the first volume we have chosen the cities of Belgrade, Bratislava, Bucharest, Budapest, Ljubljana, Prague, Sarajevo, Sofia, Vienna and Zagreb, because we are convinced that these places have compelling art scenes. A second volume including Berlin, Kiev, Krakow, Moscow, Riga, St. Petersburg, Pristina, Tallinn, Warsaw and Vilnius will follow. That Vienna as a formerly Western city is represented in an Eastern Art Guide seems logical to us, as, since the fall of the Iron Curtain, the Austrian capital has moved from the edge to the centre of a new/old cultural region. It is now in the thick of things, so to speak, and as much part of the East as all these other cities are now part of the West.

Antje Mayer and Rita Vitorelli
(editors)

Belgrade: Confectioners in Ruins

View of the mountain fortress Kalemegdan with the »victory monument«

The art scene in Belgrade counters its international isolation and nightmarish economic situation with unconventional strategies and subversive humour

By Herwig G. Höller

Monuments of the past glory of Yugoslavia are to be found all over Belgrade, but the regime of the '90s, and its opponents, have also left clear traces on the cityscape. Grass is now growing on the ruins of the military building bombed by NATO in 1999 – real estate deals for a comprehensive restoration, though already announced, are still waiting to be concluded. If the dissolution of the Milošević regime was associated with great hope, the euphoria around that historical day of October 5th, 2000, the day of the bloodless transfer of power, has long since evaporated. In 2003 the charismatic Prime Minister, Zoran Djindjić, was shot. The political establishment continues to work on the »Kosovo Complex«, which climaxed in 2008 with the province's declaration of independence.

The inconstant general political climate of recent years has not let the art business rest either, which is manifested in part by foreign policies like the EU's rigid immigration laws. For Serb artists, traveling is still associated with heavy restrictions; the word »isolation« has become a term that sums up the emotional condition of an entire generation of artists.

The ambivalent political sensitivities have spread in particular to state institutions, such as the Belgrade Muzej Savremene Umetnosti (Museum of Contemporary Art or MSU), which received a breath of artistic relevance in 2001 from a new team headed by director Branislava Andjelković. Until now they have shown such important exhibitions as *On Normality. Art in Serbia 1989–2001* or more recently a presentation of Kontakt – The Art Collection of Erste Bank Group, which concentrated on the conceptual tendencies and important artistic currents of the '60s and '70s in Central and South-Eastern Europe.

Creative circles now have a better relationship with Serb cultural politicians than they have had in the past. The well-known Belgrade art theoretician and curator Branislav Dimitrijević now functions as a top civil servant in the Ministry of Culture, where he is working on developing urgently needed international contacts.

Curators accuse the younger Post-Milošević generation of laziness

The crystal-shaped MSU building from the '60s is currently closed, however, partly due to a bomb that struck the neighbourhood in 1999. It is currently being renovated, but the state budget is tight and a reopening is not to be expected before 2010 or even 2011. In the meantime, MSU activities and exhibitions are taking place in the »Salon« of the museum in the inner city of Belgrade.

The big museum is closed, but meanwhile a small »museum« has opened. Not far from the central bus station of Zeleni Venac Boris Šribar, Maja Radanović and Milica Ružičić sit in their communal workshop, which with pleasant optimism they have dubbed »Muzej«. The artists, who have stirred up the Belgrade art scene in the past two years with projects loosely labeled *Dez Org* (Disorganisation), give exhibitions in their workshop and hold parties that help fund the »museum activities«. There is no website; information flows through an increasing number of Facebook friends. Šribar, Radanović and Ružičić drink tea and talk about some of the abstruse aspects of artistic life in Belgrade. For example, the significance of the concept »platform« – this word simply has to be used in applications for subsidies because it drastically increases the likelihood of getting public support (albeit modest).

And then there is the matter of a smoldering generational conflict. Curators, who were already active when Yugoslavia still existed, accuse the younger Post-Milošević generation of laziness. Today they have many more opportunities to exhibit and produce art but, as the accusation runs, they only complain about a lack of money. This is hard to believe when one sees projects, such as the Muzej, providing evidence that delicate institutional plants are sending out new shoots in Belgrade.

Our opportunity is to involve people who previously had no interest in art

»We have an incredible range of ideas and we think our opportunity is to involve people who previously had no interest in art in our actions « the »museum directors« proclaim self-confidently. While the charm of Muzej is in its informal nature, another new

Novi Beograd, Bulevar Mihajla Pupina
One of many skyscrapers in the most (post)modern part of the city

The Belgradian visa-question
Lines in front of the German consulate
(Birčaninova)

Radenska, a well established mineral water from Yugoslavian times advertised in Novi Beograd

Terazije, the city centre

View of old Belgrade

Legendary Hotel Moskva, a spy stomping ground during the Cold War

foundation of recent years has developed differently. The Kontekst Gallery, founded by curators Vida Knežević and Ivana Marjanović in 2006 in the centrally located Kapetan Mišin Street, has successfully committed itself to international cooperation and engaged political art. In 2008 Kontekst became a victim of the »Kosovo Complex«. When the gallery wanted to show contemporary art from Kosovo it was attacked by Serb nationalists. The police could »not guarantee the safety of visitors and curators at the exhibition«. It had to be closed.

In the same street and just a few buildings further along there is one of the rare new artworks in the public space of Belgrade. What looks like an official street sign names an intersection the *Salvador Dali Corner*. »We simply wanted to beautify the neighbourhood«, said Pavle Ćosić from the group with neo-situationist tendencies Ilegalni poslastičari (Illegal Confectioners). The group achieved international attention with a hoax press release from the Serb TV and radio station B92, asserting that the American embassy in Belgrade had demanded that an senior citizen's cafeteria called »Osama« (in Serbian »lonely« or »isolated«) must change its name for political reasons. B92, the heroic underground medium of the war in the '90s, now full commercialised and a kind of Serb RTL, is one of the Confectioner's favourite enemies.

In present-day in Belgrade any market for contemporary art exists only in a rudimentary form and better-known Belgrade artists, such as the painter Biljana Djurdjević, sell mainly abroad. Uroš Djurić, a popular artist in Serbia, not least because of his affinity for pop culture and football, has hired himself out as a permanent guest on a quiz show in commercial television, while others live patchwork lives and work on the side in »art-related« jobs such as advertising.

Even in the difficult '90s, says Jelena Krivokapić, curator of the Prodajna galerija (Sales Gallery) and who has been selling art since 1963, there were more active art collectors than there are today. The absence of an art market also has something to do with attitudes. For that reason, according to Krivokapić, it is important to promote new role models. Collectors should not just accumulate art but should, at the same time, work as art dealers, curators and critics. —

1963, there were more active art collectors than there are today

300 metres, seven different architectural languages

Mileta Prodanović, a well known Serbian writer and painter and Belgrade native, tells us where the contemporary art scene is meeting up in the city, which architectural monuments were left standing by the NATO bombardment and what John Lennon has to do with Ex-Yugoslavian President Tito.

By Herwig G. Höller

What can a visitor interested in art discover in Belgrade?

MILETA PRODANOVIĆ: The person who would come here would have to have a kind of preparation beforehand. At first glance, the current art scene is not very visible. Unfortunately the two main museums, the MSU (Museum of Contemporary Art) and the Narodni Muzej (National Museum), are in the process of reconstruction. It is very important for a person who comes here to feel the history, for example to understand that this space was inhabited even in Roman times, in the Middle Ages. Some of the current art even reflects that from time to time. If you get past this first step, you could look on the Internet and find, for example, a very active gallery called Remont – a good starting point. Of course there are a lot of galleries that are functioning, for example the MSU Salon in Pariska ulica, which was already established in the '60s, or the famous SKC, the Students' Cultural Centre, where Beuys did his performances.

One specific thing about Belgrade is the long – and also post-World War II – tradition of Modernism, something one would not expect in a former Socialist country …

Yes, there was a strong post-war wave of Modernism, but also – though less known – after World War I there was Zenitism and an avant-garde tradition. Belgrade was a very important centre for Surrealism. Mostly poets, but also artists, were in contact with André Breton and the mainstream of the international Surrealist movement. But concerning post-war Modernism, this has to do with the overall modernisation of society. All Eastern European countries had problems with that process; modernisation was never completed, almost interrupted in some stages. In a paradoxical way, Titoism brought this modernisation. And in the beginning of the '90s we had this retrograde movement all around Yugoslavia, and the term »De-Titoisation« was coined. In practise this meant a pretext for dismantling our Modernist heritage, which started with the crippling, overbuilding and destroying of good buildings and ended with the NATO-intervention in 1999, when almost all important buildings of pre- and post-war Modernism were bombed.

Belgrade has been destroyed many times and the reconstruction was almost always done in a hurry

The Tito museum wasn't destroyed, was it?

Concerning Tito: I hope that a bigger part of the collection of Tito's museum can be seen quite soon. This is one of the few personal museums in existence, and it can be very bizarre, this especially applies to the collection of gifts that Tito received in his lifetime. For example, when John Lennon and Yoko Ono got married, they sent a gift to every statesman in the world: two acorns. In Tito's museum the complete correspondence was preserved, including the report of the phytosanitary control and Lennon and Ono's letter where they ask Tito to plant the acorns for world peace. But did Tito really plant them? There is a possibility.

How do you see your city from an urban perspective?

I call Belgrade a patchwork city. It has been destroyed many times and the reconstruction was almost always done in a hurry. All these different stages left their traces. The most paradigmatic street for me is the Kralja Petra ulica. In a space of 300 meters, you can see seven different architectural languages, starting with post-Ottoman and typical Balkan houses, then a classicistic cathedral, something Neo-Renaissance, the first wave of Modernism, post-war Modernism almost in the style of Le Corbusier, Vienna Secession style and even a postmodern building. For an unprepared visitor to Belgrade this can be unexpected. From time to time the city reminds me of Istanbul. Two rivers flow through it, creating a broad skyline, just like Istanbul. In another parallel, the old port is going to be used for contemporary art. The MSU is supposed to get hold of the so-called »Beton hala« as a temporary art-space. The German army built these halls during World War II as a type of port storage. There are thousands and thousands of square metres of open space and you don't have to invest very much money, since companies used the halls when the port was still active. In any case, with some preparation you can discover a lot in Belgrade, and the art scene is definitely worth exploring. —

Mileta Prodanović, born in 1959, is a painter, fiction writer and art critic who lives in Belgrade. He has published more than a dozen books, several short stories and essays in international newspapers, and exhibits internationally. He studied architecture and painting and graduated from the University of Fine Arts in Belgrade.

Belgrade

By Herwig G. Höller

View of Zemun district

ART

❶ MSU: Muzej savremene umetnosti (Museum of Contemporary Art) — The Museum of Contemporary Art was erected in the early '60s, not far from where the Save flows into the Danube. A new team around director Branka Andjelković took over after the fall of the Milošević regime and has produced highly interesting shows. However this crystalline building (which is well worth seeing) is going to be closed for renovations until 2010. In the intervening period the MSU will use the Salon in the city centre as well as temporary locations on occasion.

MSU:
Ušće 10, blok 15, (367 62 88 or 367 62 91)
Bus 15, 84, 704, 706, 707: Bulevar Nikole Tesle, Bus 60: Muzej savremene umetnosti

Salon MSU:
Pariska 14, (263 09 40)
Tram 2,11,13: Pariska
Mon-Sun noon to 8 pm, closed on Tue
www.msub.org.rs

❷ SKC: Studentski Kulturni Centar (Student Cultural Centre) — Jacques Derrida spoke here, Niko played here, Laibach perform regularly, Joseph Beuys and Bill Viola have exhibited, and the yellow building was the location for Yugoslav Action Art of the '70s. But today, too, the SKC is a cultural »must«. Exhibition

openings in the highly contemporary gallery are a meeting point for the Belgrade scene, some of whom have their studios in the building, including the probably legendary music performer and inventor of »turbo-folk« Rambo Amadeus.

Kralja Milana 48, (360 20 36)
Tram 7, 7L, bus 31, 74
trolleybus 19, 21, 29: RK Beograd anka
Mon-Fri 11 am to 7 pm,
Sat 11 am to 3 pm (Gallery)
www.skc.org.rs

❸ DOB: Dom Omladine Beograda (Belgrade Youth Centre) — While the good years of a youth culture massively subsidised by the Yugoslav state are definitely over, the »House of Youth« is still seen as a fixed point, above all for young artists. The gallery on the ground floor is dedicated to the first exhibitions of graduates from the Academy of Fine Arts. Concerts and film presentations round off the program.

Makedonska 22, (322 04 53 or 324 82 02)
Bus 27, 27E, 32E, 35, 36, 43, 96,
trolleybus 19, 21, 22, 22L, 28, 29, 40, 41:
Trg Republike

Tue-Sat 11 am to 9 pm,
Sun noon to 6 pm (Gallery)
www.domomladine.org

❹ CZKd: Centar za kulturnu dekontaminaciju (Centre for Cultural Decontamination) — »Nomen est omen«: Milošević had little joy with this institution. During the difficult years the CZKd, founded in 1994, was a centre for cultural resistance in Belgrade. Today the '30s villa still plays an important role as a discourse oriented place for different branches of culture, which regularly attracts attention with its politically committed exhibition projects.

Paviljon Veljković, Birčaninova 21,
(361 02 70 or 361 09 54)
Bus 39, 42, 51, 59, trolleybus 22L: Slavija
Mon-Sat 11 am to 7 pm
www.czkd.org

❺ REX — This culture centre in the former Jewish district Dorćol was established in 1994 in the context of the former underground radio station B-92, which was once cult and has now grown into a commercialised media empire. REX presented a critical program for so long that it was closed down by the Milošević regime. In November 2000, the team returned and with its packed program of screenings and performances, today REX is one of the most important media art locations in the city.

Jevrejska 16, (328 45 34 or 328 43 98)
Tram 2, 5, 10, bus 24, 26, 7: Braće Baruh
Full price admission up to 100 RSD, otherwise depending on the event
www.rex.b92.net

❻ Remont Galerija — Since February 2000, this »independent association of artists« has resided on the central Trg Republike (Square of the Republic) –

however only on the second floor of a run-down Yugoslav shopping centre that should, in fact, have been demolished long ago. In addition to cooperation at an international level Remont's exhibition activity is concentrated on Serbian art from the young and middle generations.

Makedonska 5/II, (322 34 06)
Bus 27, 27E, 32E, 35, 36, 43, 96,
trolleybus 19, 21, 22, 22L, 28, 29, 40, 41:
Trg Republike
Mon-Fri 11 am to 7 pm
www.remont.net

❼ Prodajna galerija Beograd (Sales Gallery Belgrade) — Back in the days of Yugoslav state capitalism, this basement gallery with the awkward name already attempted to breathe life into the market for contemporary art and it still does today, presenting post-war Modernism as well as more current positions, and also publishing texts about art theory.

Kosančićev venac 19, (303 39 23)
Bus 15, 16, 60, 67, 71, 72, 75, 84, 95, 704E, 706, 707: Brankov Most
Mon-Fri 9 am to 7 pm, Sat 9 am to 3 pm
www.galerijabeograd.org

❽ Kontekst Galerija — In the '20s the DDSG, the Austrian Danube Steamship Company, opened a branch in the old town of Belgrade. Since 2006, the building with the striking anchor on its facade has housed this programmatic off-space. Kontekst quickly became a new fixed point in the young art scene and succeeded with fresh projects and exhibitions, some of which are also politically and socially committed.

Kapetan Mišina 6a,
Centar za kulturu Stari Grad
(639 639 or 634 652)
Bus 31, trolleybus 19, 21, 22, 22L, 28, 29, 41: Studentski trg.
Mon-Fri 4 pm to 8 pm
www.kontekstgalerija.org

❾ Muzej (Museum) — »Do something instead of just complaining« is their motto. Five artists with good contacts (Pušica, Radanović, Ružičić, Šribar, Stajčić), who formerly also appeared as *Dez Org* (Disorganisation), declared their studio a museum. And they occasionally organise exhibitions there, celebrate parties for artistic cross-subsidisation and have a lot of creative ideas.

Brankova 19/II, (328 69 52)
Bus 15, 16, 60, 67, 71, 72, 75, 84, 95, 704E, 706, 707: Zeleni Venac

Opening hours depending on the event, or by appointment
muzzej@gmail.com

ART EVENTS

Oktobarski salon (October Salon) — The October Salon, which was conceived in the '90s as an annual autumn show of contemporary Yugoslav art and saw itself as a reference point, has begun in recent years to open up to international art. Both international and Serbian curators use a wealth of locations in the city. This is the highpoint of the visual arts season.

Office:
KCB, Knez Mihailova 6/I,
(262 14 69 or 262 27 57)
October
www.oktobarskisalon.org

BELEF: Beogradski Letnji Festival (Belgrade Summer Festival) — The large Belgrade Summer Festival presents a rich diversity of cultural activities, including visual art. Reflecting the time of year when it is held, events also take place in public space.

Festival office:
Ilije Garašanina 24,
(323 841 or 323 88 59)
July/August
www.belef.org

BITEF: Beogradski Internacionalni Teatarski Festival (International Belgrade Theatre Festival) — With prominent participants such as Arianne Mnouchkine, Bob Wilson or Jurij Ljubimov as well as the creme de la creme of the Yugoslav-Serbian theatre (which can match international standards) this festival has, the organisers assert, »written theatre history« since 1967.

Festival office:
Terazije 29/1, (324 31 08 or 323 29 72)
September
www.bitef.rs

FEST: Međunarodni Filmski Festival (International Film Festival) — As the capital of a powerful »Bloc-free« state, Tito's Belgrade played an important role that also provided the basis for the reputation (at that time an international one) of the almost 40 year old Belgrade film festival. Despite the changes, FEST still remains an important major cultural event that brings numerous film-lovers into the cinemas in early spring.

Festival office:
Majke Jevrosime 20, (334 69 46)
February/March
www.fest.rs

ALTERNATIVE SIGHTSEEING

10 Novo groblje (New Cemetery) — It was not just war and protests but also organised crime that shaped life in Belgrade in the '90s. *Vidimo se u čitulji* (We look at the page with the death notices), the title of a B-92 cult documentary from 1994, became a stock phrase. By now most of the Mafia bosses portrayed in the film have met their maker. Their traces remain in the form of kitschy funerary monuments – in particular in the New Cemetery of Belgrade.

Ruzveltova 50, (207 13 33)
Bus 25, 27A, 27L, 32, 74, 202: Novo Groblje
Mon-Sun 7 am to 7 pm
www.beogradskagroblja.co.yu

11 Muzej Nikole Tesle (Nikola Tesla Museum) — The inventor and physicist Nikola Tesla, who was of Serbian origin, was born in 1856 in what is today Croatia. During his lifetime he visited Belgrade only once and just for a single day, but this fact has not affected the cult

that has developed around him. In 1999 there was talk of secret Tesla weapons that were to be used against the NATO bombers, and on the 150th anniversary of his birth, Belgrade airport was named after him. Beside Tesla's urn in the Tesla Museum there stands a warning: »It is forbidden to leave flowers and other objects beside the urn.«

Krunska 51, (243 38 86)
Bus 39, 42, 51, 59, trolleybus 22L: Slavija
Tue-Fri 10 am to 6 pm,
Sat-Sun 10 am to 1 pm
Full price admission 200 RSD
www.tesla-museum.org

⓬ Beograd Gazela — Belgrade's most visible and best-known slum has existed since 1983 beside a motorway bridge across the River Save and in the immediate proximity of the impressive conference centre Sava Centar and the smart Hotel Continental. In recent years, artists have started to show an interest in this place, for instance, in the framework of the artists' action *Under the Bridge*, which the collective Biro organised at the end of 2004.

Blok 18a
Bus 17, 18, 74, 88, 89, 94, 601:
Sava Centar

⓮ Muzej istorije Jugoslavije (Museum of the History of Yugoslavia) — The last remnants of »Titotainment« still survive. Tito died on May 4, 1980; his mortal remains rest in his beloved Kuća cveća (House of Flowers), which, since his death, has functioned as a mausoleum – nowadays without the fierce honour guard but with friendly staff members that even encourage you to take photographs of this historic place. As well as

the House of Flowers, where in addition to the sarcophagus there is a permanent exhibition on the Yugoslav »Day of Youth« celebrations, a nearby pavilion offers a small selection from the thousands of gifts that were presented to him during his lifetime: historically important weapons, musical instruments, folk costumes and far more, all things much appreciated by Tito the connoisseur.

Botićeva 6, (367 14 85)
Bus 42, 78, 94, trolleybus 40, 41:
Muzej 25. Maj
Tue-Sun 10 am to 6 pm
Full price admission 120 RSD
www.mij.rs

⓯ Zoran Djindjić — During his lifetime, Djindjić was already regarded as the »Serbian JFK«. His violent death, too, connects this democratic politician, born in 1952, with his American model: on March 12, 2003 Prime Minister Djindjić was shot dead by a sniper in front of government buildings. Unlike Dallas, so far there is no official memorial at the scene of the crime. There is only a cross at second floor level on the south side of building no. 14 Ad-

mirala Geprata , which the investigators fixed in place at that time with adhesive tape, indicating the window from which the sniper shot. But at least the restaurant Hrabro srce (Courageous Heart), once housed in the same building, has closed down in the meantime: Djindjić was hit in the heart.

Admirala Geprata 14
Bus 23, 37, 43, 58, 74,
trolleybus 40, 41: Admirala Geprata

SHOPPING

⓰ Supermarket — Once a real maxi-supermarket, since 2008, just a supermarket: the first and hippest concept store in the Serbian metropolis with a retail area of 1,400 square metres containing international designer goods,

clothing, sleeping masks, cardboard pigs, literature, exhibitions of Serbian designers' work, Asian-European cuisine, and a jazz brunch on Sundays.

Višnjićeva 10, (380 50 44)
Tram 2, 5, 10, bus 24, 26, 79: Kralja Petra
Mon-Sun 10 am to 12 am

⓱ Plato — In the '90s, Belgrade's student resistance met at the Akademski plato (Academic Plateau). The regime reacted by making three-quarters of the square disappear behind an ugly wall. This era of closure is over; in the summer months the friendly street café Plato spreads across the square and a bookshop of the same name offers not just the writings of the philosopher Plato, but also an entire range of intelligent literature, some in foreign languages.

Akademski Plato 1, (30 34 808)
Bus 31, trolleybus 19, 21, 22, 22L, 28, 29, 41: Studentski trg.
Mon-Sat 9 am to 2 am

CAFÉS

⓲ Centrala — Actually part of artist Srba Travanov's flat, but also one of the hippest cafés in the Belgrade art scene, due to the appealingly artistic interior made up in part of newspaper collages that Travanov has painted over.

Simina 17
Bus 31, trolleybus 19, 21, 22, 22L, 28, 29, 41: Studentski trg.
Mon-Sun 9 am to 1 am

⓳ Hot Spot Café — Nice café with contemporary design where you can have a reasonably priced breakfast or a cup of coffee. You can also buy a quick snack or, especially in the evening, enjoy a drink here. With Wi-Fi.

Studentski Trg 21 (263 92 05)
Bus 31, trolleybus 19, 21, 22, 22L, 28, 29, 41: Studentski trg.
Mon-Sun 8 am to 2 am

⓴ Klub Kafe Ruska Trojka — There was a time when Soviet-Yugoslav or Russian-Serbian relationships were more important. Once this was a restaurant, not just a club café in Belgrade's Ruski dom (Russian House), the Russian cultural institute. In addition to coffee, tea and vodka, piroschki, pelmeni and borscht are also served.

Kraljice Natalije 33, (3621853)
Bus 15, 16, 60, 67, 71, 72, 75, 84, 95, 704E, 706, 707: Zeleni venac
Mon-Fri 11 am to 11 pm, Sat 11 am to 3 pm
www.ruskidom.rs

RESTAURANTS

㉑ Café Ipanema — The rich, the beautiful and the hip, as well as a number of artists, meet here in what many consider their favourite restaurant, which offers excellent Mediterranean cuisine and is also famous for its desserts. Ipanema opened in 1992 as the first restaurant on Strahinjića bana Street, which in the meantime has been transformed into an area of smart restaurants and cafés. Main dishes from around 1,100 RSD.

Strahinjića bana 6,8
(328 30 69 or 328 87 22)
Tram 2, 5, 10, bus 24, 26, 79: Dorćol
Mon-Sat 9 am to 1 am, Sun noon to 1 am
Visa, Mastercard
www.ipanema.co.rs

㉒ Restoran Dačo — A Serbian village in the form of a restaurant in the middle of the metropolis. Rural ambiance, lovingly decorated, perhaps somewhat too kitschy for minimalists but this is kitsch at a high level. With a wonderful garden, Serbian cuisine of the kind cooked by Serbian mothers, which often appeals to foreign visitors. Main dishes from around 1,100 RSD.

Patrisa Lumumbe 49,
(278 10 09 or 278 24 22)
Bus 16, 23, 25, 25P: Marijane Gregoran
Tue-Sun noon to 12 am
Visa, Mastercard, American Express, Diners
www.kafana-daco.com

23 Proleće — More and more of the old established restaurants are vanishing, people in Belgrade complain. Proleće (Spring), however, still survives. The menu is dominated by Serbian dishes at reasonable prices. Main dishes from around 560 RSD.

Vuka Karadžića 11, (263 54 36)
Bus 15, 16, 60, 67, 71, 72, 75, 84, 95, 704E, 706, 707: Zeleni venac
Mon-Sun 9 am to 11 pm
Visa, Mastercard, American Express, Diners

PARTY

24 The Black Turtle Pub II — The most popular Irish pub in the city with a wide range of beers (including the speciality of the house, a beer flavoured with blueberries), located in one of the loveliest areas of the old town of Belgrade. In summer there is a garden for guests with a wonderful view of the River Save and the urban, modern Novi Beograd.

Kosančićev Venac 30,
(328 66 56)
Bus 15, 16, 60, 67, 71, 72, 75, 84, 95, 704E, 706, 707: Brankov Most
Mon-Sun 9 am to 2 am
www.theblackturtle.com

25 The Tube — Since it was decorated in 2008 by architects according to what the owner describes as a »minimalist hedonistic concept«, The Tube, with its 23-metre long dance floor, has been regarded as one of Belgrade's hippest clubs.

Simina 21 – Entrance of Dobračina,
(062 971 66 44 or 063 783 65 92)
Bus 31, trolleybus 19, 21, 22, 22L, 28, 29, 41: Studentski trg.
Thur-Sat 11 pm to 4 am
www.thetube.rs

26 Idiot — This club at the edge of the Botanical Gardens is not very large and therefore often crowded. Especially during the warmer times of the year, the small garden with a lovely view makes it particularly attractive, but a visit can be worthwhile even when the weather is less than ideal. Despite the many warning signs about high voltage the atmosphere is pleasantly relaxed. Popular with artists and students.

Dalmatinska 13
Bus 23, 77, trolleybus 28: 27 marta
Mon-Sun noon to 2 am

27 Club Plastik — A leading Belgrade techno institution in the city centre that regularly offers international DJs. One of the city's most popular clubs, above all in winter.

Ugao Takovske i Dalmatinske ulice 34,
(324 54 37)
Bus 23, 77, trolleybus 28: 27 marta
Thur-Sat 11 pm to 6 am
www.club-plastic.com

SLEEP

28 Hyatt Regency — Western journalists worked during the war in 1999 in this hotel with its classical décor, while the Serbian nouveau riche relaxed in the swimming pool – artist Vesna Pavlović recorded this in her legendary photo series *A Warm Welcome to the Hyatt Hotel Belgrade* (1999). Today the hotel in the Novi Beograd district is still regarded as one of the premier addresses for a well-heeled international public. Double rooms from € 280.

Milentija Popovića 5, (113 011 234)
Bus 68, 95, tram 7, 7L, 9, 11: Blok 21
www.belgrade.regency.hyatt.com

㉙ Hotel Balkan — Balkan – an »Oasis of Peace«? At least this is how the adwriter of the hotel describes this traditional establishment. It lies at the absolute centre of modern Belgrade, opposite there is competition in the form of the Hotel (and Café) Moskva, the pedestrian zone starts around the corner. Double rooms from € 150.

Prizrenska 2, (363 60 00)
Bus 15, 16, 60, 67, 71, 72, 75, 84, 95, 704E, 706, 707: Zeleni Venac
www.balkanhotel.net

㉚ Hotel Royal — One of the city's oldest hotels and still sometimes known under its former name Toplice. Royal may sound noble but the hotel at the edge of the central Dorćol district offers petit bourgeois prices. Double rooms from € 40.

Kralja Petra 56, (263 42 22 or 262 64 26)
Bus 31, trolleybus 19, 21, 22, 22L, 28, 29, 41: Studentski trg.
www.hotelroyal.co.rs

㉛ Arkabarka — The Internet generation lives on the water. Arkabarka, a floating hotel, offers the new experience of living on the Danube with a view of the war island, at affordable prices. From € 15 in a four-bed room.

Ušće, (064 925 35 07)
Bus 15, 84, 704, 706, 707:
Bulevar Nikole Tesle
www.arkabarka.net

KIDS

➌➋ **Zoological Gardens 1** — Like much else in the city, the Zoo has a tradition extending over decades and has repeatedly experienced difficult times. Situated in Kalemegdan Park, it offers a conventional overview with about 200 mammals, birds and reptiles. Nothing special but a nice way for kids, who might get irritated with their parents' discovery of the Belgrade art scene, to spend time.

Mali Kalemegdan 8, (262 45 26)
Tram 5, 10, 11, 13: Tadeuša Košćuška
Mon-Sun 8 am to 5 pm (Winter),
8 am to 8.30 pm (Summer)
Full price admission: 300 RSD,
kids: 200 RSD
www.beozoovrt.izlog.org

DAYTRIPS

Zemun — Zemun last appeared in headlines due to the mafia group named after this Belgrade suburb. The notorious Zemun Clan was responsible for the deaths of the Serbian Prime Minister Zoran Djindjić and the Croatian journalist Ivo Pukanić, among others. Zemun under its German name, Semlin, was once part of the Austro-Hungarian Empire. It is worth visiting, particularly in summer. Pleasant fish restaurants on the Danube, Jugendstil architecture from a bygone era, but also the tough feeling of the suburbs which produced Zemun's mafiosi.

Bus 73, 84, 707 (from Zeleni Venac):
Zemun Pošta

GOOD TO KNOW

➌➌ **Tourist Information** —
Makedonska 5, (334 34 60)
Bus 27, 27E, 32E, 35, 36, 43, 96,
trolleybus 19, 21, 22, 22L, 28, 29, 40, 41:
Trg Republike
Mon-Fri 9 am to 9 pm,
Sat 9 am to 5 pm,
Sun 10 am to 4 pm
www.belgradetourism.org.yu

Money — Although the hyper-inflation of the '90s is now a thing of the past, the Serbian Dinar (RSD) is not regarded as exactly the most stable currency. Therefore you should exchange Euro for Dinar locally and only shortly before you need them. ATM's can be found everywhere.

Alphabet/Language — Although the Latin alphabet is frequently used alongside the (more official) Cyrillic one, a knowledge of Cyrillic letters can be extremely useful as sometimes everything is written only in Cyrillic.

INTERNET

➌➍ **Lava Bar** — Kneza Miloša 77, (361 05 25), 1

Bus 15, 16, 60, 67, 71, 72, 75, 84, 95, 704E, 706, 707: Zeleni Venac
Mon-Sun 10 am to 1 am

24-hr Wi-Fi Hotspot — Studentski trg

MEDIA

www.remont.net — More than a yearbook. The Remont independent artist coalition does not only occupy itself with the exhibition happenings of the past year in it's annually appearing, and above all, in English, publication *Remont Art Files*. In addition, leading Serbian art critics publish texts pertaining to the artistic status quo, most recently this included Maja Ćirić, Ješa Denegri, and Stevan Vuković.

www.prelomkolektiv.org — The Belgrade art magazine *Prelom (Breck) Journal for Images and Politics*, has been appearing in irregular intervals since 2001, since then also in English. Intelligent texts about art and politics have brought the publication international renown. In 2008, it received special recognition with the first Igor Zabel award for Culture and Theory.

TRANSPORT

From the airport — To get from the Nikola Telsa Airport to the city take a public transport bus. The journey to the old town takes 20 minutes. Rates are 100-200 RSD for the bus, max. 1,400 RSD for taxis.

Taxis — Taxis are to be found throughout the city and are an efficient and reasonably priced means of transport. Either wave your hand at one from the side of the street, go to one of the numerous taxi stands, or call one of the many taxi phone numbers. Some drivers have a knowledge of English. The rate is 50 RSD/km. Taxis Beotaksi: 970, Beogradski: 9801, Pink Taksi: 9803, Taxi Bell: 9804.

Public transport — Tickets (»vozna karta«), which can be bought at all kiosks (Zone 1: 42 RSD, Zone 1 + 2: 65 RSD) or in the buses, trolley buses and trams (Zone 1: 80 RSD, Zone 1 + 2: 100 RSD) must be stamped/validated (»poništavanje karata«).

Car — Recently Belgrade has begun to manage its car parking spaces. Parking zones with and without time restrictions should be taken seriously. Parking permits can be bought from machines or from the inspectors, costs differ from zone to zone: red: 41 RSD/hour, yellow 30 RSD/hour, green 25 RSD/hour. The limit for driving under the influence of alcohol is 0.5 permille. There are relatively high motorway tolls, although no safety problems. —

# #

Important	Numbers
Telephone country and city code	*+386 11*
Telephone information	*988*
Police	*92*
Fire Brigade	*93*
Ambulance	*94*
24h-Pharmacy	*Prvi Maj, Kralja Milana 9, (324 13 49), bus 23, 37, 43, 58, 74, trolleybus 40, 41: Admirala Geprata*

City in	Numbers
1 Euro	*ca. 93.8 Dinar*
Inhabitants	*1.6 million*
Average income	*€ 558*
Cup of coffee	*100 RSD (ca. € 1.00)*
Bottle of beer	*35 RSD (ca. € 0.35)*
Cigarettes	*120 RSD (ca. € 1.20)*
Most talked about contemporary artists	*Marina Abramović, Milica Tomić, Mladen Stilinović*
Collectors of contemporary art	*10*
Biggest art scandal	*In 2008, an exhibition by Kosovo artists in the Kontekst Gallery had to be closed down following protests by Serbian nationalists.*

Short Art History BELGRADE

1965 As early as 1958, the Muzej Savremene Umetnosti (Museum of Contemporary Art or MSU) in Belgrade is founded as an institution, unique in this Communist part of Europe. In 1965 the crystal-shaped building is opened and the head of state, Josip Broz Tito, attends the ceremony.

1974 A few months after a performance in Edinburgh, where she attended a workshop with Joseph Beuys, the then 27-year-old Marina Abramović performs in Yugoslavia for the first time. In the courtyard of the Studentski kulturni centar (Student Cultural Centre or SKC) she lies down in the middle of a burning Communist star; during the performance *Rhythm 5* she loses consciousness.

1985 Goran Djordjević shows *The Last Futurist Picture Exhibition 0,10* in a private apartment in Belgrade. It is a recreation of the legendary exhibition with the same name, which was first shown in St. Petersburg in 1915. The postmodern Yugoslavian retro avant-garde gets into gear. But not only art history is deconstructed; Yugoslavia itself begins to break apart at the same time.

1991 – 2000 War and international sanctions on Serbia, contemporaneous with great international interest in contemporary culture and art, while Belgrade advances to become the »centre of resistance«. Artists go out into the streets, critical institutions are founded, such as the Centar za kulturnu dekontaminaciju (Centre for Cultural Documentation or CZKD) and the Cinema Rex, the centre of cultural opposition in Belgrade.

2005 The MSU in Belgrade summarises Serbian art from the turbulent '90s with a wide-ranging and skilful show – the generation from Apsolutno, through Uroš Djurić, Tanja Ostojić and Milica Tomić to Aleksandar Zograf is now ready for museums.

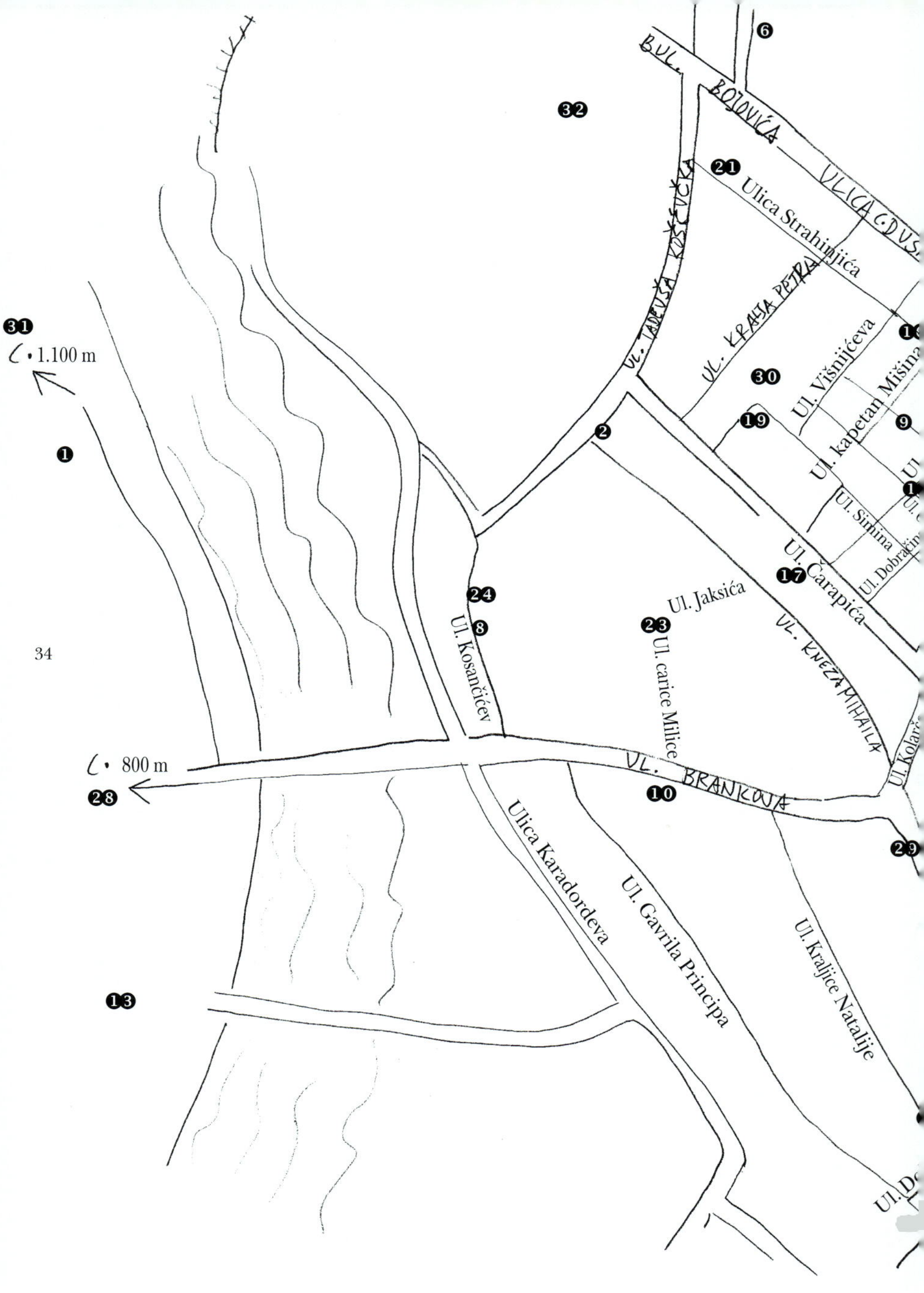

BUL. BOJOVIĆA
ULICA C. DUŠ
UL. TADEUŠA KOŠĆUŠKA
Ulica Strahinjića
UL. KRALJA PETRA
UL. Višnjićeva
Ul. kapetan Mišina
Ul. Simina
Ul. Dobračina
Ul. Čarapića
Ul. Jaksića
UL. KNEZA MIHAILA
Ul. carice Milice
Ul. Kosančićev
UL. BRANKOVA
Ul. Kolarč
Ulica Karađorđeva
Ul. Gavrila Principa
Ul. Kraljice Natalije
Ul. Do
1.100 m
800 m

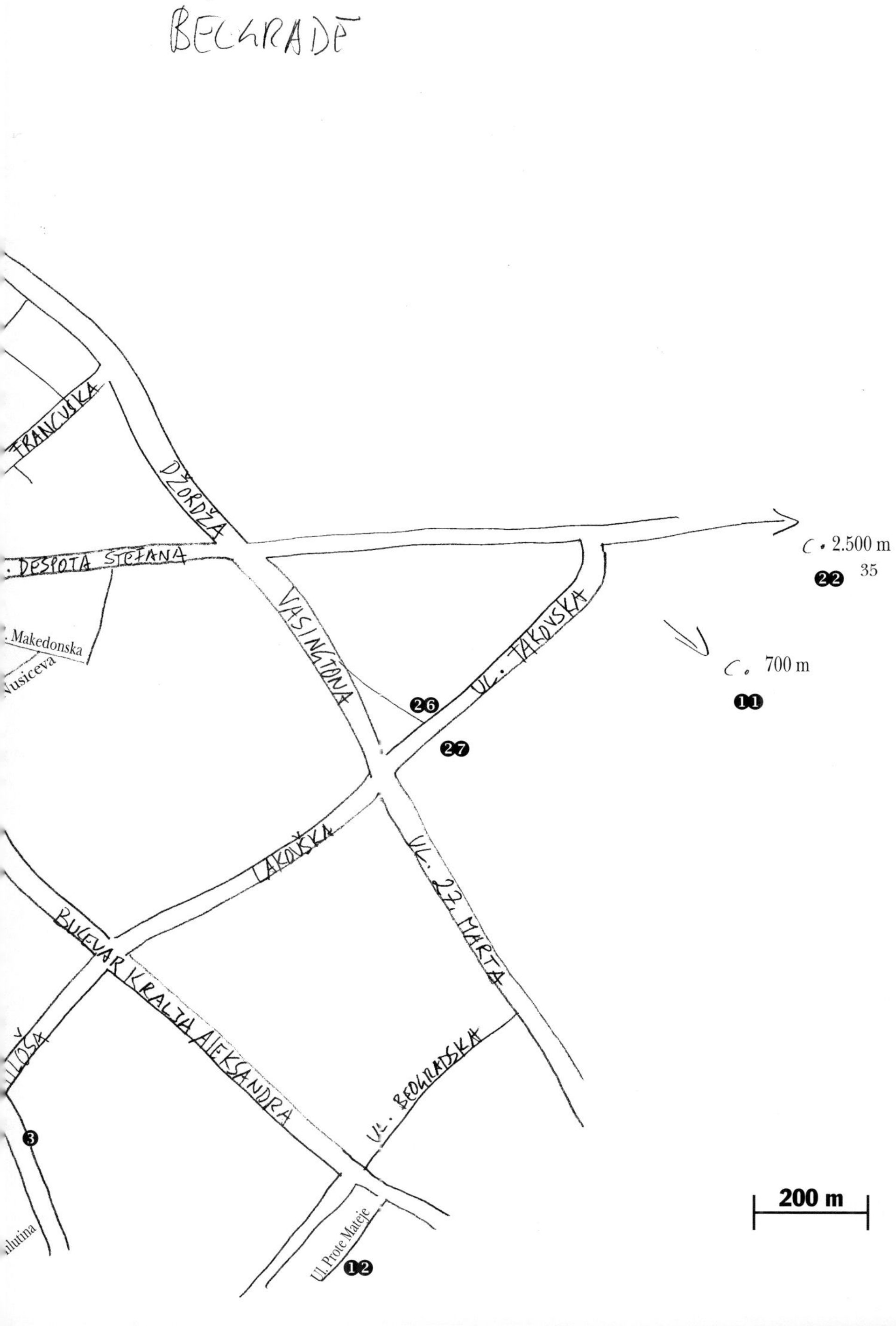
BELGRADE
FRANCUSKA
DŽORDŽA
. DESPOTA STEFANA
. Makedonska
Nusiceva
VASINGTONA
UL. TAKOVSKA
TAKOVSKA
UL. 27. MARTA
BULEVAR KRALJA ALEKSANDRA
UL. BEOGRADSKA
ILOŠA
ilutina
Ul. Prote Mateje
C. 2.500 m
22
35
C. 700 m
11
26
27
3
12
200 m

Miletičova Market

Bratislava

View of one of the biggest housing areas in Slovakia – the district Petržalka

A Seat of Honour or the Bench?

The economic situation was never overly rosy in Bratislava, which is why an art market still doesn't exist. Nevertheless, this fact frees artists and producers of culture; they don't have to live with the burden of a grand cultural heritage.

By Manuela Hötzl and Antje Mayer

»Small causes create complex phenomena«: Rarely did any thesis hit the nail on the head more accurately about the complex cultural networking that emerged from small beginnings in Bratislava. And yet! The capital of Slovakia suffers more than other former Eastern Bloc cities from a lack of dedication on the part of its cultural politicians. After 1989, they were more interested in an unswerving profit-oriented commercialisation than in any sensitive development of an emancipated cultural scene. It may also be for this reason that the past and future of any Slovak identity has always been, and continues to be, unclear. The Slovak architectural historian, Henrieta Moravčíková, expresses her scepticism over the city's future when she says, »Bratislava is lacking, as is the whole country, a vision of the future. Nobody has any idea as to what role Slovakia generally, and Bratislava in particular, are to play in the European Union. This is compounded furthermore by Bratislava's inferiority complex that it is seen as a mere suburb of Vienna on account of its size.« Jan Tabor, a Czech native who lives and works in Vienna as a curator, architecture critic and theorist and is involved as a visiting professor in the Vysoká škola vytvanrných umění (Academy of Fine Arts) in Bratislava, is generally sarcastic as regards the rapprochement of East and West. »The Viennese know the nearby new countries in the East primarily by their cheap shopping facilities. In Sopron you can get new teeth for a reasonable price, in Brno a new hip joint, or in Bratislava, inexpensive bumpers for your car.«

Viennese know the nearby new countries in the East primarily by their cheap shopping facililities

However, Bratislava, with its 450,000 inhabitants, is not merely a small town, it is the youngest capital city in the European Union, presenting itself as a very pleasant urban village with a youthful metropolitan flair. The history of the city and its buildings is marked by none of the extravagant indulgences encountered elsewhere, and the exaggerated excesses of Historicism and postmodernism prevailing in many other Eastern European cities are rarely spotted here at all. Conversely, there is to be found the odd jewel of Modernism, Functionalism or Socialist Realism. Situated on the Danube embankment, the Hotel Devin, a good example of Modernism, and the nearby Slovenská Narodná Galéria (Slovakian National Gallery), deserve special mention. The erstwhile charm of the Eastern Bloc is encountered only sporadically now, like in the shape of the grey concrete slab jungle of the district Petržalka. Investments have gone less into architecture recently, but more into an infrastructure that has been concerned less with aesthetic qualities than with the motto of »making it work«. Maintaining the city space as a symbolic reference point for the development of a local identity has been kept rather on the backburner.

Bratislava was a meeting point for the most diverse cultures of the East and West for many centuries

Manderla is thought to have been the very first skyscraper in Central Europe

Hviezdoslav Square

Bratislava was, by dint of its geographical position at the centre of Europe, a meeting point for the most diverse cultures of the East and West for many centuries. Slovakia shares borders with five countries – the Czech Republic, Austria, Ukraine, Poland and Hungary. The influence of all these cultures can be felt in Bratislava. In his book of travels entitled *Danube*, writer Claudio Magris quotes the Slovakian writer Vladimir Mináč on the occasion of his stay in Bratislava: »Over centuries, the Slovaks have been an unheeded and unappreciated people, the dark fertile ground of their own country, much like the stuff compounded of straw and dried manure that holds together the drevenice [or wooden houses that made up the rural dwellings in the country]. We have no history in terms of kings or emperors, dukes or princes, victories or conquests, deeds of violence or buccaneering raids.«

So, what history does Slovakia look back upon? What future is there to be derived from it? Two exhibitions in the past – as unalike as they may be – demonstrated the need for a search for clues or traces at various levels. On the one hand there was *Slovak Myth*, a show at the Slovakian National Gallery in 2006, which cast a telling light on the Slovak past from an ethnographic perspective, while on the other there was *Július Koller – Univerzálne Futurologické Operácie* (Universal Futurological Operations) at the Kölnische Kunstverein in 2003, where the internationally well known Slovakian contemporary artist Roman Ondák delved into the role of art in Slovakia during the '60s and '70s for the first time. Ethnographers and art historians in the West often tend to smile condescendingly on shows of this kind and this manner of coming to grips with the time before the fall of the Iron Curtain. But in Slovakia these shows are taking place for the first time, forming »the basis for a new self-discovery, which is immensely important«, says Bratislava artist, curator and musician Boris Ondreička. »The economic situation here was never overly rosy. That is why an art market still doesn't exist in Slovakia. There's no long tradition of art training, which is a pity, but it also frees us up. We're freer than the Czechs, who have to live with the burden of their grand cultural heritage. Basically, Bratislava is a small, insignificant city, barely taken note of by the world. You might say we Bratislavans like to define ourselves more from within.«

The writer Claudio Magris, however, takes an optimistic view: »Despite all, Bratislava is serene and full of life, a vital and expanding world, one that does not turn its face towards the melancholy of the past but firmly towards the challenges and developments of the future.« —

Bratislava is a small, insignificant city, barely taken note by the world

There's no long tradition of art training, which is a pity, but it also frees us up

Pyramid, home of Slovakian Radio, built by architect Stefan Svetko in the '80s

Ventúrska street becomes one big terrace in summer

We are not as spoilt as our neighbours

Slávo Krekovič, musician, journalist and »culture maker«, is an important personality in Bratislava's cultural life. He reveals the best locations and the secret of the city's vitality.

By Lýdia Pribišová

You are one of the most important people organizing cultural events in Bratislava. What is unique and specific about this town for you?

SLÁVO KREKOVIČ: In the first place, it is not such a big city, and compared to other European cities there is less of a cultural life here. But perhaps this is a positive aspect because we can appreciate it more and we are not as spoilt as our neighbours. At the same time, for me Bratislava contains a vital and experimental scene (especially a musical one) with very original personalities.

I like the extreme contrasts between old and new buildings everywhere in the centre of Bratislava, relicts of Socialist architecture like the famous Hotel Kyjev or the Slavín monument. I also have fun discovering abandoned spaces and places that are now disappearing, like the swimming pool under the castle that was never completed.

I am fascinated by the three factories Istrochem, Matador, and Tesla, the big smokestacks near the new National Theatre building. Interesting, although also a bit scary, is the rapid development of the city, also in the old, central areas – the whole new districts made of concrete and glass are almost ready to prove that they could be also used for living.

Where do you spend your spare time in Bratislava?

Concerning culture, apart from A4 – nultý priestor where I work a lot and also spend my free time, I like the alternative cultural space 13m3 in the tranzit workshop space tranzit dielne. Other popular venues include nice cafés and bars like the Kút, Verne, Exit, Next Apache, but also clubbings in the legendary Subclub – a club located in one of the many emergency military storage bunkers under the castle. A new, temporary artistic venue seems to be developing in the old Cvernovka factory, where some of the artists and designers moved their studios. Sometimes there are also interesting underground events in the punk club Intergalakticka obluda. And if one is tired of the city, the best thing to do is to go to the woods, which are not so far away – even around the charming rotating Kamzík TV Tower on the Koliba hill, which was built in the mid '70s.

Could you summarize the situation for culture and art in Bratislava in the last five years?

Coincidentally, the cultural centre A4, situated in the town centre in a state owned premises, has been in operation for the past five years. We founded it with a desire to create the first independent venue uniting contemporary theatre and dance, experimental music, alternative film, art and new media. It has proved to be a very vital concept.

A few small galleries exhibiting contemporary art have been founded and have also closed in this time frame. It is a pity that in last two years, many of the industrial spaces suitable for cultural activities have been demolished. In Bratislava, it could be said that it is not a lack of cultural potential or creative people, but a lack of space and money that is the problem. Despite this, there is still a vital and creative underground here.

Would more co-operations with foreign institutions help the scene in Bratislava?

We certainly have cooperated with institutions in the last couple of years, especially with cultural spaces in Prague and Brno – towns once a part of our common state Czechoslovakia. Contact with Vienna and Budapest? »Nicht immer, aber immer öfter« (Not always, but more often), as a famous Austrian beer advert says. A good example of uniting initiatives in the Central European region is the new media cultural festival Multiplace. The idea was created in Bratislava but, as its name suggests, it is based on a decentralised organization of activities taking place in multiple places and in cities around the world during one festival week. Last year the festival took place simultaneously not only in Prague, Brno, Budapest, Bratislava and also other Slovak towns, but also in organizations in Iceland and Germany. —

It is a pity that in last two years, many of the industrial spaces suitable for cultural activities have been demolished

Slávo Krekovič splits his official identity into the categories of cultural producer, musicologist, journalist and musician. He is editor-in-chief of *3/4 cultural magazine,* organiser and co-curator of the yearly festival of advanced music NEXT, and one of the co-founders of the media art festival Multiplace. He has been running the A4 nultý priestor for contemporary culture in Bratislava since 2004.

Bratislava

Hotel Kyjev
by night

By Lýdia Pribišová and Katarína Slaninová

ART

❶ **13 kubíkov-13m3** — The space in the tranzit workshops (see below) near lake Zlaté piesky has a unique energy. It is a meeting place for »hypermarket culture« (neighbouring shopping mall), post-Socialist summer vacation culture (nearby a lake with accommodation and summer sports facilities) and an industrial past and present. It is situated 20 minutes by tram from the city centre. 13m3 is a junction for artists, cultural activists, intellectuals and an ordinary public eager to know more about contemporary visual culture and art; it supports activities in the field of new media combining art with technology and science. Located in a former industrial barracks on the outskirts of the city, it is an attempt to move the border of cul-

tural events outside of the city centre. 13m3 is an ideal space for summer educational activities (workshops, seminars, lectures in visual culture, artist's studios on the premises). Its leading figure is the curator and art theoretician Mariša Rišková.

Studená 12, (0918 648 099)
Tram 2, 4: Zlaté Piesky
Open by appointment
www.13m3.sk

❷ **A4 –nultý priestor (zero space)** —— One of the centres of contemporary art in the heart of the capital, a meeting point and performance space with a daily program including concerts, theatre performances, lectures etc. Founded in 2004 as a non-profit, multifunctional centre with a focus on contemporary theatre, dance, avant-garde cinema, media art and experimental music. It is a cooperative partner for the international new media festival Multiplace, initiates night presentations of creative projects, named GUCHA, and operates its own experimental theatre SKRAT.

Námestie SNP 12, (0918 716 071)
Tram 13, 1: Námestie SNP
www.a4.sk

❸ **Billboart Gallery Europe** — It is run by Mira Keratová (curator) and Richard Fajnor (artist, curator)and was established in 2002 in Bratislava. It is a nonprofit organization with an extensive history of activities in the field of public art in Slovakia and all over the Europe, showing art works on commercial billboards, especially situated in the urban landscape. It operates on a network based structure. Some of the latest proj-

ects held in public spaces include the exhibition *Donaumonarchie* (2006), based on a critical reflection of the notion of Central Europe, and the exhibition project *Fantasies of the Beginning* (2008–2009), researching the specific dynamics of urban space and the social context of the housing development.

Šancova 37, (0905 511 582)
Tram 5, 3: Račianske mýto,
tram: 2, 4, 9: Trnavské mýto
www.billboart.org

❹ **Galéria Cypriána Majerníka/Project Room 14** — The reopening of one of the most important public galleries in Bratislava, dedicated to the youngest generation of artists, was one of the most important cultural activities in Old Town Bratislava in 2008. The gallery (originally founded in 1957) played a very important role in the history of Slovak art, especially during the '60s and '70s, when the gallery was a place of

polemic and critical discussions reacting to the repressions of the Communist era. Now the chief curator is Slovak art historian Richard Gregor. One part of the program is to reflect the history of the room since 1957, and the other to name the most important phenomena in emerging art in Slovakia. The Project Room 14 is part of the gallery's strategy to show work by students from art academies in town.

Ventúrska 9, Zichyho palác, (592 016 05)
Tram 5, 9: Kapucínska
Tue-Sat 2 pm to 6 pm

❺ **HIT Gallery** — This non-profit space is focused on the youngest generation of Slovak and international contemporary artists. Its basic ambition is to establish an easily accessible forum, a platform enabling young artists to present themselves in a public space and to contact professionals. The gallery follows the tradition of a venue being a gallery and a club, able to react to the impulses of the art scene and map the relevant socio-cultural phenomena in Bratislava.

Hviezdoslavovo námestie 18,
(0948 777 094)
Tram 11, 12, 13, 4: Námestie Ľudovíta Štúra
Tue-Fri 3 pm to 7 pm
www.galeriahit.com

❻ Gandy Gallery — After thirteen years in Prague, this commercial gallery, run by Nadine Gandy, also opened its space in Bratislava, a city located in the heart of a newly formed Europe and closer to the Balkan countries, which are Gandy's main artistic focus. The gallery sees itself as a laboratory for art and design, especially focused on Central European and Balkan artists (e.g. Anca Ignatescu, Zsoka Ath, Roza El-Hassan).

Panenská 30, (544 108 01)
Bus 93: Hodžovo námestie
Tue-Fri 2 pm to 6.30 pm, Sat 11 am to 4 pm
www.gandy-gallery.com

❼ Kressling Gallery — The art market in the Slovak Republic is quite sleepy, but gallery is trying to get it moving.It was founded in June 2007, and is run by artists Viktor Frešo and Martin Sedlák. It is the only gallery of contemporary art in Bratislava profiled strictly as a »commercial private gallery«, other spaces are specific combinations of non-profit and commercial models. Represented artists are among others Evžen Šimera, Kristofer Paetau or Ondřej Brody.

Zamočnícka 8, (0948 813 220)
Tram 1, 5, 9: Kapucínska,
bus 31, 39, 80, 83, 84, 93, 94: Zochova
Mon-Fri 1 pm to 7 pm
www.gallerykressling.sk

❽ Gallery M++ — This gallery is unique, based together with an adjoining theatre on a boat on the Danube River. Its special exhibition space, the interior of a boat, is predominantly dedicated to

the presentation of young emerging artists and students of art academies in Slovakia. The gallery is run by Andrea Pallang.

Ship Layuch-Lod, Tyršovo nábrežie 1,
(0915 377 663)
Bus 94, 50: Sad Janka Kráľa

Mon-Fri 10 am to 5 pm,
Sat-Sun 6 pm or 7 pm
www.galeriamplusplus.sk

❾ Galéria Medium — This gallery, founded in 1991, is a part of the Vysoká škola výtvarných umení (Academy of Fine Arts and Design) therefore its activities and exhibition plan bear very close connection to the institution. The gallery focuses on a highly professional presentation of students from various studios of the Academy in confrontation with different approaches of other foreign art academies. Thus the local students have a great opportunity to

compare and discuss their art practices with their foreign »colleagues«. The gallery also houses a design shop selling products created by students from the Academy design studios.

Hviezdoslavovo námestie 18, (544 353 34)
Tram 13: Námestie Ľudovíta Štúra,
bus 70: Nový most
Tue, Thur noon to 7 pm
Wed, Fri-Sun 10 am to 5 pm
www.vsvu.sk/galeria_medium

❿ PHOTOPORT Gallery — This gallery is focused on contemporary Slovak photography, presenting contemporary work by young emerging artists and confronting work by artists from other regions in Central Europe. The aim of the gallery is to start a market for art pho-

tography, something that doesn't currently exist in Slovakia.

Grösslingova 21, (090 337 46 03)
Tram 13, bus 50: Šafárikovo nám.
Wed-Fri 1 pm to 7 pm
www.photoportgallery.com

⓫ Plan B — This old sewing factory has transformed itself into a sub-cultural epicentre, an always necessary space for people to meet, talk, inspire, create and exchange. Apart from providing space for artist's studios (photographers, designers and architects), Plan B is a multifunctional, creative environment open to concerts, dance, festivals, cinema, conferences, workshops and exhibitions. Extraordinary factory feeling with a panorama view, bar (open only during events), all on 230 m², run by young Slovak artists Martin Mistrík, Šimon Kliman, Radana Valúchová, Viktor Szemzö, Juraj Kuchárik and Emília Jesenská.

Páričkova 18
(plan.b.bratislava@gmail.com)
Bus 50, trolleybus 205, 207: Páričkova

⓬ Satelit — Satelit is an exhibition space and meeting point for the institution Slovenské centrum dizajnu (Slovak Design Centre). Its poster, typography and fashion exhibitions present the current Slovak design scene. They run a design library and offer design related workshops. There is also the chance to encounter interesting design from abroad.

Dobrovičova 3, (529 201 84,
Bus 95, 78, tram 4, 12, 13, 14:
Šafárikovo námestie
Tue-Sun 1 pm to 6 pm
www.sdc.sk

⓭ SPACE Gallery — The gallery, founded by curator Juraj Čarný in 1999, is undoubtedly the most visible among non-profit spaces in Bratislava, having already established its name and that of a number of its artists in international circles (Marek Kvetán, Anetta Mona Chisa & Lucia Tkáčová, Stano Masár or Otis Laubert). It focuses on a permanent scanning and presentation of the

most innovative and experimental forms of art, presenting predominantly video art, sound art, light art, installation, and site-specific art as well as painting. Currently the gallery is carrying on with its activities in an alternative exhibition space, a van called nomad SPACE, which latches itself onto various cultural events.

Štefánikova 21, (0911 33 11 87)
Bus 83, 93: Hodžovo námestie
www.crazycurators.org

⓮ tranzit dielne (tranzit workshops) — Tranzit workshops, a long-term initiative supported by Kontakt the arts and civil society program of Erste Bank Group in Central Europe, is a large and dynamic environment for production and dialogue in the fields of contemporary art, curating, music and literature, philosophy and intellectual discourse in general. Its vivid and creative character is emphasised by artist's studios located on the premises. The interdisciplinary nature of tranzit is reflected in a variety of events ranging from exhibitions and music concerts to lectures, symposia and workshops. Set in an old warehouse, with a huge garden-like courtyard, it is, especially in summer, a pleasant and creative meeting place for artists, curators, students, musicians and intellectuals. Since 2002 the project has been led by Boris Ondrejička, an artist, poet and musician.

Studená 12, (090 820 15 07)
Tram 2, 4: Zlaté piesky
Wed-Sat 3 pm to 6 pm
www.tranzit.org

ART EVENTS

Crazycurators Biennial — This biennial was founded in 2006 by the SPACE Gallery and is one of the smallest biennials in existence. It is a type of constructive critique of the megalomaniac biennials that have been emerging steadily all around the world. Thus the conception is based on a narrow selection of renowned curators actively working in the framework of gallery practice. Each of the curators chooses one artist for the biennial. Paradoxically, they lose a chance to be curators in the real meaning of the word, and curate their own exhibition in the framework of the biennial. Likewise the biennial has no ambition to adjust the selection of an artist to a given theme, extremely abstract, which is usually a part of such events. One of the participating artists is awarded the »Crazycurators Award« selected by a jury consisting of the curators.

Biennale office:
Štefánikova 21, (0911 33 11 87)
Bus 83, 93: Hodžovo námestie
Autumn
www.crazycurators.org

Multiplace Festival — Taking place each spring since 2002, this festival for the media arts and network culture brings together several independent organizers in cities in Slovakia and other countries, presenting networked events, concerts, workshops, clubbings, video screenings, lectures and seminars (among the organizers: Atrakt Art, SPACE Gallery, Burundi, HIT Gallery, tranzit etc.).

Festival office: Nám. SNP 12,
(090 386 09 23)
Tram 13: Námestie SNP
Spring
www.multiplace.org

Pecha Kucha — This informal and very lively event presenting artists, designers, architects has been in Slovakia since 2008. Participants have a limited time, as well as number of slides, for their presentation; with 20 slides each on the screen for 20 seconds, they have to fill the 6 min 40 sec timeframe. In Bratislava (Pecha Kucha also occurs in the city of Žilina) the event takes place approximately every three months in the Kyjev hotel – a jewel of '70s Slovak architecture. The Pecha Kucha was founded in Japan in 2003 and aims to let artists, designers and architects present themselves in a fast, entertaining way.

Contact: info.ba@pechakucha.sk
Tram 4, 1: Mariánska Organized on regular basis four times a year, start time 8.20 pm
Full price admission € 5
www.pechakucha.sk

ALTERNATIVE SIGHTSEEING

15 Chair lift to the Železná studienka — This park and green recreation area is a favourite place among Bratislava residents and is a perfect place to relax, enjoy pleasant nature walks in the fresh air, recharge your batteries, or for children's games and sports. The chair lift gives you the chance to enjoy a comfortable ascent from Železná studienka to the Kamzík TV tower on the Koliba hill, which offers a marvellous view of the forests and peaks of the Little Carpathians.

Bus 43: Železná studnička
March-Sept, Thur-Sun 10 am to 6 pm
Oct-April, Thur-Sun 10 am to 4 pm
Full price admission € 3.20

⓰ Kamzík TV Tower — The highest point in Bratislava is the TV tower, which was constructed in 1974 by architect Marco Klatt. It is 200 metres high. Here you can see the entire city from the comfort of the slowly-rotating restaurant (with quite affordable prices), 68 m above the base of the tower. If you don't want something to eat or drink, you can just visit the observation desk.

Restaurant: Cesta na Kamzík 14,
(444 62 774) Bus 206, 212: Kamzík
Mon-Sun 11.30 am to 11 pm
Full price admission € 3
www.veza.sk

⓱ Chatam Sofer Tomb — This architecturally remarkable memorial is the

tomb of Moshe Schreiber, a renowned Orthodox rabbi and scholar, and also part of a Jewish cemetery dating back to the 17th century. It can be entered with a guide from the Bratislava Jewish Religious Community. Appointments must be made at least two working days in advance.

Nábrežie arm. gen. L. Svobodu, (593 491 42)
Tram 12, 4, bus 39: Chatam Sofer
www.chatamsofer.com

⓲ Slavín — Slavín is a memorial to the liberation of the city by the Soviet army in World War II, built in 1957–1960, situated on top of a hill near the Bratislava city centre. It is a unique military cemetery with a beautiful panorama view of the city.

Trolleybus 203: Búdková

54

⓳ Medzijarky (UFO) — If you are a fan of sci-fi films and space ships you should definitely visit Bratislava's Medzijarky district. Amidst Socialist blocks of flats, in the middle of a grass plain, aliens have landed and left behind an abandoned metal space ship.

Bus 75, trolleybuses 201, 202: Komárovská

DAYTRIPS

Jaskyňa Driny (Driny Cave) — This beautiful cave near the western Slovakian village Smolenice has 450m of walking paths and offers guided tours. It is formed of brown-grey Lower Cretaceous chert-limestone and is the only cave open to the public in the western part of Slovakia. By car take route 502 northeast from Bratislava to Smolenice or get a bus from Bratislava to Smolenice, the ticket costs € 2.50. The departure times of the buses can be found on the website cp.atlas.sk/vlakbus/spojenie/. The trip takes about an hour from Bratislava by car or bus.

Smolenice, (033 558 62 00)
September-May, Tue-Sun admission every 1.5h from 10 am to 2.30 pm
June-August, Tue-Sun admission every hour from 10 am to 5 pm
Full price admission € 5
www.ssj.sk/jaskyne/spristupnene/driny/

National Park Donau-Auen — An area in Lower Austria between Vienna and Bratislava contains the last major river floodplains in Central Europe still unspoilt by construction. It is full of botanical treasures and precious species that have found a refuge here. Yearround national park staff offer a wide range of activities for adults and children alike such as activities on foot, by boat, in horse-carriages or by bike. Guided tours in English/Slovakian and in German are offered. The National park is freely accessible from several entry points in Austria. The best bet is to start from the Austrian village of Orth or from the wien-lobAU National Park House in Vienna (you can reach both destinations in about one hour by car from Bratislava). Take your passport with you.

schlossORTH
Nationalpark-Zentrum
2304 Orth/Danube, Austria
(+43 (0)22 12 35 55)
www.donauauen.at

Modra and Pezinok — These historical villages are rich with winemaking tradition, full of comfortable cellars with a path that wanders through the surrounding vineyards. Modra is also famous for its very original ceramics with peculiar design patterns. Both places organize a traditional wine-picking festival in autumn, full of stalls selling wine and homemade specialities. Try lokša, something like a pancake served with duck fat or sauerkraut. The villages are situated approximately 30 km from Bratislava and are accessible by car on route 502 or by bus. The buses leave approximately every half an hour from the main station in Bratislava. Check out details on the website: cp.atlas.sk/vlakbus/spojenie/.

The trip takes about 45 minutes by car or bus.

The City Information Center in Modra:
Štúrova 59, (033 647 23 12)
Mon-Fri 8 am to 6 pm, Sat 9 am to 2 pm
www.modra.sk

Information Centre in Pezinok:
Radničné Square 9, (033 641 25 50)
Mon-Fri 8 am to 6 pm, Sat 9 am to 2 pm
www.pezinok.sk

KIDS

⓴ Bibiana – medzinárodný dom umenia pre deti (Bibiana – International House of Arts for Children) — This institution, founded in 1987, focuses on introducing and promoting art among children and youth using experimental and interactive methods. With its activities it addresses children of all ages, nationalities, religious and ethnic backgrounds. It co-organizes the Biennial of Illustrations Bratislava presenting illustrations from children's books. When coming to Bratislava with your children do not hesitate to visit this »magic« place full of interesting exhibitions, theatre performances, workshops and other attractions with a very friendly (and English speaking) staff.

Panska 41, (544 313 08)
Tram 4, 12, bus 70: Nový most
Tue-Sun 10 am to 6 pm
Family ticket € 1.66, children € 0.33
www.bibiana.sk

㉑ Zoo and Dino Park — The zoo in Bratislava houses a unique Dino Park consisting of 22 models of life-sized dinosaurs. This place is a great opportunity for children to discover and explore about life on Earth in the Mesozoic Era. A paleontological playground, a 3D cinema about life on Earth and a knowledge path are a part of the complex, offering plenty of creative and educational space for young explorers.

Mlynská dolina 1, (601 021 11)
Bus 30, 31, 32, 37, 39, 92: Mlynská dolina
April-October, 9 am to 6 pm
November-March, 10 am to 3 pm
Full price admission € 4.30
www.zoobratislava.sk & www.dinopark.eu

SHOPPING

㉒ Artfórum — This bookshop was founded 17 years ago and has slowly become a chain of shops with branches all around Slovakia. Apart from books, it houses a music store and organizes evenings with writers and musicians. You can choose from a wide range of books in English on art and culture as well as novels.

Kozia 20, (544 118 98)
Bus 93: Zochova
Mon-Fri 10 am to 8 pm, Sat 9 am to 1 pm
www.artforum.sk

㉓ Ex Libris — This bookshop offers a wide range of books on art, photography and visual culture (even in English). Located in the Stredoeurópsky dom fotografie (Central European House of Photography) with a small cafe, right in the city centre, it is a nice opportunity to sit down for a while, read a good book or a magazine, have a cup of coffee or visit a photo exhibition.

Prepoštská 4, (544 109 90)
Tram 1, 5, 9: Kapucínska
Mon-Fri 8 am to 10 pm, Sat 10 am to 10 pm

㉔ Design Shop (in the Medium Gallery) — If you are bored of ready-to-wear clothes and crave something unique, or you want to buy an original present, visit this place located in the heart of downtown. By shopping here you support the young emerging artists and designers, who create the products.

Hviezdoslavovo nám. 18, (594 285 70)
Tram 11, 13, 12, 4: Námestie Ľudovíta Štúra
Tue, Thur noon to 7 pm,
Wed, Fri-Sun 10 am to 5 pm
www.vsvu.sk/galeria_medium/

CAFÉS

㉕ Café Verne — Café Verne offers excellent light fare, drinks at affordable prices and a particular atmosphere, as almost 90 per cent of the visitors are people dealing with art. It is an important meeting point for Bratislava's art scene and a very useful source of backstage information and gossip. Situated in the Old Town pedestrian zone.

Hviezdoslavovo námestie 18, (547 717 67)
Tram 4, 12: Nový most
Mon-Thur 8.30 am to 12 am,
Fri 8.30 am to 1 am,
Sat, Sun 11 am to 1 am

㉖ Café Kút — A favourite meeting place for artists, musicians, and actors characterized by a pleasant atmosphere, furnished with quirky antique furniture and offering original cocktails, mixed drinks and snacks together with cool music. Situated in the Old Town pedestrian zone.

Zámočnícká 11, (544 349 57)
Tram 1, 5, 9: Kapucínska
Mon-Fri 8 am to 11 pm,
Sat-Sun 4 pm to 11 pm
www.kut.prasnabasta.sk

㉗ Next Apache — This is not only a café and bar run by Ben Pasce, it is also a second-hand English bookstore and a meeting place for artists, writers and intellectuals. The name of the place is derived from the Slovak »Nech sa páči« (Here you are). In the bar, exhibition after-parties continue into the night. You can also see film screenings, presentations of books and small concerts.

Panenská 28, (0903 818 169)
Bus 83, 93: Hodžovo námestie
Mon-Fri 9 am to 10 pm,
Sat-Sun 10 am to 10 pm

RESTAURANTS

㉘ Malecon Bar & Restaurant — Malecon, situated in the Slovak National Gallery building, is a Cuban restaurant and bar with a wide spectrum of drinks, cocktails and hot Cuban music. Every Friday there is a Latino disco. Main dishes from € 8.

Nám. Ľudovíta Štúra 4, (0910 274 583)
Tram 4, 12, 11: Nám. Ľudovíta Štúra
Mon-Wed 11 am to 1 am, Thur-Sat 11 am to 3 am, Sun 11 am to 11 pm
American Express, Diners Club,
MasterCard, Visa
www.malecon.sk

㉙ Prašná Bašta — This restaurant, situated in the old historical centre of Bratislava, is certainly one of the best restaurants in the city with a wide range of wines and typical Central European specialities. It is characterized by a slightly nostalgic atmosphere, good live music and a very friendly staff. In the summer it is possible to sit in a quiet garden at the back of the building and drink refreshments. Main dishes from € 6.

Zámočnícka 11, (544 349 57)
Tram 1, 5, 9: Kapucínska
Mon-Sun 11 am to 11 pm
American Express, Diners Club,
MasterCard, Visa
www.prasnabasta.sk

㉚ Leberfinger — A 250 year old traditional tavern on the quieter right side of the Danube (Bratislava – Petržalka) in a typical Slovakian one story building with a rustic interior and garden with a lovely view of the castle. This restaurant is known for its authentic Slovakian cuisine. Nearby is the Janko Kral Park, ideal for a postprandial walk. Main dishes from € 7.

Viedenská cesta 257, (62 31 75 90)
Bus 50: Sad Janka Kráľa
Daily 11 am to 12 pm
American Express, MasterCard, Visa
www.leberfinger.sk

㉛ 1st Slovak Pub — A venue popular with university students, and probably the only place in the world where you can get free soup for getting an A on an exam. It offers specialities from traditional Slovakian cuisine and tries to present Slovak traditions and history in

14 separate rooms that encompass old pagan times up to the revival era of the 19th century. Main dishes from € 4.50.

Obchodná 62, (529 263 67)
Tram: 1, 5, 9: Obchodná
Mon-Thur 10 am to 12 am,
Fri-Sat 10 am to 2 am, Sun noon to midnight
Diners Club, Visa, MasterCard
www.slovakpub.sk

㉜ Lacinka — This is not a restaurant, it is a cult créperie with a long tradition located near the main railway station offering hundred types of tasty crepes. It is famous not only for its crepes but also for its friendly, smiling staff. It looks a little bit like a cafeteria in a kindergarten. Without doubt it is a good place to visit when you have a long wait for your train.

Šancová 18, (524 974 14)
Tram 3, 8,bus 21, 63,
trolleybuses 201, 204, 209:
Kooperativa
Mon-Fri 10 am to 9 pm, Sun 2 pm to 9 pm

PARTY

Ufo — This venue is in an UFO-like object on top of the New Bridge and houses a trendy restaurant and bar with a spectacular view of the city. There is a fee to use the lift to get the view.

Novy Most 1, (0905 499 108)
Tram 4, 12, bus 70, 37: Nový most
Mon-Sun 10 am to 11 pm
Full price admission for the lift € 6.60
www.u-f-o.sk

㉝ Nu Spirit Bar — If you like jazz, funk and soul, this bar is the right place for you. It is located just a short walk from the historical centre and the Opera. DJs and live bands play cool music six days a week, including hip-hop, house and drum'n'bass. There are excellent drinks including different kinds of tea and free Wi-Fi Internet.

Medená 16, (0905 865 566)
Tram 4, 12, 11: Nám. Ľudovíta Štúra
Mon-Fri 10 am to 4 am
www.nuspirit.sk

㉞ Pivnička (Beer tavern) — A very lively bar and party place, with a rich program of concerts and DJ sets. Reggae music nights alternate with electronic music and live concerts. A place for fans of good beer and table soccer.

Palackého 2, (0915 796 487)
Tram 4, 11, 12: Nám. Ľudovíta Štúra
Mon-Sun 4 pm to 4 am
www.rockgarden.sk

❸❺ Mark Twain — Mark Twain is situated on an inactive river channel of the Danube [called Karloveske rameno], near the Botanicka zahrada (Botanic Garden). It's a pub with a special holiday atmosphere on a boat open from spring to autumn. You can also have a barbecue, see an exhibition of photographs of old steamships, or catch a glimpse of the occasional beaver in the river channel.

Karloveske rameno, shipyard
Tram 1, 4, 5, 9, 12, bus 32:
Botanicka zahrada
May-October, Mon-Fri 2 pm to 12 am,
Sat-Sun 1 pm to12 am

❸❻ Sonáta — Situated near the Opera in the town centre this venue features good food, drinks and a friendly staff. A must if you want to experience old time entertainment with a quirky older DJ dressed in a glitter suit, playing disco tunes from the '70s and '80s.

Palackého 14, (0904 652 191)
Tram 4, 11, 12: Nám. Ľudovíta Štúra Mon-Thu, Sun 9 am to 12 am,
Fri-Sat 9 am to 2 am
www.restauracia-sonata.skg.sk

❸❼ Subclub (formerly the U-Club) — If you want to go out in (cool) style in Bratislava, this is where you must head

in the evening, located in a former air raid shelter below the castle mountain situated directly in the centre of Bratislava. This dance club was mainly known for many years as a regional centre for techno and electronic music, but also for its punk and gothic sounds.

Nábrežie arm. gen. L. Svobodu,
(544 111 83 or 0904 949 105)
Tram 12, 4: Nový most
usually daily 9 pm to 4 am
www.subclub.sk

SLEEP

❸❽ Hotel Devin — This is a very special tip for a hotel in the luxury range. It is

an architectural pearl from the period between Functionalism and Socialist realism. Located directly next to the Danube River. Double rooms from € 125.

Riečna 4, (599 858 56)
Tram: 4, 12, bus 70, 37: Nový most
www.hoteldevin.sk

㊴ Botel Gracia — This hotel often serves as accommodation of festival guests, artists and people who look for something unusual. Botel Gracia on the Danube River is situated directly across from the Slovak National Gallery, very close to the New Bridge and the Cirkus Barok, a famous disco on the river where foreigners look for young beautiful Slovakian girls. The Bratislava Castle completes the panorama view from the Botel outlook. A three-minute-walk from Botel Gracia takes you to the historical city centre and all the important city institutions. Wi-Fi internet connection is available. Double rooms from € 96.

Rázusovo nábrežie, (544 32 132)
Trams: 4, 12, bus 70, 37: Nový most
www.botelgracia.sk

㊵ Hotel Kyjev — Kyjev is a hotel with the spirit of the Communist era, with a specific interior and a nostalgic atmosphere. It is one of the most important symbols of Socialist architecture's heritage, built in the '70s for Communist business people. In the near future it might be torn down by a powerful developer who is intent on constructing something in uniform architecture on the site. This particular hotel was also the set for a film by Polish artist Katarzyna Skupny in which a lot of Slovak artists participated. These days,

Hotel Kyjev is a place of Pecha Kucha Nights (see »art events«). There is a quite good restaurant in the hotel, with good prices and a unique interior. Double rooms from € 56.

Rajska 2, (596 411 11)
Tram 4, 11, 14:
Kamenné námestie
www.kyjev-hotel.sk

㊶ Downtown Backpackers — This is a hostel with dorm rooms and a limited number of private rooms, a trendy restaurant and bar with friendly staff situated in a historical building just a few steps from the Presidential Palace. It offers wonderful possibilities for exploring Bratislava Old Town at a reasonable price. Gandy Gallery and Café Next Apache are situated nearby. Double rooms from € 30.

Panenská 31, (546 411 91)
Bus 34, 83, 84, 93:
Hodžovo námestie
www.backpackers.sk

GOOD TO KNOW

❹❷ Tourist Information —
Klobučnícka 2, (544 337 15)
Tram 4, 11, 12, 13: Nám. Ľudovíta Štúra
October-May: Mon-Fri 8.30 am to 6 pm,
Sat 9 am to 4 pm, Sun 10 am to 3 pm
June-September: Mon-Fri 8.30 am to 7 pm,
Sat 9 am to 5 pm, Sun 10 am to 5 pm
www.visit.bratislava.sk

INTERNET

❹❸ Internet café: Štefánka —
Palisády 59
Bus 93, 83: Hodžovo námestie
Mon-Fri 9 am to 10 pm,
Sat 10 am to 10 pm

MEDIA

www.spectator.sk — This magazine offers valuable information about life in Slovakia for expats living here. It brings the latest information about politics and society, the economy, business, culture and regional news helping the English speaking community to break the information barrier.

www.bratislavaguide.com — Provides the largest overview of exhibitions, concerts, operas and other tourist-friendly events in Bratislava.

www.bkis.sk — The Bratislava information and cultural centre provides information on life in the capital in the form of regularly issued periodicals and information points in the city centre. It also organizes cultural events.

Twin City Journal and Enjoy — Periodicals predominantly focusing on foreign visitors offering information about culture, accommodation, food and sports facilities in the capital.

BA! From UFO To UFO — An alternative tourist guide compiled by cultural activists, artists, designers and architects introducing the capital from a different perspective by focusing on »cultish«venues, derelict, abandoned or soon- to-be-demolished places with unique atmospheres. The »guide« offers an insider's view of Bratislava.

TRANSPORT

From the airport — The international airport M.R. Štefánik is 9 km outside the city centre. You can get to the main railway station by using bus 61. Bus 96 brings you to Petržalka, Prokofievova street. The price for a one-way ticket valid for 15 minutes is € 0.50, a 60 minute ticket costs € 0.70. You can find the timetable on www.airport-bratislava.sk/51/32.html

A taxi (cabs are standing outside the arrival hall of the airport) from the airport to the centre should cost around € 25. When calling a taxi company, prices are slightly lower.

Taxis — Taxis are cheap in Bratislava, though when you hail a cab in the street it is slightly more expensive than ordering one by phone. ABC Taxi (161 00), Fun Taxi (167 77).

Dispatchers at ABC Taxi and Fun Taxi speak English. As a foreigner, you might find that your drive is a bit more expensive. The usual charge for about 5 km is around € 3-4. Always ask for a receipt.

Public transport — Single-trip tickets for the bus, tram and trolleybus lines are valid in 15, 60 and 70 min increments and cost from € 0.50–0.80. Ticket machines are at the bus stops. You can also buy tickets at a tobacco/Noviny (newsagent). Night buses numbered N21 – N99 run between 12 am and 4 am; a night bus ticket costs € 1.40. It is recommend that visitors obtain 1, 2, 3 or 7-day tourist tickets, which can be purchased from ticket machines. A 1 day ticket costs € 3.50, 2 day tickets cost € 6.50, 3 day tickets cost € 8 and a 1 week ticket costs € 12.

Car — Driving a car in the Bratislava centre can be a nightmare as there are not many parking spaces, and some are very expensive, especially in underground parking garages. If you decide to rent a car, or drive to Bratislava in your own, you can park on the streets in the centre during the day from 8 am to 4 pm after buying a 1-hour parking card for € 0.70. They can be purchased from sellers in reflective vests or at newsstands, or you can go to underground car garages or find a parking lot. You can rent a car at the airport or go to: www.comparecarrent.com

Ship — Do you enjoy travelling by boat? Then Twin City Liner is the best option for you. This city centre to city centre service depart from Bratislava (close to the Propeller house) to Vienna Schwedenplatz/Marienbrücke and vice versa, from one city to another in just 75 minutes.

Twin City Liner Entrance Station
Rázusovo nábrežie,
(0903 610 716 or 544 102 35)
Tram 4, 13, 11: Nám. Ľudovíta Štúra
April-September: Daily 10.30 am, 2.30 pm, 5 pm, 6.30 pm and 10.30 pm
(but not in April, October)
November-December-March: Daily 6 pm
Tickets from € 17 up to € 30
www.twincityliner.com

#

Important Numbers

Telephone country and city code	*+421 2*
Telephone information	*1181*
Emergency	*112*
Police	*158*
Fire Brigade	*150*
Ambulance	*155*
24h-Pharmacy	*Lekáreň Pokrok, Račianske Mýto 1/A, (444 552 91), Tram 5, 3: Račianske mýto*

City in Numbers

Inhabitants	*427,000*
Average income	*€ 697*
Cup of coffee	*€ 1.20*
Bottle of beer	*€ 1.50*
Cigarettes	*€ 2.79*
Most talked about contemporary artists	*Stanislav Filko, Július Koller, Roman Ondák*
Collectors of contemporary art	*3*
Biggest art scandal	*The withdrawl of Richard Gregor from his post as head of the Cultural Department of the Bratislava Old Town Council because he was accused of a »pornographic« exhibition in Galéria Cypriána Majerníka.*

Short Art History BRATISLAVA

1928 The founding of the Secondary School of Applied Arts and Crafts (ŠUR), inspired by the German Bauhaus.

64

Early 1930s Ľudovít Fulla and Mikuláš Galanda release *Súkromné listy Fullu a Galandu* (The Private letters of Fulla and Galanda), a manifesto calling for new forms of artistic representation. It is the first theoretical reflection by Slovak artists on art practice.

1948 Foundation of the Slovenská Národná Galéria (Slovakian National Gallery). In the following years politically engaged art, serving the ruling Communist party, starts in the form of Socialist realism. Art life, as such, is concentrated in partly illegal, underground artistic groups.

1960s Contact with the European art scene, Actionism, conceptual art.

1970s The period of »Normalization«, the government's persecution of artists not complying with »mainstream« forms of art.

1993 Founding of the Soroš Centre of Contemporary Art/SCCA, today known as Foundation – Centre for Contemporary Arts, which is the first institution systematically supporting contemporary art.

1996 The SOGA auction house is founded, the first institution in Slovakia organizing auctions of both modern and contemporary art.

2006 First issue of *Flash Art,* the Czech and Slovak edition.

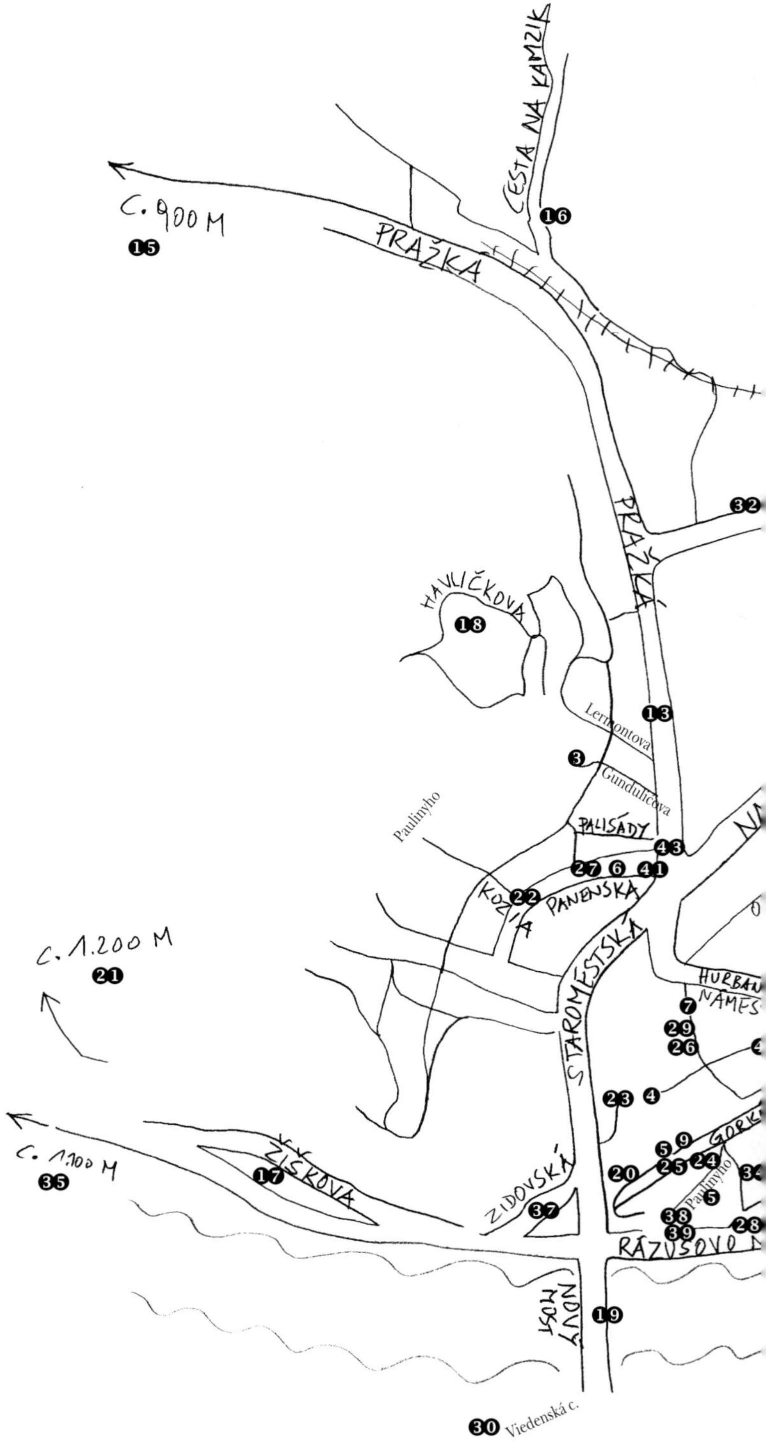
CESTA NA KAMZIK
16
C. 900 M
15
PRAŽKA
32
PRAŽKA
HAVLIČKOVA
18
13
Lermontova
3
Gundulićova
Paulinyho
PALISÁDY
43
27
6
41
KOZIA
22
PANENSKÁ
STAROMESTSKÁ
C. 1.200 M
21
7
29
26
23
4
C. 1.100 M
35
ŽIŽKOVA
17
ŽIDOVSKÁ
37
20
5
9
25
24
Paulinyho
5
38
39
28
NOVÝ MOST
19
30
Viedenská c.

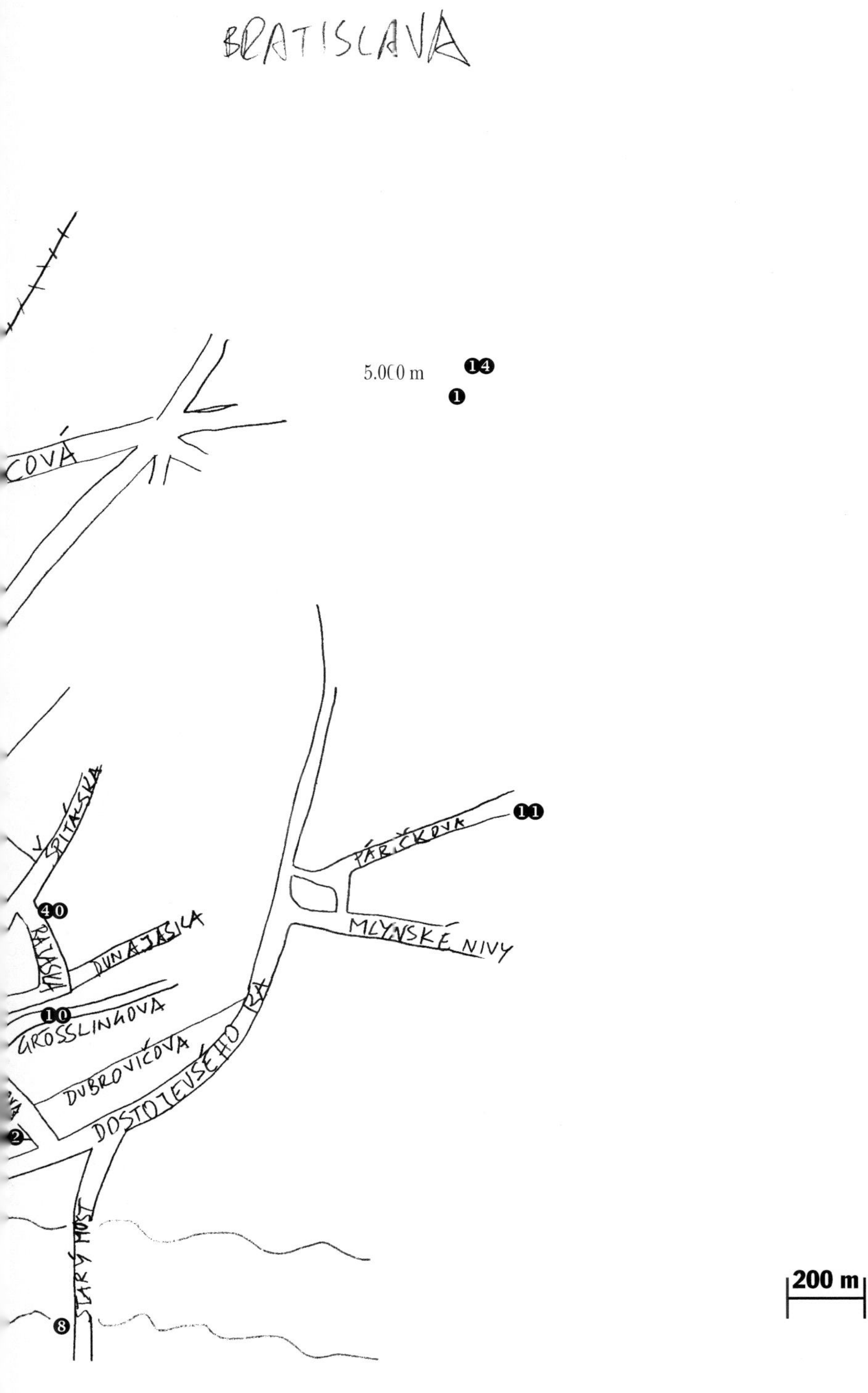
BRATISLAVA
5.000 m
14
1
COVÁ
SPITÁLSKA
PÁRIČKOVA
11
40
MLYNSKÉ NIVY
DUNAJSKÁ
10
GROSSLINGOVA
DUBROVIČOVA
DOSTOJEVSKÉHO RA
2
STARÝ MOST
8
200 m

Bucharest

City of Records

The former shine of the »Paris of the East« has disappeared in the bitter charm of its post-Communist capitalistic present. The contemporary art scene is small, however in the past five years a number of interesting spaces and projects for contemporary art have been created.

By Raluca Voinea

Romania is one of the most original destinations for Western European travellers and the like. Indeed it is a big country of numerous possibilities and even greater projections. Having been among the most isolated people in the entire former Eastern block, Romanians are today unconditionally embracive of Western values, which are in most cases over-translated there, and only countered by the ultra-orthodox return to so-called »national spirit«, which takes different public manifestations. The Romanian artists Cristi Pogacean and Dan Acostioaei, for example, have both realized short videos in which one can see people in the city making the sign of the cross when passing by a church, a habit still widely spread. The mix of primitive and emancipated behaviours, the relativity of borders separating private from public space, and the disordered urban development are some of the most immediately striking characteristics of Romanian cities.

The capital in particular offers as much as an entire country in unforgettable experiences, although »it is not a city which lets itself be easily unveiled«, as Fernando Klabin, a translator and tourism guide in Bucharest puts it »The speedy visitor who is discouraged by the dust, the chaotic traffic and the confused effervescence of people, who seems to want to compensate all at once for the 42 years of Communism through a too intense consumerism, will miss the opportunity of knowing a city full of charm, which gathers in one place influences as diverse as the Byzantine and French.« Indeed, the city appears to be first a puzzle, albeit one which doesn't need solving, for there isn't a complete image that each fragment should fit into, but everything is developed according to an inner logic, and diverse strata coexist. A city of contrasts, intense aggression and inestimable charisma define Bucharest and make most people not like it, but eventually fascinates them, and they end up loving it.

The city appears to be first a puzzle, but everything is developed according to an inner logic

Vasile Ernu, the author of the Romanian bestseller *Born in the USSR* and a recent Bucharest inhabitant, (he declares it his 7th city-home), explains this eclecticism: »A city with an oriental savour, in a geographical area under European influence, over which came waves of Turks, Greeks, Jews, Russians, Hungarians, and, not just recently, Gypsies. Among all of them, there were also many Romanians. This mix and these cultural and identity gaps are noticeable everywhere, in the architecture, in everything that moves in the city. Even people, without necessarily having the memory of this history, carry its direct fingerprint.«

Horse-driven carriages at the beginning of the 20th century in Bucharest moved faster than cars there do today

Sometimes one can get the feeling that Bucharest's residents are so fond of the city that they live in that they take all their time to admire every inch of it judging by the time they spend in traffic. According to police statistics, horse-driven carriages at the

Herastrau Park

E-URANUS
outdoor cinema

beginning of the 20th century in Bucharest moved faster than cars there do today. However, traffic is only one of numerous records that seem to take Bucharest out of its oriental haven and situate it directly on the map of paradoxical metropolises, found in constant competition for something »big«. We not only have the biggest parliament building in Europe and the biggest diversity of European architectural styles in our city, the mayor put Bucharest in the Book of Records with the biggest cake ever baked, the city is proud of its »biggest« Christmas tree and the nouveau riche's cars grow bigger with each passing year. One could continue this enumeration with peculiarities from the art field, such as the biggest museum in the country, the MNAC, the National Museum for Contemporary Art, in the biggest building in town, Ceausescu's most famous architectural accomplishment. There are the three international biennials for contemporary art, all happening in the same year: Periferick in Iasi, the Bucharest Biennale and the Biennial of Young Artists, also in Bucharest. This all does not mean that our art scene is ready for the cabinet of curiosities. There are certain anomalies that were determined by the long time needed to unlearn dependency on the state, by some missed opportunities and unfavourable political conjunctures, as well as by the exacerbated egos of most actors active on this stage.

Since then however, the increasing number of opportunities which have arisen, and the »professionalisation« of the generation who has »die Gnade der späten Geburt« (the mercy of late birth), those who are said to be old enough to understand the chronic mistrust acquired during the Ceausescu epoch, but also young enough to have almost completely escaped its contamination, determined the development of a much more flexible and nuanced situation today.

The platforms in Bucharest that exhibit and promote contemporary art are multiplying and diversifying

For artists it is essential that, in the last five years, the platforms in Bucharest that exhibit and promote contemporary art are multiplying and diversifying, for there was a long period in which the only alternative they had was to join the obsolete and almost bankrupt National Artists Union, the centralized structure which, once upon a time, provided artists with everything from social status to studios, teaching positions to travels abroad. The alternative was to use their creativity in the service of the advertising industry, the booming business of the late '90s, alongside real estate and plastic thermo-framing for windows.

People have actually learned more than sheer survival techniques

Today the spectrum of opportunities available is much broader. For example, artists can participate in the decoration of the metro stations with the project *I love Bucharest,* an initiative dedicated to community art and urban intervention. They can design the trendy coffee shops or stores in the capital in the newly refurbished streets

no smoking area

Caru' Cu Bere
(Beer Wagon)

Obor fish market

Stefan cel Mare Boulevard

of the historic centre Lipscani. They can have their works sold by commercial galleries such as Andreiana Mihail, a gallery which the eponymous owner tries to keep »consistent with the dynamic and intensity of the city«, bringing together some of the most successful artists of the young generation while at the same time confronting the international standards of the art scene. The artists can also »feed on the capital of cool«, as the Romanian curator Stefan Tiron would say, by attending the parties on the terrace of MNAC, overlooking a wasteland where the biggest (!) Orthodox cathedral in the country may one day be erected.

The fact that structures which functioned, until now, informally have become institutionalized, enjoying a large public visibility, proves that people have actually learned more than sheer survival techniques. Lia Perjovschi's Contemporary Art Archive, which has functioned for years in her studio, is now partially moving into a new centre for contemporary art, the Pavilion Unicredit, which is initiated by the creators and organizers of the Bucharest Biennale, Razvan Ion and Eugen Radescu. Located in the former offices of a bank, which is also the supporter of this ambitious project, the new space promises to be a white cube for exhibitions and a resource centre.

However, beyond these examples (and keeping in mind that there are not many others), Bucharest remains a city of hopes and dreams, where the most rewarding experience is walking at a slow pace through the fast-changing urban maze, preferably accompanied by a local guide who can tell you all the intrigues and histories of the past 20 or 200 years, depending on which route you decide to take. —

Bucharest remains a city of hopes and dreams

Bus in wintertime on Stefan cel Mare Boulevard

Villacrosse passageway

Little Calcutta and the official chic

An Interview with Bucharest cultural worker *Stefan Tiron*, who calls himself »a paranoid double agent, information dealer, dirty data miner, info broker, shady somatic recipient and damaged cortical data retriever.«

———

By Raluca Voinea

What is it in Bucharest that gives you such pleasure in »dissecting« it when talking about it?

STEFAN TIRON: There are many mixed feelings one can have when thinking or speaking about Bucharest. This city, as it sits here, in a semi-desert area, where people came with their sheep and cut all the forests down and eroded the land, has now become a sort of little Calcutta. In the summer it is impossible to live here; the asphalt gets liquefied and everybody leaves the city, going to the seaside or the mountains. Of course, this destroys any potential elsewhere, but it's an expansion determined by the city's intolerable atmosphere. Naturally, people react. I can say a new suburbia exists, which is emerging around the city, people are commuting, there are many families; this suburbia is growing in all the little nice villages that have been incorporated by the city.

Let's start talking about the suburbia around Bucharest. One is formed by the Communist housing blocks and the most recent one is defined by neo-capitalist villas and architectural improvisations.

On one hand it's a life lived in segregation, with racist environments and close-knit communities. On the other, there are the new neighbourhoods where you have police, guards, entrance passes, all these artificially maintained standards. But there are not so many differences between them. Also in the old neighbourhoods where there are the so-called »good blocks« in which there are no intruders, they have had the same administration for the last 30 years, everybody knows everybody, and they check out the newcomers. Of course they cannot really control the influx of people but they would surely like to. So people put intercoms at the entrance, all sorts of barriers that make them feel guarded, protected. The most symbolic one is the door. It doesn't matter the state in which the buildings is in (some often don't have electricity in the stairwell) the door to one's private flat needs to be really imposing – some of them are quite luxurious, and most look like safe-doors, with several locks, so that it gives the impression that people are barricaded inside the flat, or that they are under house arrest.

Bucharest's city centre, beyond its first impression as a very crowded place and a heterogeneous mix of architecture and lifestyles, has its particularities, which are at the same time odd and spectacular. For example, the night car races, do they still take place?

For sure this is not going to end very soon. Let me tell you something that I saw recently. I was waiting for the trolley shortly before midnight when a huge cortege of cars and motorbikes started to pass by. A famous racing club boss had hit a pole at 210km/h and had died. All these cars had his picture stuck on their windows, and they were a slowly moving funerary cortege. The interesting thing was that there were also Romanian cars, Dacia, very old, but which had been customized for the races. There are some of the race's participants who can't really afford it but they are crazy for the phenomenon, and so they adapt their cars and join the flow.

Where does this come from? Is there a need for a community, for participating in something?

There is a certain nomadic feeling within communities; each one absorbs from the other one. It's true that there are no social centres or an infrastructure for young people, who don't have a space for expressing themselves as groups; on the other hand this makes them determined to invent their own places to gather.

What about the artistic community, does it have such spontaneous spaces?

There are all sorts of temporary phenomena. For example, there was the summer derelict and abandoned Cinema Capitol, in a hidden garden, which at some point was »administered« by some young artists, coming mainly from the graffiti and VJ background. They tried to clean the space and keep it functioning as a sort of temporary Utopia, which one could use for as long as possible.

Now, a more recent phenomena is the »General school« which takes place at the National Centre for Dance. It is a platform for informal discussions, organized mainly by Vlad Nanc, Cristi Neagoe, Constantin Vica and others. In a way it synthesizes all sorts of ideas that have been around for a long time, related to a free school. It has this pedagogical aspect, but is mainly determined by the needs of an already existing group to restructure and reinvent itself, after it has functioned in other formats.

There is a certain nomadic feeling within communities; each one absorbs from the other one

Are there some cool places that are more official, where one can go without being an insider?

Two of the places where everybody goes, sooner or later, either as a local or foreigner, are the clubs Ota and Fabrica. Ota is kept going by its owner and has been in vogue for some time now, with little changes being made from time to time in the old charming house which hosts it and with the help of his famous soup. Fabrica, in a former factory, as its name implies – was a completely fucked-up squat in the beginning, with generators for the electric equipment and no toilets, whereas now it has become a trendy industrial kind of club, which attracts a lot of people.

I would say the future is secure. The density of new art spaces will grow

How do you see this scene developing in the coming years?

I would say the future is secure. The density of new art spaces will grow, mostly on commercial grounds, powered by a massive PR internal combustion engines promising and designing art hierarchies, art value at home being equated with international top selling names. A long list of obscenity scandals (such as the ones which have recently taken place, with artists being accused of defaming national and religious symbols) and publicity stunts will certainly attract new waves of censorship backed up by an outraged public. Enthusiastic underground communities will feed the »capital of cool« into the mainstream with the help of the advertising industry, making it all look fresh and radical chic. —

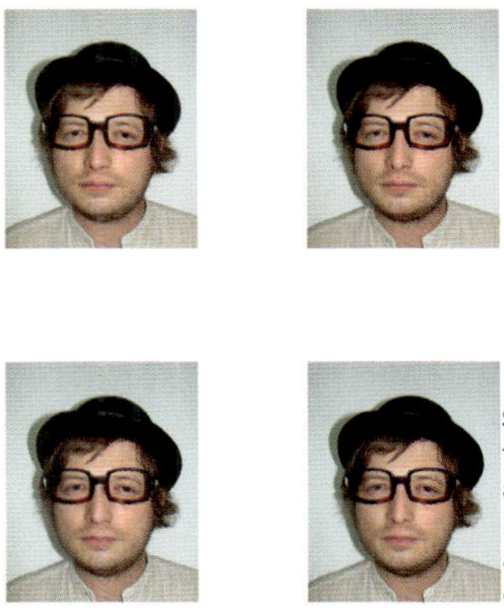

Stefan Tiron is a ubiquitous figure in the underground art and the cultural scenes in Bucharest. He is trained as an art historian and is now a curator and writer, coordinating the programme of a new art space called *ParadisGaraj* with Claudiu Cobilanschi.

Bucharest

By Maria Farcas

ART

❶ **MNAC: Muzeul National de Arta Contemporana (National Museum of Contemporary Art)** — It's hard not to think about the ironic and controversial location of the National Museum of Contemporary Art during the 30-minute walk around its endless fences. It sits at the back of Ceausescu's infamous piece de resistance, still known as the Casa Poporului (The House of the People), the second largest building in the world and it certainly is in competition for the most provocative location that a museum of contemporary art ever had. At its opening in 2004, there came a flood of critique and outrage. While still accused of lacking cultural vision, pushing young artists towards the margins and lacking cultural grants or creative and research scholarships, the museum has held numerous internationally focused exhibitions as well as some by Romanian artists.

Str. Izvor 2-4, (021 318 91 37)
Metro 1, 2, 3: Piata Unirii
Wed-Sun 10 am to 6 pm
Full price admission 5 RON
www.mnac.ro

❷ **Pavilion Unicredit** — In a time when venues for contemporary art are closing down or being pushed to the margins, a permanent centre for contemporary

art has been founded with the support of a bank. Apart from the three or four exhibitions every year, Pavilion Unicredit functions as an important source of information with its Contemporary Art Archive (created by the artists Lia and Dan Perjovschi) and Pavilion Resource Room (a non-archive by Razvan Ion and Eugen Radescu). By promoting critical thinking and the understanding of art and cultural institutions, Pavilion Unicredit hopes to dissipate the stress and ignorance that prevents the general public from confidently entering any space dedicated to contemporary art. Only time will tell whether their ambitious plans will turn into reality.

Sos. Nicolae Titulescu 1, (031 103 41 31)
Metro 2, 3, tram 20, 24, 45, bus 300: Piata Victoriei
Tue-Fri noon to 7 pm, Sat-Sun 2 pm to 9 pm
www.pavilionunicredit.ro

❸ **Centrul de Introspectie Vizuala (Centre for Visual Introspection)** — Proclaiming itself an interdisciplinary laboratory aiming to stimulate the cultural scene in Bucharest, the newly founded Cen-

tre for Visual Introspection is set to explore Romanian cultural production. While questioning the contemporary social and cultural space, the centre also subjects itself to the less introspective task of developing projects with direct social potential. Alina Serban, the director and also Romanian pavilion curator of the Venice Biennale brings a strong theoretical and curatorial support to the gallery, which is rare in most art spaces in Bucharest.

Str. Biserica Enei 16, (021 314 22 98)
Metro 2: Universitate
Wed-Thur 2 pm to 6 pm, Fri-Sat noon to 5 pm
www.pplus4.ro

❹ **Galeria Posibila** — It's not a white cube and it's not easy to find in the maze of streets in old Bucharest, but if you

want to buy good Romanian art, Galeria Posibila is the place to visit. Since opening in 2003, owner Matei Ciltia has embarked on the difficult journey of improving art awareness among the public and of regulating the backward art market. The gallery enthusiastically promotes, exhibits and sells work by young Romanian artists including, among others, Roman Tolici, Gheorghe Fikl and Gili Mocanu.

Str. Popa Petre 6, (021 211 79 33)
Trolleybus 66: Eminescu
Opening times depend on events
www.posibila.ro

❺ **Galeria Karousel** — Nowadays nearly everyone owns a photo camera and alas, too many think of themselves as artists. With a gallery in Bucharest exclusively dedicated to art photography, owner Violeta Sarbu took up the daring mission of educating the public about not necessarily matching the photos on the walls with the sofa upholstery and actually paying for good contemporary photography. The gallery exhibits established Romanian and international photographers – many involved in fashion and commercial photography, as well as emerging talents.

Str. George Calinescu 5A, (0742 055 888)
Bus 301, 331, 131: Piata Dorobanti
Mon-Fri noon to 8 pm, Sat 11 am to 4 pm
www.karousel.ro

❻ **H'Art Gallery** — Dan Popescu founded the Gallery in 2002 in the space of a former Communist grocery store. Neither an entirely non-conventional venue nor a white cube, the gallery managed successfully to shock and shake the still inert and conservative contemporary market with several controversial shows. In a scandal-surrounded exhibition, proving once again that any bad publicity is good publicity, the Romanian Orthodox Church scornfully accused H'Art of blasphemy.

Str. Mihai Eminescu 105-107,
(021 210 83 51)
Metro 2: Piata Romana
Mon-Fri 1 pm-to 6 pm, Sat 2 pm to 6 pm
www.hartgallery.ro

❼ **ParadisGaraj (Paradise Garage)** — There's always a garage hidden somewhere in the underground of Bucharest ready to be invaded by people who want to flash around creatively. The tiny courtyard-cum-garage became a guerrilla project-space open to loads of activities involving information and »intelligence« trafficking, from various presentations, screenings and exhibitions to simply as a friendly place for networking and any kind of cultural exchange. Enthusiastic initiators of, and guides through, this experimental safari are Stefan Tiron and Claudiu Cobilanschi.

Str. Batistei 20, (0728 374 007)
Metro 2: Universitate
Opening times depend on events
www.feeder.ro

❽ **Galeria Andreiana Mihail** — Andreiana Mihail runs this eponymous gallery engaged in the crusade of promoting promising Romanian artists beyond the boundaries of a country in which several decades of severe Communism didn't do much good to contemporary art's status. In the successful commercial awakening that followed, this gallery was among the first to participate at the Nada Miami and Art Basel.

Str. Pandele Tarusanu 4, (0722 650 221)
Metro 3, 4: Gara de Nord
Wed-Fri 2 pm to 6 pm, Sat 1 pm to 4 pm
www.andreianamihail.com

❾ **Galeria Laika** — This gallery is an artist-run-space that opened in 2008 in Cluj-Napoca and Bucharest (artists Mircea Suciu and Serban Savu), which generously seeks to promote very young emerging artists as well as atypical, »problematic and fragile« projects by already internationally established artists. With their experimental nature, hinted at by the name of the gallery (the first dog launched into space), Laika Gallery is a freshly independent alternative to commercial galleries and successfully avoids art managers, dealers and gallery owners in its relationship with art.

Str. Christian Tell 21, (0723 320 931)
Metro 2: Piata Romana
By appointment
www.laikaars.blogspot.com

⑩ CND: Centrul National al Dansului (National Centre of Dance) — The third and fourth floors of the Teatrul National (National Theatre) witness some of the most edgy movements in Romania, with developments in dance, performance,

choreography, conceptual or theatre-dance shows. Founded in 2004, the National Centre of Dance is one of the few examples of a viable state institution, having a coherent program and fresh, interesting artistic discourses that invite reflection and dialogue. In warm weather, check out La Motoare, the rooftop terrace in the same building. It's huge and lively, with a more than welcome breeze.

B-dul Nicolae Balcescu 2, (021 318 86 76)
Metro 2: Universitate
www.cndb.ro

ART EVENTS

BB: Bienala Internationala de Arta Contemporana Bukaresti (Bucharest International Biennial for Contemporary Art) — This event takes place in various sites every two years in Bucharest and was founded by the art magazine *Pavillion* in 2005. The continuously changing curators show the latest and, above all, young international positions in contemporary art (from video to painting), although until now, Romanian artists have only played a limited role. The extensive accompanying program with discussions, readings and performances constitutes an important focal point. The curator of the 10. Biennial for 2010 is the German Felix Vogel (born in 1987!).

Festival office:
PO Box 26 03 90, (031 103 41 31),
www.bucharestbiennale.org

Bienala Tinerilor Artisti (Biennial of Young Artists) — This biennial is one of Bucharest's largest periodic events in the domain of visual arts, aiming to display and promote the art of young contemporary artists in a regional and international context. The project was designed to combine theoretical and artistic discourses and brings together artists, curators, art critics, journalists,

cultural operators, researchers, and visual culture theoreticians. The META Cultural Foundation has organised the biennial since 2004. Held in October.

Festival office:
META Cultural Foundation
Str. Luiggi Galvani 61-63,
(0722 381 243)
www.metacult.ro

Rokolectiv Festival — Don't be misled by the »rok« in the name; amazingly, it has nothing to do with rock music, quite the contrary. It's a cornucopia of everything electronic: genres, approaches and techniques as well as the visual arts born in relation to it. The festival is held every spring at several locations.

www.rokolectiv.ro

Cinema E-Uranus — Perfect for the torrid Bucharest summers, E-Uranus is a charming, laid-back open-air cinema that suddenly sprang to life in 2008 in the middle of a derelict courtyard surrounded by 19th century industrial architecture. Every evening after sunset, you can have a beer and watch an excellent, usually European, film (subtitled). Films are shown every summer after sunset.

Str. Uranus 144, (031 345 27)
Metro 1, 2, 3, tram 32: Piata Unirii
Full price admission 11 RON

ART OUTSIDE OF BUCHAREST

Plan B Gallery — Many of the successful young names in Romanian contemporary art were first exhibited by this smart gallery in the provincial town of Cluj, in the heart of Transylvania, but Plan B really has nothing to do with the provinciality of the Romanian art market. It's alive, connected to the international scene and has recently opened a second Plan B in Berlin. Mihai Pop, the friendly owner, will happily chat with you about hot young Romanian artists, about Cluj, Berlin, art and other stuff.

Str. Albert Einstein 14, Cluj, (0742 504 901)
Tue-Fri 4 pm to 7 pm
www.plan-b.ro

Periferic – Bienala de Arta Contemporana Iasi (Biennale for Contemporay Art Iasi) – – Initiated in 1997 by Romanian artist Matei Bejenaru, Peripheric started as a performance festival and then developed into an international art biennial organized in Iasi. Apart from putting the sleepy Moldavian town on the international map of contemporary art, the biennial aims at involving and educating the public in order to grant it a dynamic access and understanding of contemporary art events. Approximately a six or seven hour train ride from Bucharest.

Biennial office:
Of. Postal 7, Iasi, (023 223 7486)
www.periferic.org

Anonimul International Independent Film Festival — Sfantu Gheorghe is a remote village deep into the Danube Delta, where the river embraces the sea through murky and beautiful canals. If you're there in August, you can easily bump into pink pelicans, huge sheatfish and various famous actors/directors. Don't expect any tourist facilities; everything is stripped to bare necessities, with a lot of fish meals, accommodation in the Anonimul camping site or fishermen's guesthouses. There is access only by boat, from the port town of Tulcea.

www.festival-anonimul.ro

For ship schedules check
www.navrom.x3m.ro
www.sfantugherghe.ro

ALTERNATIVE SIGHTSEEING

❶❶ Manastirea Cernica (The Cernica Monastery) — For a view of the imagery and customs of the Romanian Orthodox Church, or at least for a glimpse at the gloomy black frocks and long beards of monks flapping against the dazzling white of the monastery's fortified walls, visit Cernica Monastery (it is located about 20km southeast of the city centre). Surrounded by forest and nestled in the middle of a small island in Lake Cernica, the beautiful compound was built at the beginning of the 17th century and contains two churches, several chapels, a cemetery and a museum. A peaceful retreat, though not on weekends or religious holidays.

Cernica: Ilfov, (021 351 17 37)
Bus 410 or 459 from metro 1: Pantelimon to the monastery gates (approx. 20 minutes)
www.cernica.go.ro

❶❷ Insula Lacul Morii (Lacul Morii Island) — A manmade island on a manmade lake built on a cemetery and surrounded by Communist blocks of apartments. That's the stuff urban legends are made of. In summer, bold swimmers ignore the dirty waters and the multitude of crosses, marking the earthly departure of other bold swimmers, and dare take a plunge in Lake Morii. The island was one of those Socialist wonderful-on-paper projects, an ideal place for the contended Communist masses to spend their Sundays at leisure. It now remains an interesting place for a picnic among recent Neo-classical Communist ruins: a monumental pavilion, some fountains, some columns and occasionally, peacefully grazing sheep.

Metro 3: Crangasi

DAYTRIPS

Palatul Mogosoaia (Mogosoaia Palace) — Built by Prince Brancoveanu as a summer residence at the end of 16th century, this palace (15 km northwest of Bucharest) is an interesting mixture of Wallachian and Byzantine styles with traces of Italian Renaissance influences. It was seized by the Communists in the '50s and turned into a museum until 1970 when Ceausescu closed it down. It again serves as a museum. If you walk around the compound, you might stumble into Lenin's huge feet, knocked down and abandoned after having been proudly erect in front of Bucharest's Press House, an eloquent example of Soviet architecture.

Str. Valea Parcului 1,
(021 350 66 19 or 021 350 66 20)
Tram 20 from Gara de Nord to the end station, then bus 460: Mogosoaia
Tue-Sun 10 am to 6 pm
Full price admission 5.50 RON

Region of Sinaia — For a mouthful of fresh air after the dusty streets of Bucharest, the 120 km distant Sinaia, the »Pearl of the Carpathians« as Romanians proudly call it, might be a good idea. It has magnificent mountain scenery, breathtaking hiking trails and the Peles Palace, the summer residence of Romania's royals. Eclectic in style, the Peles Palace was built at the end of the 19th century in a Romantic Neo-Renaissance style, boasting Italian elegance, German aesthetics and French Baroque excessiveness.

Peles Palace:
Pelesului 2, Sinaia, Judet Prahova,
(0244 310 918)
Many trains from Gara de Nord to Sinaia (approx. 1.45h):
Summer (15 May-15 Sep): Tue 11 am to 5 pm, Wed-Sun 9 am to 5 pm
Winter (16 Sep-14 May): Wed 11 am to 5 pm, Thur-Sun 9 am to 5 pm
Full price admission 17 RON
www.peles.ro

SHOPPING

⓭ Muzeul Taranului Roman Shop (Romanian Peasant Museum Shop) — If you're into folk art or at least have a fancy for the heavily embroidered hippie blouses that were the trend in the '70s, then this shop is a must. Apart from a small, negligible offering of inescapable kitschy souvenirs, the shop has the most marvellous selection of authentic old handicrafts and traditional costumes, splendid rugs and beautiful icons, painted eggs and pottery from different Romanian provinces. Upstairs you can have tea in the well-endowed Carturesti bookshop. Of course, the museum itself is touchingly lovely, indisputably the best in Bucharest.

Sos. Kiseleff 3, (021 317 96 61)
Metro 2, 3: Piata Victoriei
Tue-Sun 10 am to 6 pm
www.muzeultaranuluiroman.ro

⓮ Libraria Carturesti (Carturesti bookshop) — The Carturesti bookshop (actually a chain) has beautifully and tastefully conquered two formerly rundown, now exquisitely restored, aristocratic villas in the heart of Bucharest. It's a sheer pleasure to amble among rows of stylish, high-ceilinged rooms full of books, travel guides, art books, CDs, rare wine, tea tableware and postcards. There's also an atmospheric tea-room as well as underground exhibition spaces. There's a good selection of English books.

Str. Arthur Verona 13, (021 317 34 59)
Metro 2: Piata Romana
Mon-Fri 10 am to 9 pm,
Sat-Sun 11 am to 9 pm
www.carturesti.ro

⓯ Babaluna — Lodged in a typical Bucharest bourgeois villa on a sleepy street in the middle of town, Babaluna will tempt you with a good selection of young Romanian designers, some small international designer labels as well as an interesting pick of vintage items. Owners DJ Sleek and designer Irina Marinescu will happily chat with you if around. In the same building on the first floor, you can visit the freshly launched Laika artist-run space (see »art«). Slowly but surely, a creative community is building a nest here.

Christian Tell 21, (0724 132 241)
Metro 2: Piata Romana
Mon-Sat 12 am to 8 pm
www.christiantell21.blogspot.com

⓰ Târgul de vechituri Drumul Taberei (Drumul Taberei Flea Market) — To visit the weekend flea market on the western margin of Bucharest is to marvel at the involuntary and often humorous creativity fuelled by kitsch and scarcity. You can't but be amazed at what people will sell: used toilet seats to rusty technical parts to shoes worn-out beyond salvation to decent antiques to a fabulous 80's leather blouse. Even if you don't emerge with a great find, the market remains an interesting anthropological window into Romania's recent past. Most of the sellers are dirt poor, so don't be dispirited if bargaining can become rather grim. If you get the »flea fatigue«, you can smell your way to one of the kiosks that sell the famous »mici« – sausages of pork, lamb and garlic.

Valea Cascadelor
Tram and bus 137: Frigocom
Sat, Sun 6 am to noon
Full price admission 2 RON

⓱ The ARK — Recently opened in a rundown, but nevertheless fascinating, area of old Bucharest, The Ark is the first sign of a neighbourhood revival. It's an admirable project that saved a wonderful historical building from col-

lapse and created a new contemporary space that is going to host exhibitions, concerts, fairs and events. One of its first residents was Rozalb de Mura, a fashion label that stormed the scene with its nonconformist attitude, intriguing storytelling and clothes. There is a shop on the ground floor. Within the Romanian Peasant Market every Saturday and Sunday (8 am to 12 noon) the courtyard turns into a heaven for organic-seeking freaks: tomatoes that taste of tomatoes, home baked bread, walnut and basil goat cheese in fir bark, etc.

Calea Rahovei 196 A, (0752 218 555)
Metro 1, 2: Piata Unirii, then tram 32: third stop
Mon-Fri 11 am to 6 pm
www.theark.ro

CAFÉS

⓲ Ceainaria La Metoc (La Metoc Teahouse) — The best thing about the teahouse is that there's nothing contemporary about it. It's a wild, peaceful garden of lilac and fig trees in a charming street, with tables and sofas cuddled under bushes, good tea and muffled conversation, lazy cats and an out-of-time atmosphere. A true oasis, this teahouse is a nostalgic reminder of what Bucharest would have looked like without the Communist demolition craze.

Str. Popa Rusu 21, (0722 725 533)
Trolleybus: Armeneasca
May-October
Daily noon to 12 am (call in advance)

⓳ French Bakery — It's a Bucharest patisserie chain that one would want multiplied by the thousands. The eight cafe-patisseries are extremely stylish (their owner Venera Arapu is a fashion and interior designer) and sell mouth-watering, sinfully delicious desserts. How could one resist the sound, let alone the taste of something like this: feuillantine mousse, religieuse au chocolat, cake aux fruits rouges? These cafes are the perfect place to have a quick, light lunch of salad, quiche or pie. French Bakery the Restaurant, in the centre of the city, even comes with a more sophisticated lunch menu.

Piata Romana, (021 310 33 02)
Metro 2: Piata Romana
Daily 9 am to 9 pm
Visa, Mastercard, American Express
www.frenchbakery.ro

⓴ Planters Café — Huge windows, high ceilings, low chairs and during the summer, Persian carpets on the front lawn. Located in the city centre, near Cismigiu Park, Planters Café has a comfortable, laid-back atmosphere with good coffee and quick sandwiches for those who missed breakfast and lunch.

Str. Stirbei Voda 68, (0722 200 072)
Metro 2: Piata Romana (Cismigiu park)
Daily 8.30 am to the last client

RESTAURANTS

㉑ La Mandragora — Mandragora is the Latin for mandrake and it is obviously a bold gesture to name a restaurant after a poisonous plant used by ancient sorcerers in magic rituals. The restaurant has a classy but nevertheless edgy ambiance, a contemporary decor and discreet, efficient service. German chef Paul Peter Kopij will enchant you with his superbly sophisticated dishes. For the grande finale, try the creme brulee with homemade green apple ice cream. Bewitching! Main dishes from 40 RON.

Str. Mendeleev 29, (021 319 75 92)
Metro 2: Piata Romana
Mon-Fri noon to 3 pm, 6 pm to 12 am;
Sat 6 pm to 11 pm
Visa, Mastercard, American Express

22 Count Dracula — Here you can step into the realm of His Highness of Supreme Kitsch. You can have some sanguinary supper surrounded by a wolf, a wild boar, an antlered stag and a Carpathian bear grinning stiffly at you from the walls in the Hunting Lodge, or from your plate. You might try the Evil salad or some blood-red Transfusion, Crucifix or Children of the Night cocktails in the Medieval room, among armour, crossed halberds and Vlad Tepes portraits. If you're lucky enough to be seated in the Chapel – an impressive cross-breed of Medieval prison and hardcore brothel, you'll have the chance to meet the man. Pushing back the cobwebs of his coffin, Dracula himself emerges with typical demonic laughter, black-cloaked, white-faced, red-lipped, the whole lot. Your wallet might bleed a little after this vampiresque experience, not lethally though. Main dishes from 35 RON.

Splaiul Independentei 8A, (0720 21 12 01)
Metro 1, 2: Piata Unirii
Daily 1 pm to 12 am
Visa, Mastercard, American Express
www.count-dracula.ro

23 Balthazar — It's a joy to dine at the flashy Balthazar restaurant, from the beautiful villa to the sophisticated décor, the designer furniture and above all the refined French-Asian fusion cuisine. Lit with candles, it has a stylish atmosphere and impossibly chic female customers. Put on something nice and enjoy the salmon with mascarpone and truffles, bathed in red orange sauce. Main dishes from 34 RON.

Str. Dumbrava Rosie 2, (021 212 14 60)
Metro 2: Piata Romana
Daily noon to 12 am
Visa, Mastercard, American Express
www.balthazar.ro

24 Il Gattopardo Blu — If you want to have a taste of mediocre cuisine in one of Bucharest's most beautiful mansions, don't miss Il Gattopardo Blu. This villa, with a charmingly decrepit air, features marble columns, crystal chandeliers, dim gilded mirrors, putti-painted ceilings and poorly dressed writers sipping a coffee here and there. In spite of its beauty and probably due to its mediocrity, the restaurant is almost always deserted. The shaded garden at the back is a welcome break away from the impossible heat of a summer's day in Bucharest. Main dishes from 25 RON.

Calea Victoriei 115, (021 319 65 95)
Metro 2: Piata Romana
Daily noon to midnight
Visa, Mastercard, American Express

25 Papa la Shoni — Bucharest is definitely not a shining star on the world gastronomic firmament. Therefore when you stumble upon the delicious Transylvanian delicacies such as chicken with sour cherry sauce or pork soup with tarragon within Papa la Shoni's menu, you treasure them dearly.

Due to the locale's anonymous entrance, its unreliable opening hours and the fact that no one answers the phone, managing to eat there is equal to a sort of culinary victory. Main dishes from 17 RON.

Str. Sfintii Voievozi 13, (0771 437 152)
Metro 2: Piata Romana
Daily 1 pm to 11pm
www.papalasoni.ro

㉖ Caru' cu bere (Beer Wagon) — Built in the late 19th century, Caru' cu bere used to be a favourite hangout for Romanian inter-war intelligentsia. When you are pushed through the revolving doors into the opulent Neo-Gothic interior, you might think for a second that you have inadvertently stepped into a cathedral. You're quickly brought down to earth by the loud chatter and the blaring traditional music and in the evenings, by some live pseudo-traditional dance. The Romanian/German cuisine is not as flamboyant though. If you like meat, you'll be all right. Home-brewed beer, of course. Main dishes from 16 RON.

Str. Stavropoleos 3, (021 313 75 60)
Mon-Thur, Sun 8 am to 12 am,
Fri, Sat 8 am to 2am
Visa, Mastercard, American Express
www.carucubere.ro

PARTY

㉗ Ota's bar — Thursday night soups at Ota's became so famous within the young creative Bucharest crowd and beyond, that it soon became clear it was no longer possible to eat the soup, have an audible conversation or breathe for

that matter in the stuffy underground bar. Ota, owner and occasional chef, brilliantly anticipated the need for an after-hours bar with hip DJs, good cocktails and an unpretentious atmosphere. He sensibly decided to prepare the soups for quieter Wednesday nights.

Dr. Staicovici 26, (0721 840 723)
Metro 1, 3: Eroilor
Wed-Thur 10 pm to 4 am

㉘ Expirat / The Other Side — When the small underground Expirat club became so crowded it was evident that taking a plunge there was synonymous to a suicidal attempt, it was blessedly expanded with some more equally smoke-choked rooms. Simply named The Other Side, it's practically another club, heavily electronica oriented, much posher and with a trendier public. Same place, one admission fee, two clubs. On the downside: air still hardly breathable. On the upside: stand-up acts or readings by the Hydra Literature Society in the evenings.

Str. Ion Brezoianu 4, (0726 80 41 42)
Metro 2: Universitate
Wed, Fri, Sat 10 pm to 5 am
Full price admission 10 RON
www.expirat.org

㉙ Fabrica club — Three years ago, Fabrica was only a big space in a former leggings factory where underground parties were held. Now it's the best club in town in terms of concerts, from electro to hip-hop, funk, new wave, dub and all the permutations in between. The fresh design of the ground floor kept the raw, industrial feel and enlarged the chill-out area, allowing the space to be used as venue for other events as well including exhibitions, conferences, etc.

Str. 11 Iunie 50, (0753 227 422)
Metro 1, 2, 3, tram 32: Piata Unirii
Daily 11 am to1 am
www.fabrica-club.ro

㉚ Studio Martin — If God is a DJ, then Studio Martin in Bucharest is the ultimate heaven where the world's most famous DJs enrapture crowds from the shrines of their turn tables. Since 1993, the club has relentlessly set trends on Romanian electronica dance floors. It claims to have created a phenomenon in bringing house music to the bewildered Romanian masses.

Iancu De Hundoara 61, (021 230 32 43)
Metro 2: Piata Romana
Sat-Sun 10 pm to 5 am
www.studiomartin.ro

㉛ B52 — Underground, clouded with smoke, cheerful and with no claims whatsoever as to posh décor, B52 used to attract almost exclusively student-like crowds, so young that you might have heard a sincerely astonished »Do people still go out over 30?«. Due to the new program of live bands and DJs, the age limit has expanded a bit, so that you can spot people that look like they actually go to work the next day. Creative industries, mainly.

Str. Popa Tatu 4, (021 311 65 86)
Metro 2: Piata Romana
Thur-Fri 4 pm to 5 am, Sat-Sun 6 pm to 5 am
Full price admission 10 RON
www.clubb52.ro

㉜ Control Club — When Control Club arrived in 2008 to fill the enormous gap in rock, alternative and indie currents on the Bucharest music scene, hundreds must have cried »Halleluja!« It's big, it's boisterous, it's central, not too expensive, has frequent Romanian and international live acts and an unexpectedly clean toilet for a rock venue.

Str. Academiei 19, (0733 927 860)
Metro 2: Universitate
Mon-Sun 6 pm to 4 am
Full price admission 10 RON
www.control-club.ro

KIDS

33 Blue Servicii — This service offers a database with 350 potential employees who offer babysitting, occasional house keeping and adult daycare in Bucharest. The company provides babysitter courses for their staff and has its own psychologist who tests and helps sitters and parents.

Str. Batistei 5, et. 5, apt. 12b,
(0727 007 799)
Metro 2: Universitate
Mon-Fri 8 am to 6.30 pm
www.blu.ro

34 Arlechino Club — An indoor playground of approximately 200m² for kids from 2 years up to the age of 12 situated in the very centre of the city, only a five-minute walk from the Casa Poporului (People's House). The club offers a multilevel labyrinth, tunnels, ball-pools and so forth, babysitting for children over 4 years old and operates a snack and espresso bar for parents and hungry kids. Attention: Crowded on the weekend!

B-dul Unirii 9, (021 335 43 99)
Metro 1, 2: Piata Unirii
Mon-Sun 10.30 am to 9.30 pm
Admission for the play area: 17 RON (Mon-Fri), 19 RON (Sat-Sun)
www.arlechinoclub.ro

SLEEP

35 Carol Parc Hotel — If you are a king or suddenly feel the urge to be treated like one while in Bucharest, then the Carol Parc Hotel (even the name comes from Romania's first king) is the place to indulge yourself. It's the definition of luxury: king-size beds, marble, LCD TVs, Bulgari-Armani cosmetics, enormous rooms, sumptuous décor and a royal breakfast with Persian caviar and Moet&Chandon champagne. In the elevator you might bump into Sting or France's president – movie and pop stars, politicians and top executives prefer it for its grandeur and secluded location. Double rooms from € 250.

Str. Aleea Suter 23-25, (021 336 33 77)
Metro 1, 2: Piata Unirii
www.carolparchotel.ro

36 K+K Elisabeta Hotel — This recently opened hotel boasts a great location in the middle of town, good taste and flawless service. Minimalist design with flashes of red and yellow here and there, very small but all in all comfortable rooms with TV, internet and minibar. Other amenities include a small sauna and fitness room and a ground floor bistro. For night owls: The hotel offers breakfast until 11am, on weekends even to 12 noon. Double rooms from € 100.

Str. Slanic 26, (021 311 86 31)
Metro 2: Universitate
www.kkhotels.com

❸❼ **Rembrandt Hotel** — The owner who bought and restored the Rembrandt Hotel understood the quintessence of travellers' needs. A thoughtful, soothing atmosphere that combines ultimate comfort, sleek design, discretion and a central location. The mattresses are excellent, the floors and furniture are made of real wood, the linens are crispy white and the staff is friendly and eager to please. If you like panoramic views, ask for the top-room floor with balcony: a splendid view of the city with the Casa Poporului (People's House) like a huge cherry on top. Double rooms from € 99.

Smardan 11, (031 393 15)
Metro 2: Universitate
www.rembrandt.ro

Apartments — Renting an apartment in Bucharest is a thrifty and perhaps unusual alternative to the usual hotels, especially when one is travelling in a large group or with family, or when the planned trip is a little longer than usual. These agencies offer apartments in all the city districts with various accommodations, in villas as well as in apartment houses. Many offer similar amenities to hotels: airport transfer, laundry service, internet, spa services, etc. From about € 40 a night.

(021 314 55 56), www.efectcapital.ro
(0741 24 34 30), www.princeresidence.it
(0722 36 75 68), www.for-rent.ro

GOOD TO KNOW

Tourist Information
Unfortunately there is none

INTERNET

37 Cafepedia — A café in the center of Bucharest which offers free Wi-Fi internet, coffee, sandwiches, newspapers. A friendly and helpful stuff. Three other places in town. You find the adresses on the website.

B-dul Regina Elisabeta 11-13 (021 10 44 51)
Metro 2: Universitate
www.cafepedia.eu

MEDIA

www.idea.ro/revista — It presents relevant events and institutions on the local and international scene and functions as an archive of very importantcontemporary texts on art theory. Romanian/English.

www.omagiu.com — Young urban Romanians have long been yearning for an *ID*-cum-*Dazed&Confused* sort of magazine. *Omagiu* readily came to fulfil that need. It's cool, it's flashy, it's artsy, and a bit chaotic here and there; each issue is grouped around a theme, with contributions about art, design, photography, illustration, fashion and everything in between, scanning the creative Romanian reality and proclaiming itself a »guide through the aesthetic jungle of mass market consumerism«. Romanian/English.

TRANSPORT

From the airport — Baneasa Aurel Vlaicu International Airport is located north of the city centre and can be reached by taxi or by bus. Take a Fly Taxi (9411) to the centre for approx. 70 RON. The Express Bus 783 leaves from the international departure terminal every 30 minutes from 5.23 am to 11.53 pm and takes approx. 40 min to the city centre. A ticket costs 7 RON.

Taxis — Always get into trusted taxi companies (even though it's a bit difficult to spot the difference). Don't get into any taxi whose tariff exceeds 2 RON per kilometre. The best way to get a taxi is by calling one of the following: Alfa (9481), Leone (9425), Meridian (9444), Prof Taxi (9422), Taxi 2000 (9494).

Public transport — There is an efficient public transportation system in Bucharest. It operates between 5 am and 11.30 pm. Tickets have to be purchased ahead of time (at any kiosk displaying the RATBI logo) and stamped upon boarding. Single tickets cost 1.30 RON, 1-day-tickets 8.00 RON, 7-day-tickets 17 RON.

Car — Traffic in Bucharest is infernal! The speed limit if not otherwise marked is 50 km/h. No alcohol is allowed when driving. Parking lots are rare in this city. Most drivers don't respect traffic rules so be aware even as pedestrian!

Important Numbers

Telephone country and city code	*+40 21 or +40 31 (there are two different phone companies)*
Telephone information	*931*
Police	*955*
Fire Brigade	*981*
First Aid	*961 or 973*
Anti-corruption unit	*982 22 22*
24h-Pharmacy	*Farmacia Dona, Magheru 32-34, (021 316 54 07) Metro 2: Piata Romana, bus 126, 131, 168, 226, 301, 331, 368, trolleybus 79, 86*

City in Numbers

1 Euro	*ca. 4.30 RON (Leu)*
Inhabitants	*1.9 Mio*
Average income	*€ 474*
Cup of coffee	*8 RON*
Bottle of beer	*7 RON (ca. € 1.65)*
Cigarettes	*6.30 RON (ca. € 1.50)*
Most talked about artists	*Mircea Cantor, Jon Grigorescu, Dan Perjovschi,*
Collectors of contemporary art	*2*
Biggest art scandal	*The location of the MNCA in former dictator Ceausescu's monstrous palace , today under the same roof with the Romanian parliament*

Short Art History BUCHAREST

1966 The 111 Group is founded in Timisoara, later to become the Sigma Group. The group was multi-disciplinary, promoting art pedagogy, constructivist and kinetic ideas and was highly influential in changing the aesthetic vocabularies of the time.

1975 Ion Grigorescu takes the photographs for the series *Electoral Meeting,* in which members of the secret police are observed alongside the participants at the Communist Party meeting they were infiltrating and supervising.

1986 Alexandru Antik performs *The Dream Hasn't Perished* for a small group of colleagues in the basement of a pharmacy in Sibiu. The action is interrupted by the secret police before it can be finished.

1993 The Zona Festival for performance art, organized by Ileana Pintilie in Timisoara, takes place for the first time. The artist Dan Perjovschi has »Romania« tattooed on his arm, which he has removed with a laser ten years later, without being able to erase it completely. As if in acknowledgement, he still lives in Bucharest.

1997 The fourth annual exhibition of the Soros Centre for Contemporary Art Bucharest is the comprehensive *Experiment in Romanian Art since 1960,* curated by Alexandra Titu. The '90s seem to also underline the fact that an art history dominated by male artists is written mainly by women critics and curators like Ileana Pintilie, Alexandra Titu, Magda Carneci, Liviana Dan, Irina Cios and others.

2003 The Periferic 6 Biennial – *Prophetic Corners,* curated by Anders Kreuger, takes place in Iasi. In 2006, Iasi-based artist Cezar Lazarescu creates a picture with three identical mirrors and a written line: »Mirror mirror on the wall/ Which is the fairest biennial of all?« as a response to the three equally ambitious events of this kind taking place in Romania all in the same year.

2007 Romania joins the EU, more money flows in. *Spatiul Public Bucuresti | Public Art Bucharest 2007* takes place, a project curated by Marius Babias and Sabine Hentzsch. Agendas change, stakes are higher, art needs to reach beyond the narrow confines of its traditional institutions.

100

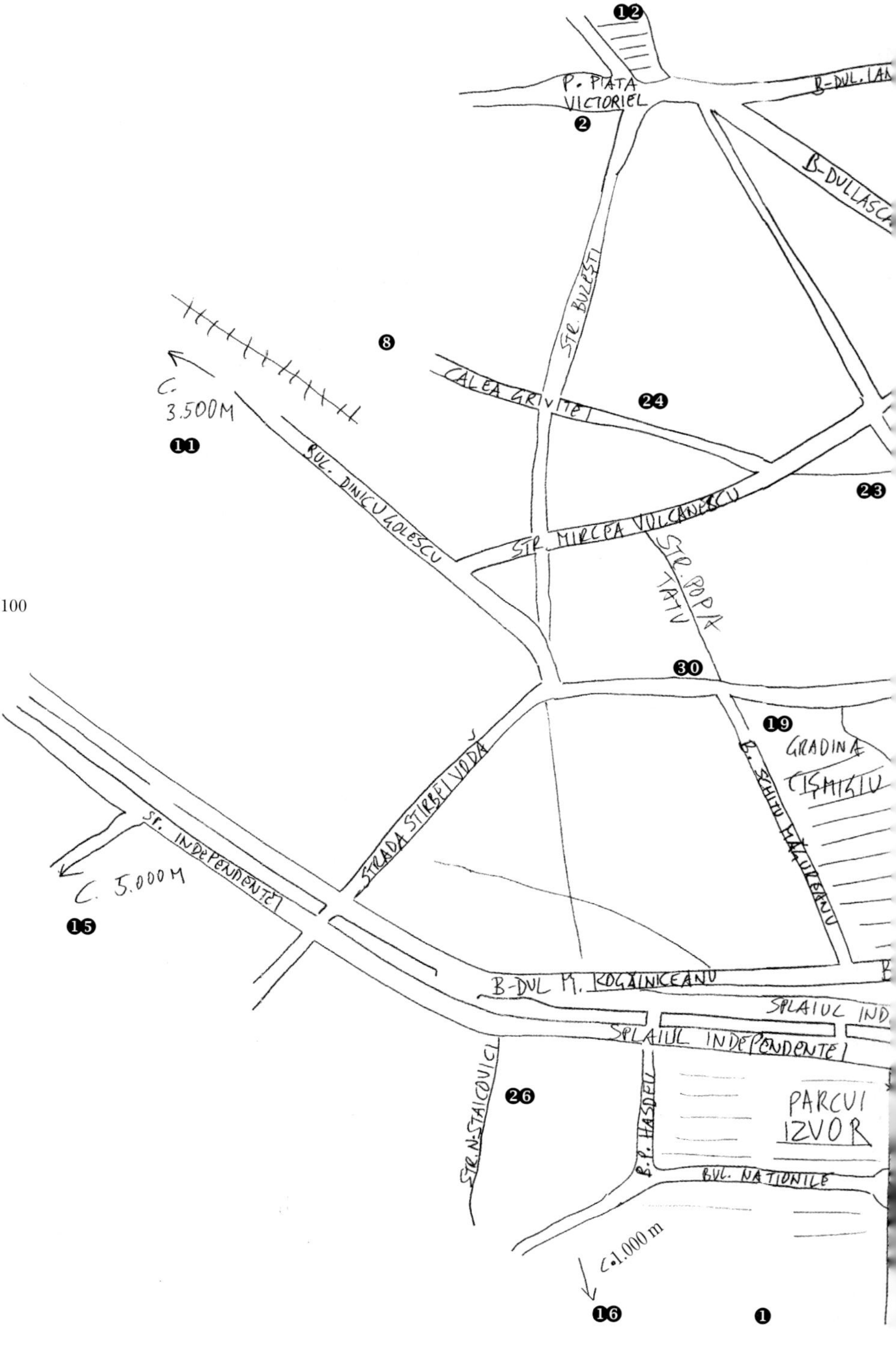

12
P. PIATA VICTORIEI
2
STR. BUZESTI
8
CALEA GRIVITEI
24
C. 3.500M
11
BUL. DINICU GOLESCU
STR. MIRCEA VULCANESCU
23
STR. POPA TATU
30
19
GRADINA CISMIGIU
B. SCHITU MAGUREANU
STRADA STIRBEI VODA
STR. INDEPENDENTEI
C. 5.000M
15
B-DUL M. KOGAINICEANU
SPLAIUL INDEPENDENTEI
STR. N. STAICOVICI
26
B. P. HASDEU
PARCUL IZVOR
BUL. NATIUNILE
c.1.000 m
16
1

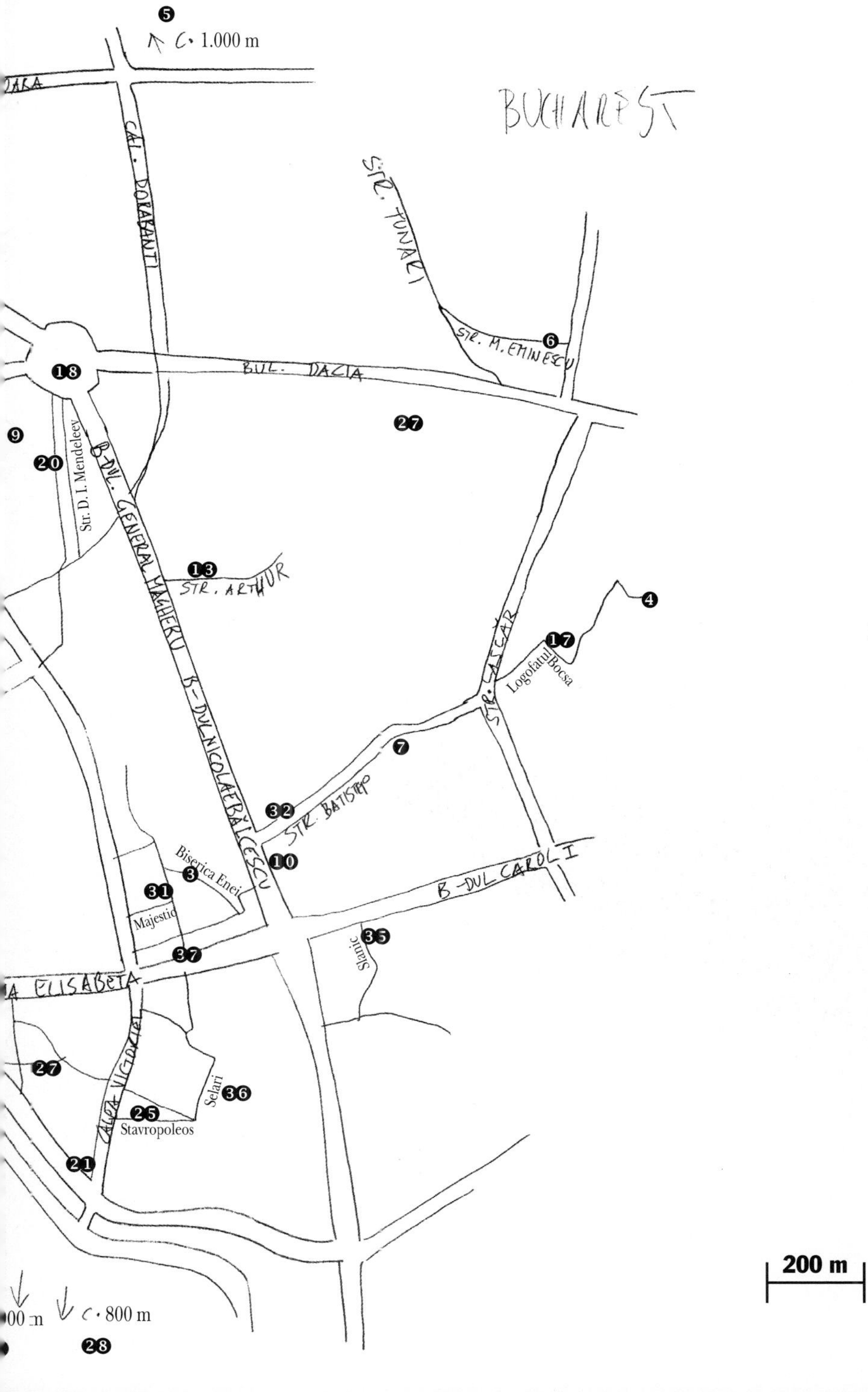

c. 1.000 m
BUCHAREST
CAL. DOROBANTI
STR. TUNARI
STR. M. EMINESCU
BUL. DACIA
Str. D. I. Mendeleev
B-DUL GENERAL MAGHERU
B-DUL NICOLAE BĂLCESCU
STR. ARTHUR
STR. LASCAR
Logofatul
Bocsa
STR. BATISTEI
Biserica Enei
B-DUL CAROL I
Majestic
Slanic
ELISABETA
CALEA VICTORIEI
Selari
Stavropoleos
c. 800 m
200 m

Budapest

Dunapart

Andrássy Avenue

The West Balkans – A Genie in a Bottle

Why Budapest is a city of copies, of paraphrases and an essentially eclectic concentration.

By József Készman

As an Eastern European metropolis, Budapest experienced its heyday during the fin de siecle and, in their heart of hearts, many of its residents would prefer to still live in that period. Thanks to nostalgia and a peculiar relationship to the past, Budapest is a city of copies, of paraphrases, an essentially eclectic concentration. It is a city that seeks to find its identity in the past and is nevertheless blind to its own microcosm and unable to shape it consciously. The cityscape, defined by historicization, Art Nouveau and eclecticism, is host to important modernist initiatives. Similarly indelible is the mark of decades of Socialism, of Socialist realism, the mediocre reinforced-concrete architecture, the sprawling housing estates and industrial plants. This strange fabric provides a spectacular backdrop: the Hungarian capital has served as the set for many world famous films. The oversized centre of what was once »the most cheerful barrack« in the Soviet camp, used to offer a number of alternative scenes and lifestyles for its city dwellers (music clubs, like Black Hole, which were unique in Socialist countries), but it barely seems original now in a global context.

The annual Sziget Festival is nonetheless the largest popular music event in Central and Eastern Europe. A few figures, if you please. The largest professional association of Hungarian creative artists, MAOE, has 7.000 visual artist members, 200 to 300 of whom belong to the contemporary scene. 60 to 80 of the latter can claim to produce art that makes a contribution to the contemporary discourse, but only eight or nine can lay claim to international renown.

What is the reason? Literature and music were always more dominant than the visual arts in Hungarian education and culture, and this is true of the contemporary milieu as well. The visual arts

Tram in Budapest's 10th district

Erzsébet Square at night

Christmas market in Vörösmarty Square

National Theatre

are not very present in the public mind, and its makers are barely unified in their vision of its position. For decades, artists were cut off from the chance to network, to inform themselves about current problems and theoretical issues. Contemporary Hungarian art has been characterized by a craving for information, an eagerness to comply with Western standards, a compulsive desire to be avant-garde, thanks perhaps to an unacknowledged set of values, and an outlook in which conceptualism is considered the apex of art. The opinion-makers of the art scene exert their influence through printed and electronic media *(Balkon, Új Müvészet, Praesens, Artmagazin, Műértő*, and the online magazine *exindex)*. The most important institutions for contemporary art in Budapest are Műcsarnok (Kunsthalle), Ludwig Múzeum – Museum of Contemporary Art, the Stúdió Galéria (run by F.K.S.E. – Association of Young Fine Artists), Trafó, the ICA-D (which may be in Dunaújváros, 60 kilometres away, but is certainly still within the capital's sphere of influence), and a number of for-profit exhibition spaces and private galleries.

Before the political transition in 1989, the commissions and regular purchases of the paternalist state provided artists with a livelihood. What succeeded state patronage, namely the present system of competitions and grants, is unable to sustain the scene itself. There is little method in the support offered to culture; what is given is distributed inefficiently, and no government to date has come up with a strategic concept to settle the issue. There are uncovered areas, and artistic production itself has changed in character. Works are very often projects, processes that branch into any number of directions, and often have the profundity of academic research. After the transition, a tradition was revived which had been in suspended animation for forty years: art collecting. At present, about fifty galleries in this city of two million deal with contemporary art. Only five or six of them, however, can lay claim to professionalism or international repute. Restricted as the market is, it is the area where the most dynamic development is to be expected and in fact a new style, technorealism, already owes its success to these galleries. Most of those active on the Budapest scene seem to live in a state of expectation, in hope that a curator may emerge, a god who will save them and give them their place on the map of world art – as a city that is looking for its place in the region. The way out is cooperation, based on an active dialogue and made possible by artist-in-residence programs and grants. True inspiration may come from the new generations, who, if they circumvent the wrong questions posed by their predecessors, may overcome compulsions and constraints and establish natural links with the universal discourse concerning contemporary art. —

Most of those active on the Budapest scene seem to live in a state of expectation

Hot springs, hot prices

The Hungarian art market is booming like never before, despite the financial crisis. The collector couple *Katalin Spengler* and *Zsolt Somlói* explain why and what they cherish most about Budapest.

By Antje Mayer

How big is the art scene in Budapest?

KATALIN SPENGLER: In the listings of the biggest Hungarian art magazine *Műértő* you can count 75 contemporary galleries in Budapest alone with temporary exhibitions. Furthermore we have approximately 25 non-profit exhibition spaces run by companies and local municipalities in the city. In Hungary there are around 200 serious collectors active. The biggest collection can claim 10,000 pieces, including Modern and contemporary Hungarian art, as far as I know.

When you compare the situation of contemporary art in Hungary to other former Communist countries you can count yourself lucky, can't you?

ZSOLT SOMLÓI: Hungary already had a deep-rooted tradition of art collecting before the first World War. According to sources from that time, Budapest was the third art market in Europe after Paris and Rome. During the Communist area, no official art market existed, but a lot of people, mainly doctors, lawyers, teachers and private entrepreneurs, continued to collect and in this manner they maintained the collecting culture.

Did the art scene forge ahead in the last three years?

ZSOLT SOMLÓI: Absolutely. There was a change of generations in the management of big art institutions. Young, new, dedicated directors came on board: László Baán for the Szépművészeti Múzeum (Museum of Fine Arts), Zsolt Petrányi for the Műcsarnok (Kunsthalle) and Barnabás Bencsik for the Ludwig Múzeum, all of them in their mid-forties. Only the director of the Magyar Nemzeti Galéria (Hungarian National Gallery) has remained the same for the last 28 years. The art scene in Budapest is improving. Some private collectors in Hungary are starting to be interested in the international art market whereas before they were collecting mainly Hungarian artists. The importance of private collections is continuously growing. On the other hand, a lot of foreign exhibitions help us to see beyond our own nose; at the Kunsthalle there were exhibitions with Luc Tymans, Wim Delvoye, the Leipzig School or Thomas Ruff, while at the Ludwig Múzeum, with Katarzyna Kozira and Katharina Sieverding.

As far as I know, the prices of Modern and classical Hungarian masters prices have increased steeply lately ...

KATALIN SPENGLER: Recently the Hungarian contemporary painter Judith Reigl, born in 1923, realised a price of 28 Million HUF (approx. € 90,000) at Erdész & Makláry Fine Art in December 2008. From the '90s on, more and more Hungarians started to collect art and then, after a while, there began to be a

There was a change of generations in the big art institutions

Even though the financial crises has barely hit the Hungarians yet, passionate collectors are still buying

shortage of high quality twentieth century masterpieces. The biggest auction houses were seeking new territory and all of them finally found contemporary art to be the solution for the high demand. This process made contemporary art works in Hungary pricier and more and more people now see an alternative business opportunity in selling contemporary art. This is why in 2008, at the Budapest Art Fair, the exhibiting galleries showed more contemporary art than Modern art for the first time since they were founded, and why more and more galleries run by former businessmen and businesswomen are opening now in Budapest. Even though the international financial crisis has barely hit the Hungarians yet, passionate collectors are still buying. Local stars from the 20th century have made records at auction and their prices are, in the meantime, on a parallel with the prices of well-known international artists.

What about the photographers Hungary is famous for?

KATALIN SPENGLER: Although Hungary is very well known for it's famous photographers, Moholy-Nagy, André Kertész, Capa, Brassai, Martin Munkácsi, Lucien Hervé and so forth, until now photography was not considered a part of the art market in our country. This situation changed dramatically in last two years. The global problem of the contemporary art market is that young artists are often overvalued compared with those from the middle generation. We paid less for an Academy teacher's work than for his student's work not because the young artists are overvalued, but because the senior generation is undervalued.

Katalin, you collect contemporary jewellery and have a passion for contemporary design. Do people like you find what they are looking for in Budapest?

KATALIN SPENGLER: Definitely. Beside the old charm of the city, its beautiful buildings and picturesque historical places, it offers plenty of design spots like Eclectick, a young fashion designer's shop, the Fazekas Valéria hat shop and all the galleries which recently opened, especially the Sterling Ékszergaléria (Sterling Gallery) and the Eventuell Galéria (Eventuell Gallery) which sell jewellery and interior and textile designs by Hungarian designers. I can also recommend WAMP, a design market that takes place on Sunday once a month in downtown Budapest. The ambiance is open minded, cool and funny. You can listen to concerts, watch happenings and spectacles not only for adults but for children as well. Most of the quality designers in Budapest sell their stuff there: bags, jewellery and fashion accessories.

What do you personally love about your hometown, Zsolt?

ZSOLT SOMLÓI: What I treasure is that Budapest had, and still has, one of the most extensive art cinema networks in Europe that still enjoys huge municipal support. These cinemas air solely independent and non-profit movies. There are 13 cinemas alone in downtown Budapest. In the twentieth century, the film industry played a very important role in Hungary's cultural life. There were and still are excellent filmmakers in Hungary or with Hungarian origin: George Cukor, George Halas, Alexander Korda, István Szabó, Vilmos Zsigmondy, Lajos Koltai and so forth. What I also like is the fact that Budapest is the city of spas and thermal water. You can find thermal baths and fountains with spring water in downtown. There are some houses in the city that use thermal hot water for heating. When I was a young boy there were a lot of public spring water squares with fountains. Most of them are closed now and dry due to cost cutting. —

Budapest has one of the most extensive art cinema networks in Europe

Katalin Spengler (43) and **Zsolt Somlói** (41) were born in Budapest where they both live and work. She has been a journalist and editor since 1996. He is a businessman in the communication field. Both started collecting in 1992 with Hungarian Modern, and twentieth century art and then in 1996 turned to Hungarian contemporary art. In 2002, their collection opened itself up to international artists and consists of approximately 500 paintings, photos, installations, sculptures, and videos.

Budapest

By József Készman

Republic of Councils
Monument in Memento
Park

ART

❶ Szépművészeti Múzeum (Museum of Fine Arts) — This Museum is not only an exhibition space for classical art but also for historical Modernism. The most successful museum in Hungary, it often attracts hundreds of thousands of visitors with blockbuster exhibitions that feature world-famous star artists. With excellent public relations and services, the museum has managed to achieve a breakthrough in the Hungarian museum landscape. Less well known is the fact that some of the most important treasures of the museum, including a serious collection of contemporary art, are kept from public view in its storerooms.

Hősök tere, (469 71 00)
Metro 1: Hősök tere, trolleybus 75, 79: Dózsa György út or Hősök tere, 72: Szondi utca, bus 20E, 30, 105: Dózsa György út or Hősök tere
Tue-Sun 10 am to 17.30 pm, every odd week Thur 10 am to 10 pm
Full price admission 1,400 HUF
www.szepmuveszeti.hu

❷ Műcsarnok (Kunsthalle Budapest) — First opened in 1896, the Budapest Műcsarnok originally followed the model of the German Kunsthallen. A »stronghold of conservatism« (András Török) until well into the '80s, it was only gradually transformed into a professional exhibition space for contemporary art. Since the '90s it has become more and more open to work from abroad, has put on shows of international art and invited guest curators to organise exhibitions. Large art bookshop.

Hősök tere, (460 70 00)
Metro 1: Hősök tere,
trolleybus 75, 79: Benczúr utca,
bus 20, 30, 105: Dózsa György út
Tue-Sun 10 am to 6 pm, Thur noon to 8 pm
Full price admission 1,200 HUF
www.mucsarnok.hu

❸ Ludwig Múzeum – Kortárs Művészeti Múzeum (Ludwig Museum – Museum of Contemporary Art) — Also known as the LUMÚ, the museum is based on dona-

tions from the German Ludwig Foundation. Since the '90s, the museum has collected and exhibited contemporary art, primarily from Hungary and Eastern Europe, from the '60s to the present day. The permanent collection also focuses on American Pop art (Andy Warhol, Claes Oldenburg, Robert Rauschenberg, etc.). The museum presents the permanent collection but also temporary exhibitions of international contemporary art. In addition, they offer a huge program with discussions, seminars, screenings, workshops etc. Formerly accommodated in the Castle, it has found its new home in the Palace of Art, where the reorganized collection of contemporary art is now on permanent display.

Komor Marcell u. 1, (555 34 44)
Tram 1: Lágymányosi híd-pesti hídfő,
Tram 2: Millenniumi Kulturális Központ
Tue-Sun 10 am to 8 pm
Full price admission 600 HUF
www.ludwigmuseum.hu

❹ Magyar Fotográfusok Háza (Hungarian House of Photography) — A museum of photography with a specialist library and bookshop in a wonderful fin-de-siecle building, built by the famous Hungarian photographer Mai Manó. His family lived here. You can visit Manó's original daylight studio. The museum makes a significant contribution to the support of young Hungarian art photography.

Nagymező u. 20, (473 26 66)
Metro 1, bus 105: Oktogon or Opera, tram 4, 6: Oktogon, trolleybus 70, 78: Andrássy út
Mon-Fri 2 pm to 7 pm,
Sat-Sun 11 am to 7 pm
Full price admission 700 HUF
www.maimano.hu

❺ acb Galéria — Lead until recently by János Szoboszlai (former director of the Dunaújváros Contemporary Art Institute) and backed by the owners of the Irokéz Collection, this is at present one of the most important galleries for contemporary art in Budapest. The strength of the gallery, which is located in a flat in an old apartment building, lies in the fact that it is almost the only gallery that has been able to present new media commercially. Artists include Attila Csörgő, Atilla Szücs, Zoltán Ádám, András Braun, or Soós Nóra.

Király u. 76, (413 76 08)
Tram 4, 6: Király utca,
trolleybus 70, 78: Teréz körút
Tue-Fri 2 pm to 6 pm
www.acbgaleria.hu

❻ Knoll Galéria — This is the Budapest branch of the Viennese gallery, whose owner helped to make Roza El-Hassan, among others, a big success in the '90s. Hans Knoll, who opened his gallery in 1989 in Budapest, has played a key role in the development of the contemporary art market in Hungary (art fairs, events, discussions, open studio program). The gallery represents Ákos Birkás, Csaba Nemes, as well as other artists from various Eastern European countries.

Liszt Ferenc tér 10, (267 38 42)
Metro 1, tram 4, 6, bus 105: Oktogon
Tue-Fri 2 pm to 6.30 pm, Sat 11am to 2 pm
www.knollgaleria.hu

❼ Deák Erika Galéria — Owner Erika Deák honed her skills in New York and boasts extensive international relationships. The gallery represents Imre Bak, IRWIN and Szabolcs Kisspál, among others.

Jókai tér 1, (302 49 27)
Metro 1, tram 4, 6, bus 105: Oktogon
Wed-Fri noon to 6 pm, Sat 11 am to 4 pm
www.deakgaleria.hu

❽ **Várfok Galéria** — One of the first private galleries to be founded immediately after the political transition. Owner Károly Szalóky's exhibition program originally concentrated on the »second generation of the Hungarian neo-avant-garde«, while today he prefers so-called technorealist painting. Várfok

is actually a conglomerate of galleries and the owner would like to transform the street, which leads to the Castle, into a gallery walk, giving the area the profile of an artist's quarter. The works of younger artists are exhibited in the XO Hall (Várfok u. 8), Café Alkoholos Filc is an artist's cafe, while opposite is the Gallery Ponton, the exhibition space of the Moholy-Nagy University of Art and Design.

Várfok u. 14, (213 51 55)
Metro 2, tram 4, 6, 18, 41, 59, 59A, 61, bus 22, 22E, 90, 128: Moszkva tér, bus 10 castle bus (Várbusz): Várfok utca
Tue-Fri 11 am to 6 pm
www.varfok-galeria.hu

❾ **Vintage Galéria** — A gallery specialising in Modern and contemporary photography, Vintage Gallery also publishes texts on this subject, and regularly participates at various international art fairs and exhibitions.

Magyar utca 26, (337 05 84)
Metro 2, tram 47, 49, bus 7: Astoria
Tue-Fri 2 pm to 6 pm
www.vintage.hu

❿ **Lumen Galéria** — A small, independent space for current art photography, surrounded by the flair of the alternative scene. Governed by the Lumen Photography Foundation, the gallery aims to present works by young artists and to open them up to a wider public.

Mikszáth Kálmán tér 2
Trolleybus 70, 78: Teréz körút, tram 4, 6: Király utca
Mon-Fri 8.30 am to 7 pm, Sat 10 am to 6 pm
www.photolumen.hu

⓫ **Stúdió Galéria** — The exhibition space of the F.K.S.E (Fiatal Képzőművészek Stúdiója Egyesület), Association of Young Visual Artists. Here, young Hungarian artists can show their work, often at solo exhibitions. In addition, it stages theme exhibitions and events

such as »Gallery by Night«, when a different artist is presented on each night of the week. A place for progressive contemporary Hungarian art.

Rottenbiller u. 35, (342 53 80)
Trolleybus 70, 78: Lövölde tér
Tue-Fri 4 pm to 8 pm, Sat noon to 4 pm
studio.c3.hu

⓬ Labor — A joint initiative of C3 (Center for Culture & Communication), F.K.S.E and Magyar University of Fine Arts. This open exhibition platform was established in September 2007 in the space formerly occupied by Stúdió Galéria. The aim of the space is to promote research in the visual arts, the exchange of information between institutions and the support of students and young emerging artists in conjunction with the University's educational program. With occasional evening programs like lectures, discussions, happenings, etc.

Képíró u. 6, (411 02 35)
Metro 3, tram 47, 49, bus 15: Kálvin tér
Tue, Thur 4 pm to 8 pm
www.labor.c3.hu

⓭ Trafó: Kortárs Művészetek Háza (House of Contemporary Art) — Once a squat, this former factory building was bought by the Budapest City Council to accommodate an open arts centre, which hosts programs in all the arts: dance, theatre, literature, the visual arts and music. It is also home to Trafó Gallery, which organises performances and discussions, as well as exhibitions specializing in socially conscious, political art.

Liliom u. 41, (215 16 00)
Metro 3, tram 4, 6: Ferenc körút
Tue-Sun 4 pm to 7 pm
www.trafo.hu

⓮ Tranzit.hu — Tranzit is a long-term initiative supported by Kontakt – the Arts and Civil Society Programe of Erste Group. The Hungarian section and the so called »Free School for Art Theory and Practice« in Budapest is led by Hungarian curator and art historian Dóra Hegyi. tranzit.hu does not hold exhibitions very often, but regularly has lectures, seminars and discussion for which the initiative invites mostly well known art theorists, artists and philosophers from abroad. Check out the program on the website!

Ezredes u. 13, (office@tranzitinfo.hu)
Metro 1: Moszkva tér
www.tranzit.org

ART EVENTS

Budapest Art Fair — The successor to the former Budapest Art Expo (BAE) is always held at Műcsarnok Kunsthalle, with two very different sections: the building hosts the displays of galleries specializing in antique and Modern art, as well as art from auction houses, while private Hungarian galleries of contemporary art are featured in a large tent set up outside.

Hősök tere, (460 70 00)
Metro 1: Hősök tere, trolleybus 75, 79: Benczúr utca, bus 20, 30, 105: Dózsa György út

Office: Várfok u. 16, (319 33 69)
Metro 2, tram 4, 6, 18, 41, 59, 59A, 61, bus 22, 22E, 90, 128: Moszkva tér, bus 10/ castle bus (Várbusz): Várfok utca
www.budapestartfair.hu

ALTERNATIVE SIGHTSEEING

⓯ Sziklakórház (Hospital in the Rock) — A hospital under the city – a journey into the past. A military infirmary and fall-out bunker, this air-raid shelter and hospital was built during the Second World War and later reconstructed as nuclear-proof. It was maintained until the end of the Cold War. Today, it hosts the odd theatre production or performance. Safety gear, operating rooms and wardens – with a great many wax figures with tormented faces.

Lovas út 4/c, (306 898 775)
Bus 16 A, 116: Szentháromság tér
Tue-Sun 10 am to 7 pm
Full price admission 3,000 HUF
www.sziklakorhaz.hu

⓰ Memento Park Budapest — Where did those emblematic sculptures and monuments of Budapest's Socialist past go? They ended up in a theme park on the edge of the city. Removed from their original contexts, these pieces of stone and metal carry on representing past ideals. A favourite haunt for tourists, the park introduces those who grew up in democracies to how an unimaginable regime communicated in its public spaces. An incredible concentration of Marx, Engels and Lenin, together with the heroes and stories of the Hungarian workers' movement.

Corner of Balatoni út and Szabadkai utca, (424 75 00)
Bus 150: Szoborpark-Memento Park, direct transfer from Deák tér daily at 11 am (and 3 p.m. in July and August), fare includes ticket for Memento Park
Mon-Sun 10 am until dusk
Full price admission 1,500 HUF
www.mementopark.hu

Budapest Beyond Sightseeing Tours — These English guided tours in the 8th district of Budapest are a socio-cultural discovery in the heart of the city. Organized by two young people (Manó Domján and Gyuri Baglyas), who show visitors the human face of one of the most rundown districts of Budapest. Their motto: »Fall in love with the real Budapest. Small groups and enthusiasm are guaranteed!« Different themes are offered: 1. Socio-cultural walking tour – in the slummy 8th district, 2. Night ride – Palaces in the Twilight, 3. Contemporary Art Instant – in the legendary 8th district. Booking via email only.

Price from 2,500 HUF to 4,000 HUF
beyondbudapest@gmail.com
www.beyondbudapest.hu

17 Margitsziget (Margit Island) — Margit Island is the green heart of Budapest, the best choice for sports activities. On its perimeter stretches a 5,300 metre riverside running track. You can also find the Olympic-sized Alfréd Hajós swimming pool here, housed in a stylish early Modernist building. The restaurant Holdudvar occupies the former casino building, near the fountain. It is located in a splendid environment, has a garden by the river, and besides food and drink, they also have ping-pong tables.

Tram 4, 6: Margitsziget, bus 26:
any stop on the island

18 Király gyógyfürdő (Király Thermal Bath) — The King's Bath in Budapest is a colourful and unusual gem, seldom crowded by tourists. Begun in 1565 during the Turkish reign and renovated for the last time in '50, this minor bathhouse contains a large octagonal main bath and several smaller pools, interspersed with quiet niches and imposing pillars. Located away from natural hot springs, the water is piped in from the Lukács bath pipes. Király is one of the few baths in Budapest where nude bathing is the norm, and therefore the week is split between men's days and women's days. Subdued lighting and thick steam mean that reading or chess is eschewed in favour of quiet conversation. The bath is also a favoured meeting place for the gay community.

Fő u. 84, (202 36 88)
Tram 4, 6: Margit-híd/budai hidfő,
bus 86, 160: Bem József tér.
Men: Tue, Thur-Sat 9 am to 8 pm,
Women: Mon-Wed 8 am to 7 pm,
Mixed: Sun 9 am to 8 pm
Admission from 1,800 HUF
www.spasbudapest.com

SHOPPING

19 Rododendron — Young graduates of the Moholy-Nagy University of Art and Design founded this shop of designer ware, which also sells clothes and hosts exhibitions. The works of art and designer stuff on display and in the artist's portfolios are available for purchase.

Madách Imre út 3, (419 53 29)
Metro 1, 2, 3, tram 47, 49,
bus 9, 105: Deák Ferenc tér
Mon-Fri 11 am to 7 pm,

Sat 11 am to 3 pm
www.rododendron.hu

⓴ Tisza Cipő — Tisza Cipő is a truly Hungarian brand and the ultimate retro trip. In 1971, behind the Iron Curtain, »the Hungarian Adidas« was created. Branded with its distinctive logo, the products of Tisza Cipő soon became popular in the Socialist bloc countries. Today, a corps of young designers and graphic artists work to make the traditional products suitable for today and tomorrow.

Károly körút 1,(266 30 55)
Metro 2, tram 47, 49, bus 7, 9: Astoria
Mon-Fri 10 am to 7 pm, Sat 9 am to 1 pm
www.tiszacipo.hu

WAMP — This market was created in 2006 to enable artists and audiences to find each other under the aegis of art that can be used in everyday life, and to offer a forum for applied art that is unique and modern, has quality and is affordable. Today, WAMP's monthly design market is one of the most important agorae for culture and design. You can find work by goldsmiths, graphic and textile artists, potters, glass and recycling artists, and toymakers. Represented are respectable galleries, as well as designers of international renown. Since 2007, WAMP events have had thematic foci, with the intention to reveal the points of connection between design and other fields.

Office:
Hattyú utca 16. IV. 5.,(784 84 75)

Market places:
Erzsébet tér or Gödör Klub,
(both near to Deák tér) ㉑ ㉒
Metro 1, 2, 3, tram 47, 49, bus 9, 105:
Deák Ferenc tér.
One Sunday a month,
10 am to 6 pm
www.wamp.hu

KIDS

㉓ Csodák Palotája (Palace of Miracles) — The Palace of Miracles is one of the two outstanding permanent exhibitions in the Millenáris (House of Future Centre). You can enjoy the miracles of nature and understand the rules of science, for example, how it is possible to lie down on a fakir's bed of nails. It offers joyful hands-on experiences both for children and adults in an exciting, entertaining way.

II. Fény u. 20-22, (350 61 31)
Tram 4, 6: Széna tér
Mon-Fri 9 am to 5 pm,
Sat-Sun 10 am to 6 pm
Full price admission 1,200 HUF
www.csodakpalotaja.hu

㉔ Fővárosi Állat- és Növénykert (Budapest Zoo and Botanical Garden) — The Budapest Zoo was founded in 1866 and is one of the oldest in the world. Many of the buildings are protected landmarks, such as the famous Jugendstil elephant house.

Állatkerti krt. 6-12, (273 49 00)
Metro 1: Széchenyi Fürdő, trolleybus 72, 75, 79: Állatkert, bus 4, 30, 20: Hősök tere
Opening hours depend on the season
Full price admission 1,850 HUF

kids 1,290 HUF
www.zoobudapest.com

CAFÉS

㉕ New York Cafe — The New York Cafe, inside the New York Palace, used to be the meeting place of the Hungarian intelligentsia in the early 20th century. Lately it has returned to its original function and been restored to its original glamour together with the palace, which now belongs to the Boscolo chain of hotels.

Erzsébet krt. 9-11, (886 61 11)
Metro 2, tram 4, 6, bus 7, 7E: Blaha Lujza tér
Mon-Fri 10 am to 12 am,
Sat-Sun 9 am to 12 am
www.boscolohotels.com

㉖ Szóda — Situated in Wesselény Street, near the Dohány Street Synagogue, Szóda is the place to have the first cappuccino of the day and drink the first shot of the evening. There is free Wi-Fi access, a dance hall in the cellar, and you can rent a bike. The special interior design features original sofas from the '70s, xerox prints on the ceiling and spritzer bottles everywhere.

Wesselényi utca 18, (461 00 07)
Metro 2, tram 47, 49, bus 7: Astoria
Mon-Sun 8 am to 5 am
www.szoda.com

Mai Manó Café 4 — There is a wonderful small coffee house in the Magyar Fotográfusok Háza (Hungarian House of Photography) with a cosy Moroccan style interior (see »art«). In summer you can sit outside and watch the people passing by. A meeting point for artists, intellectuals and creative souls.

Nagymező u. 20, (473 26 66)
Metro 1, bus 105: Oktogon or Opera, tram 4, 6: Oktogon, trolleybus 70, 78: Andrássy út
Mon-Fri 2 pm to 7 pm,
Sat-Sun 11 am to 7 pm
www.maimano.hu

RESTAURANTS

❷❼ Bock Bisztró — The winner of *Dining Guide's* 2008 competition for best restaurant in Hungary. Located on Nagykörút (Grand Boulevard), it is run by Bock, a producer of fine wines known around the world. Their motto is: »No one has gone bankrupt by pleasing customers.« Main dishes from 3,100 HUF.

Erzsébet körút 43-49, (321 03 40)
Tram 4, 6: Király utca, trolleybus 70, 78: Teréz körút
Mon-Sun 10 am to 12 am
Visa, Mastercard
www.bockbisztro.hu

❷❽ Abszint Étterem és Kávézó (Absinthe Restaurant and Café) — Founded by three friends, this small, pleasant French restaurant is in the middle of the city centre, on elegant Andrássy Ave., near the Opera House. Main dishes from HUF 2,190, daily menu from 1,290 HUF.

Andrássy út 34, (332 49 93)
Metro 1, bus 105: Opera
Mon-Sun 11 am to 11.30 pm
Visa, Mastercard, Eurocard
www.abszint.hu

❷❾ Sípos — Sípos would be the perfect choice for those keen on tasting traditional spicy Hungarian fish dishes. It is situated in the historic old town centre of Óbuda. Main dishes from 2,100 HUF.

Lajos u. 46, (250 80 82)
Tram 17, bus 86, 206: Kolosy tér
Visa, Mastercard
www.regisipos.hu

❸⓿ M — It is a restaurant on an intimate scale, where European cuisine is enriched by such traditional Hungarian dishes as the lecsó casserole (hard to come by anywhere else in Budapest), and where you are allowed, or even requested, to draw on the tablecloth – which is in fact made of recycled paper. Main dishes from 1,900 HUF.

Kertész u. 48, (342 89 91)
Tram 4, 6: Király utca
Mon-Fri 6 pm to 12 am,
Sat-Sun noon to 4 pm
and 6 pm to 12 am
Visa, Mastercard
mrestaurant.blogspot.com

❸❶ Kőleves Étterem — The Kőleves (Stone Soup) borrowed its name from the legend of King Matthias, according to which the disguised king exchanged a soupstone for gold. The tale can be read on the homepage of the restaurant. Kőleves refreshes the weary wanderer with the best in food and drink. Main dishes from 1,460 HUF.

Kazinczy u. 35, (322 10 11)
Tram 4, 6: Wesselényi utca
Mon-Sun noon to 12 am
Visa
www.koleves.com

❸❷ Menza — Menza is a restaurant with an interior design that recalls the atmosphere of the '60s, with high-quality European cuisine, an unforgettable bouillon and vegetarian dishes not to be missed. It is situated in Liszt Ferenc Square, facing Knoll Gallery and surrounded by a dozen fashionable bars and restaurants. Main dishes from 1,890 HUF, daily menu for 890 HUF.

Liszt Ferenc tér 2, (413 14 82)
Metro 1, tram 4, 6, bus 105: Oktogon
Visa, Mastercard
www.menza.co.hu

33 Kiadó (For Rent) — Whether you choose its rooms in the cellar or the garden, which in the summer are located on Jókai Square, beside Erika Deák Gallery, it would be a shame not to taste the grilled vegetables, the zucchini filled with cottage cheese and spinach, or the spicy oven-fried potatoes. Main dishes from 1,300 HUF.

Jókai tér 3, (331 19 55)
Metro 1, tram 4, 6, bus 105: Oktogon
Downstairs: Mon-Sun 5 pm to 2 am,
Upstairs: Mon-Fri 10 am to 2 am,
Sat-Sun noon to 2 am
Visa, Mastercard

34 Szeráj — Turkish restaurants are the best alternative to fast food and Szeráj has one of the longest menus in town. Main dishes from 800 HUF.

Szent István krt. 13, (311 66 90)
Tram 4, 6: Jászai Mari tér.
Mon-Sun 9 am to 4 pm

PARTY

Szimpla (Mocha) — Szimpla is smoky, trendy and atmospheric – a good bet almost any night. Also visit Szimpla kert, a nice place in the garden.

35 Szimpla: 1
Kertész u. 48, (352 41 98)
Tram 4, 6: Király utca
Mon-Fri 10 am to 2 am,
Sat-Sun noon to 2 am

36 Szimpla Kert: 2
Kazinczy u. 14, (352 41 98)
Metro 1, bus 105: Opera
Mon-Sun noon to 2 am
www.szimpla.hu

CINETRIP spaRTY — Cinetrip is a speciality of Budapest that relies on the spas of the city. The monthly »swimsuit parties« are popular with adventurous and fun-seeking young people. The venues are always special and feature dazzling visuals. Started as ambient music for silent films screened in Rudas Spa, the series has come to include all sorts of special parties over the years.

Admission 6,000 HUF
www.cinetrip.hu

37 A38 — The boat A38, originally a Ukrainian freighter, is moored next to the Buda bridgehead of Petőfi Bridge, and is used as an alternative venue for parties, concerts and other cultural events. It also houses an excellent restaurant, with a very special view of the Danube.

Pázmány Péter sétány 3/11, (464 39 40)
Tram 4, 6: Petőfi híd/budai hídfő
www.a38.hu

❸❽ **Pótkulcs** — No sign marks the location of Pótkulcs (The Spare Key), but you'll be sure to hear the happy folks and live music at this hidden bohemian gem.

Csengery u. 65/b, court, (269 10 50)
Metro 3, tram 4, 6: Nyugati pu.
Sun-Wed 5 pm to 1.30 am,
Thur-Sat 5 pm to 2.30 am
www.potkulcs.hu

❸❾ **Corvintető** — Budapest from a bird's eye-view, underground on the top: the second chance for a Socialist realism department store. The summer's hippest hotspot with a groovy vibe to get you moving on top of the city.

Blaha Lujza tér 1-2, Corvin Department Store, 4th floor, (20 77 22 984)
Metro 2, tram 4, 6, bus 7, 7E:
Blaha Lujza tér
Mon-Sun 6 pm to 5 am
www.corvinteto.hu

❹⓿ **Zöld Pardon** — Open from April to September, this open-air bar is situated close to the bridgehead in the Buda-district of Petőfi Bridge, with A38 a ship/bar moored nearby. Zöld Pardon offers concerts every night, with the schedule heavy on Hungarian bands, but the odd international group occasionally takes the stage (recent rockers include the Sex Pistols). Listen to the music either near the stage or hovering by the cocktail bar, and fuel your dancing with a snack from the terrace grill.

1117 Goldmann György tér, South Side, (061 279 1880)
Tram 4, 6: Petőfi híd, budai hídfő
Mon-Sun 9 am to 6 am
www.zoldpardon.hu

❹❶ **West-Balkán Garden** — One of the few places that truly lives up to the moniker »kert« (garden), the outside area is positively horticultural and, on warm weekends, packed with a laid-back student crowd. Indoors, West-Balkán is much more urban, but no less arty and agreeable, in a dingy-cellar-sort-of-way. Reasonably priced, tasty international beers on tap and a grill window for snacks.

Nagytemplom u. 30, (204 733 651)
Metro 3, tram 4, 6: Ferenc körút
Mon-Sun 5 pm to dawn
www.west-balkan.com

SLEEP

❹❷ **Four Seasons Hotel Gresham Palace** — This is a landmark on Roosevelt Square! Good old Art Nouveau is paired with contemporary design. The view is amazing: 360° Budapest as its best. Double rooms from € 260.

Roosevelt Tér 5-6, (268 6000)
Metro 1: Bajcsy Zsilinszky út
www.fourseasons.com/budapest

43 New York Palace — The building of the New York Palace is a great mixture of opulent Italian Neo-Renaissance style and contemporary interior design. If you like marble and décor a lot, you should go there! Don't miss visiting the New York Café (see »cafés«). It's a sensational place full of glamour. Double rooms from € 200.

126

Erzsébet krt. 9-11, (866 111)
Metro 2, tram 4, 6, bus 7, 7E:
Blaha Lujza tér
www.boscolohotels.com

44 Hotel Palazzo Zichy — This impressive historical palace was built in the 19th century for an Hungarian aristocrat and was adapted into a hotel in 2008. The interior, protected as an historic landmark, is paired with very elegant contemporary design in the middle of the Pest villa quarter. Double rooms from € 120.

Lőrinc pap tér 2, (235 4000)
Metro 3: Kálvin tér, tram 6: Baross utca
www.hotel-palazzo-zichy.hu

45 Residence Izabella Budapest — Centrally located in the Andrassy Radial Street, this accommodation offers 36 individually designed apartments and has a fitness room, sauna and garden for the guests. Double rooms from € 110.

Izabella utca 61,
(475 59 00)
Metro 1: Vörösmarty utca
www.residence-izabella-budapest.com

46 Danubius Grand Hotel Margitsziget — Nature and urban life rolled into one. This hotel in the middle of the Margits Island has a prospect of the Danube, surrounded by the landscape of a botanical park with ancient trees and a jogging path along the river that offers an impressive view of the Budapest skyline. The basement of the hotel has a well-planned thermal water spa and a medical centre where you can book everything from dental treatments to plastic surgery, or from a mudpack to a massage. Especially worth recommending are the incredible Thai massages. Be aware: You can book a room in the old or new part of the hotel, though the newer part is more advisable. The staff is very friendly. Take advantage of the reduced price packages offered on the website. Room price does not include breakfast, which is an additional € 14. Double rooms from € 90.

Margitsziget,
(889 47 00)
Bus 26: Szabadtéri Színpad
www.danubiushotels.hu/grandhotel

47 Hotel Kulturinnov — Actually part of the Hungarian Cultural Foundation, housed in an old Neo-Gothic palace next to the Church of St. Matthew in the centre of the castle district. Simply furnished rooms, but at € 64 for a double-room, very reasonably priced for the location.

Szentháromság tér 6, (355 01 22)
Bus 16: Disz ter
www.budapest-hotel.hu/budapest_en/hotels/HotelKulturinnov-hotel.htm

48 Easy Hotel — This incredibly centrally located hotel near the Nagy Korut Boulevard is exactly as named: easy. Everything is simply maintained, and though one has to pay for extra services, the rooms are clean, new and practically designed. The staff is friendly and ready to help. By Budapest standards, the price is right. Double rooms from € 30.

Eotvos utca 25/a,
enquiries@budapestoktogon.easyhotel.com
Metro 1, bus 105: Oktogon or Opera,
tram 4, 6: Oktogon,
trolleybus 70, 78: Andrássy út
www.easyhotel.com

GOOD TO KNOW

49 Tourist Information
V. Sütő u. 2,
(near Deák Ferenc tér)
Metro 1, 2, 3,
tram 47, 49, bus 9, 105:
Deák Ferenc tér.

INTERNET

50 Internetcafé
V. Kecskeméti 5
Metro 3, tram 47, 49, bus 9, 15:
Kálvin tér
Daily 10 am to 10 pm

MEDIA

www.ikon.hu — The best tip for art lovers is the *index-places of art*, a small guide freely available in museums and galleries. Two visual artists, Attila Menesi and Cristoph Rauch, realized it in 1999. If the art event is not here, it doesn't exist! Unfortunately only in Hungarian.

www.funzine.hu — Hungary's freshest English program magazine (for free)

TRANSPORT

From the airport — A transfer from the main airport Ferihegy 1 and 2 to the centre should not be more than around

4,000-5,000 HUF. Cheaper than a cab is the Airport Minibusz service, the 8-11 seaters will pick you up, or will drive you to any destination in Budapest (www.bud.hu/english/transport/airport_shuttle). A single ride with the mini bus to the Airport costs 2,990 HUF, a return ticket is 4,990 HUF. WizzAir (mogyoro.hwstudio.hu/pair/index.php?town=1) also runs its mini-vans between Madách Square (that's in the centre) and Terminal 1, at 2,200 HUF for a single ride.

Taxis — Make sure to choose a cab that is marked with logos, not just anything with a »Taxi« sign on top! By far the most common complaint from tourists in Budapest is being »taken for a ride« in a taxi and charged exorbitant fees. You will need to call the taxi company, give your name and the address or approximate location to be picked up. Taxi companies in Budapest: City Taxi (211 11 11), Taxi 2000 (200 00 00), 6x6 Taxi (266 66 66), Tele 5 Taxi (555 55 55), Főtaxi (222 22 22)

Public transport — Budapest offers metro, bus, tram and trolleybus services from 4.30 am to 11 pm. Night buses run along the major routes, at roughly 25-minute intervals. A standard ticket costs 290 HUF, or you can buy it from bus drivers for 400 HUF. A 10-ticket book costs 2,600 HUF, a one-day travel card, 1,500 HUF, a three-day travel card, 3,700 HUF, a seven-day travel card, 4,400 HUF, A daily family ticket 2,100 HUF, a short section metro ticket for 240 HUF or a transfer ticket for 450 HUF. Tickets are available at underground stations, tobacco and news-agents, or from vending machines at many bus and tram stops in the city centre. (www.bkv.hu/english)

Car — Drinking and driving is not allowed in Hungary (0.00%). To use the Hungarian motorways you have to pay a fee. (4-day ticket for the average car costs between 1,170 and 1,530 HUF, depending on the season.) You can buy highway stickers at petrol stations and at some kiosks, or in the internet: www.motorway.hu.

The capital is sectioned into several parking zones, where different parking fees are charged (between 120 and 400 HUF per hour). Charges apply on week-days, from 8 am to 6 pm.

Get your tickets at the ticket machines. The shortest period you can buy a ticket for is 15 minutes, the longest 2 or 3 hours. For longer periods, you are better off leaving your car in a P+R car park. They are generally found at metro stations and bus terminals (Pest side of Árpád Bridge, Nagyvárad Square, Örs Vezér Square, Népliget etc.).

#

Important | Numbers

Telephone country and city code	*+36 1*
Telephone information	*191*
Police	*107*
Fire Brigade	*105*
Ambulance	*104*
Central emergency	*112*
24h-Pharmacy	*Teréz krt 41, (311 4439), metro 1: Oktogon*

City in | Numbers

1 Euro	*ca. 302 HUF (Hungarian Forint)*
Inhabitants	*1.7 mio*
Average income	*€ 791*
Cup of coffee	*300 HUF (ca. € 1)*
Bottle of beer	*260 HUF (ca. € 1)*
Cigarettes	*500-1000 HUF (ca. € 2-4)*
Most talked about contemporary artists	*Róza El-Hassan, Little Warsaw, Attila Szücs*
Collectors of contemporary art	*50*
Biggest art scandal	*2006 Kriszta Nagy (a.k.a. Tereskova, a.k.a. X-t) relieves herself on the wall of the Hungarian Parliament.*

Short Art History BUDAPEST

1949 –1968 Progressive art finds itself in an impossible situation under the Communist regime, it develops its own strategy for survival. This is the so-called »secondary public sphere«: art takes place in small clubs, the privacy of homes, the web of informal communities – while Big Brother is watching (often through spies).

1968 – 69 *Iparterv:* Freshly graduated art historian Péter Sinkovits invites eleven young artists to the exhibition that is held in the banquet hall of a construction firm, and follows the organization principles of the 1968 Documenta 4. It is not a classic group exhibition, but selects from almost all of the current progressive trends.

1970 – 73 Exhibitions in the Balatonboglár chapel. In 1968, a fifteen-year lease agreement is made about the artistic use of the structure, and in the summers that follow it serves as a studio and alternative institution for Hungarian artists.

1978 – 86 Indigo Group: An informal alliance of artists, whose name is both a reference to the artistic medium and an acronym of interdisciplinary thought. Based on the findings of creative research, this workshop could be considered the playground of the second generation of the Hungarian neo-avant-garde.

1989 – 90 The Iron Curtain comes down. The first private commercial galleries are founded, new artistic associations are formed, private collections are established.

1996 The Ludwig Múzeum opens. It is based on a donation of artwork from the Ludwig family, and has temporary and permanent exhibitions on its program.

2005 The Ludwig Múzeum moves to the newly built cultural complex, the Palace of Arts.

2007 In a drive to reform the state budget, government subsidies for culture are reduced. The Műcsarnok becomes a non-profit organisation.

2010 The Hungarian city Pécs is named to be the European Capital of Culture for 2010. So far, not so good: no developments or other projects have been started, and 2010 promises to be a Hungarian Year of Ignominy, one of European dimensions.

Deák Square

17
46
C. 700 M
C. 2.100 M
29
MARGIT HÍD
SZENT
C. 300 M
23
BEM JÓZSEF UTCA
18
MARGIT KÖRÚT
14
C. 400 M
8
11
VÁRFOK UTCA
PESTI ALSÓ RAKPART
AKADÉMIA UTCA
UTCA
47
LOVAS ÚT
15
TÓTH ÁRPÁD S.
TÁRNOK UTCA
VÉR-MEZŐ
Széchenyi-Lánchid
42
BUDAI ALSÓ RAKPART
ERZSÉBET HÍD
900 m
16

132

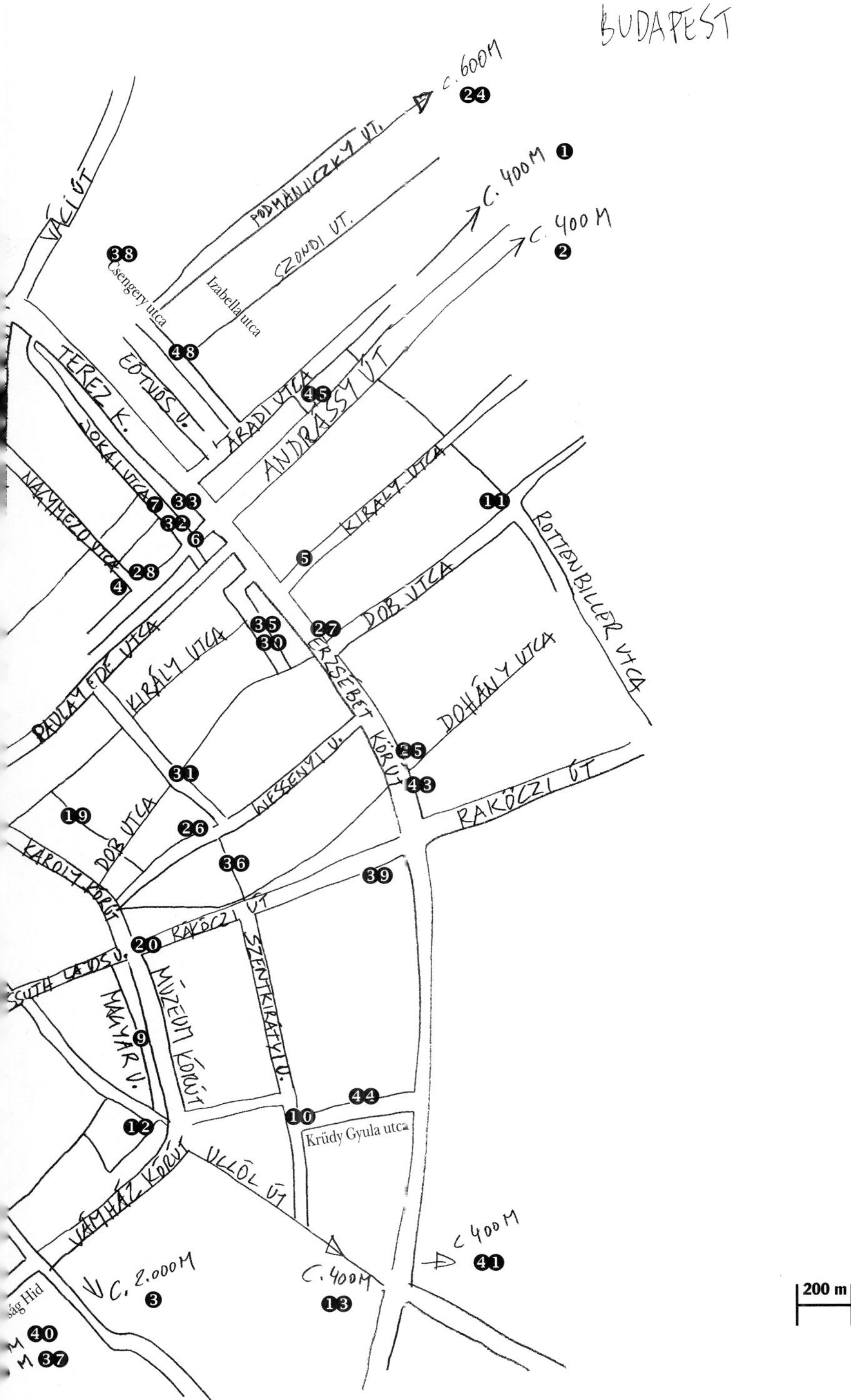
BUDAPEST
C. 600M
24
C. 400M
1
C. 400M
2
PODMANICZKY ÚT.
SZONDI ÚT.
VÁCI ÚT
38
Csengery utca
Izabella utca
48
TERÉZ K.
EÖTVÖS U.
ARADI UTCA
45
ANDRÁSSY ÚT
JÓKAI UTCA
NAGYMEZŐ UTCA
33
7
32
6
28
4
11
KIRÁLY UTCA
ROTTENBILLER UTCA
5
DOB UTCA
27
35
30
KIRÁLY UTCA
PAULAY EDE UTCA
ERZSÉBET KÖRÚT
DOHÁNY UTCA
25
43
WESSELÉNYI U.
RÁKÓCZI ÚT
31
19
DOB UTCA
26
KÁROLY KÖRÚT
36
39
RÁKÓCZI ÚT
20
SZENTKIRÁLYI U.
MÚZEUM KÖRÚT
MAGYAR U.
9
44
10
Krúdy Gyula utca
12
ÜLLŐI ÚT
VÁMHÁZ KÖRÚT
C 400M
41
C. 400M
13
C. 2.000M
3
40
37
200 m

Ljubljana, the Capital Village

Metelkova mesto's alternative art scene

The Alps right in front of you, the salty tang of the Adria in your nose, the Balkans at your back. The small capital of a small country with a big cultural scene.

By Antje Mayer

In the cultural scene everyone knows everyone

The sun is shining, the alpine peaks are glittering in the sun, the sky hints at the nearby Slovenian Riviera. It is so small, according to a Slovenian joke, that you have to carry your passport in your mouth if you go for a swim. The innumerable open-air coffee houses and bars are full to the last seat and radiate a Mediterranean warmth. I meet the Slovenian Maja Vardjan at the weekly market so that she can show me her Ljubljana. She is an architect, journalist and the manager of her own design gallery, the T5 Project Space. »The nicest thing about my city is that you only need to drive for an hour to get to Trieste for an Italian cappuccino«, she laughs. With just under 280,000 inhabitants, Ljubljana is small, and in the cultural scene everyone knows everyone else. »You have to go away often, for example to Vienna, to see international exhibitions. Here, sadly, no museum can afford them, if only because of high insurance costs. We are really a ›capital village‹.« We go to the Moderna Galerija (Museum of Modern Art), which celebrated its 60th birthday in 2008 but has been being remodelled for quite a while. In addition to Slovenian Modern art it also houses the Arteast 2000+ Collection, an excellent collection of contemporary art from Central and Eastern Europe from the '50s to today, which has been collected by curator Zdenka Badovinac. The collection, which focuses mainly on conceptual art, has already been shown several times internationally. The museum also has an external branch, the Mala Galerija (Little Gallery), for more innovative exhibition projects

Nebotičnik is a prominent high-rise located in the centre of Ljubljana, built in the '30s by Vladimir Šubic

Triple bridge by Josef Plečnik

At Tovarna Rog

The young architecture scene is very lively in Ljubljana

and young artists. In the legendary Galerija Škuc we meet the artistic director Alenka Gregorič. At the unusually early age of 26, she took over as director of the gallery in 2003, replacing Gregor Podnar, an important figure in the Ljubljana art world, who had startet to find it too quiet. Now Podnar runs a commercial gallery with Slovenian and Scandinavian artists in Berlin and is active in Ljubljana only sporadically.

The gallery, now partly commercial, is still one of the most important places for contemporary art in the city. It was founded in 1978 as a protest against established art institutions. In the mid '80s it was the centre of a sub-culture, where many legendary exhibitions (such as *Homosexuality and Culture* in 1984), performances and happenings took place. Between the death of Tito in 1980 and the 10-day war in 1991 actions critical of the state, punk concerts and also gay and lesbian bars characterised the underground. Important impulses came from the platform NSK – Neue Slowenische Kunst (New Slovenian Art) which was founded by three groups in 1984: Laibach (music), IRWIN (painting and graphic art) and Noordung (theatre). In those exciting times many personalities emerged who are still influential and internationally known, including many women such as the co-founder of NSK, Eda Cufer, now an expert in cultural theory and a dramaturge, the artist and architect Marjetica Potrč, the philosopher Marina Gržinić, who was also artistic director of the Škuc Gallery, and her even better-known philosopher-colleague Slavoj Žižek. The Industrial band Laibach, which created a furor partly because of its use of Nazi aesthetics and was banned by the Yugoslavian government.

We cross the Ljubljanica River over the Triple Bridge, a work by Jože Plečnik, and buy cigarettes at the tobacco kiosk nearby that he also designed. Hardly anyone has had such an influence on the image of the city as he has had with his general urban plan and more than two dozen monuments, squares, public buildings, villas, gardens and religious buildings. His most beautiful building is by many believed to be the Narodna in univerzitetna knjižnica (National and University Library), with its famous reading room. Not far from the library Maja shows me her » favourite Plečnik«: a street lamp with two strangely rolled-down phalli. A »Column of Double Impotence« is what the German architectural theorist Andreas Ruby calls them, one of those many interventions in the city area that are examples of the architect's idiosyncratic sense of humour. Even today, the young architecture scene is very lively in Ljubljana. »In the '90s the competitions were still open. As a result, a few small firms could establish themselves in their formative years with major projects.«

Maja leads us to an old, abandoned tobacco factory called

Tobačna Ljubljana, one of the many old industrial sites from the Yugoslavian period, which are now being restructured into offices and loft apartments for the country's »creative industry«. Fashion designers, new architecture firms, graphic artists and galleries have already moved in. The art scene views commercially oriented project like this with scepticism. After all, people have grown accustomed to anarchic scenarios such as the Metelkova, a barracks occupied by the autonomous art scene since 1993, with state-supported galleries, clubs, studios, social institutions and a youth hostel in a former military prison. It is situated in the inner city, fiercely fought over by real-estate sharks, not far from the main railway station. The city authorities have tried repeatedly to tear the building down or at least to cut off the electricity, until now, without success.

Maja and I end our walk at the market again, over a Slovenian coffee. »It tastes almost as good as in Trieste«, jokes Maja. When we say goodbye, I ask her whether the Slovenians have any problem with the term »Balkan country« »No, at worst we make jokes about it. The Slovenian media artist Igor Stromajer once told me the following story: during the Balkan wars people wanted to transfer bears that had been driven out of their habitat to areas in the French Pyrenees. The local people protested: bears from the Balkans, they claimed, were too bad mannered.« —

At worst we make jokes about the term »Balkan country«

Next stop: Future

Collective spirit and Safari Curators

Alenka Gregorič, the young artistic director of the legendary Škuc Gallery in Ljubljana, on the lively scene of the '80s, an ambitious generation of young artists and the Balkan label.

By Antje Mayer

What do you like about your hometown Ljubljana?
ALENKA GREGORIČ: That I can recommend visitors who are not coming just to see the Plečnik buildings and churches to go off the beaten tourist path and visit the alternative cultural district Metelkova city, which has a huge range of cultural institutions.

What do you think about the contemporary art and architectural scene in Ljubljana when you compare it to other cities?
Ljubljana is a small city, we like to call it the »capital village«, but for such a small size it has a really energetic and vibrant contemporary art and architectural scene. There are a number of protagonists who are active and internationally well known IRWIN, Marjetica Potrč, Marko Peljhan, Vuk Ćosić, Vadim Fiškin to name just a few; there are museum and gallery spaces with international programming, which can be easily compared to other spaces that play an important role in the network of contemporary art (Museum of Modern Art, P74 Centre and Gallery, Alkatraz Gallery etc.), which some might find surprising for a city of this size.

And yet Slovenia can look back on a rather lively recent history of art?
Of course there was lively scene, especially if we look back to the '80s. This period was very important for us from many different perspectives. I am, as a curator and art historian, especially interested in the phenomena of collectives such as NSK, FV or Borghesia, that were practising different cultural genres like visual arts, video, music, theatre at the same time. These collectives were pillars of the sub-cultural movement. They were inter-connected and played an extremely important role in forming and collabo-

rating with non-governmental institutions. What I see as a phenomenon, not even talking about the impact of these movements, is that these protagonists shared the common collective spirit, which is almost impossible to imagine today, and this is also true for other Ex-Yugoslav countries. This vivid decade, with all its different art and civil movements, is still playing an important role in influencing the contemporary art of today.

Is there an interesting generation of artists coming up now in Slovenia?

At present, in fact, I see a noticeably strong generation of internationally active artists in their 30s, who combine a wide range of genres and are dealing with different issues like social and political realities, science, social sciences and so forth. Artists are likewise permeated with the bitterness of the geopolitical, social and artistic systems, and this is communicated through individual artistic acts. Their radical, critical and sometimes ironic positions are presented through various types of artwork, ranging from new media installations, drawings, paintings and photography to videos.

Slovenian artists are very often subsumed again and again under the »Balkan« label, especially by Western curators. Artists don't like to hear that, do they?

Talking about things »Balkan« was extremely trendy a few years ago but now it has almost ended. So called »safari« curators moved further on to countries in the Middle East and Asia. I must say that we are (luckily) almost out of a certain geographic stereotyping and calcification since the region is not so popular any more. We almost forgot how we felt about these labels. —

These protagonists shared a common collective spirit, which is almost impossible to imagine today

I see a noticeably strong generation of internationally active artists in their 30s

Art historian **Alenka Gregorič** was only 26 years old in 2003 when she took over the legendary Škuc Gallery from Georg Podnar. Today she directs it as its leading curator.

Ljubljana

By Tina Smrekar

The City Museum

ART

❶ Galerija Škuc — The foundation of the Škuc Gallery at the end of the '70s created a counterpart to the dominant exhibition policy of the established national institutions in Slovenia; in the '80s

it became the centre of (sub)culture in Slovenia and remains one of the most visited exhibition spaces in the country. The focus on local Slovenian and regional developments represents a significant segment of the gallery's program while on the other side the involvement in the international art scene also plays an important role. The gallery has been representing its artists at international art fairs since 2000.

Stari trg 21, (421 31 40)
Bus 2, 3, 11, 20, 27: Gornji trg
Mo-Fri noon to 8 pm
www.galerija.skuc-drustvo.si

❷ Galerija Kapelica — The Kapelica Gallery, housed in a former chapel, has been following a profiled and exciting concept since its creation in 1995. Kapelica has had what many would consider a controversial program throughout the '90s with a focus on installation and performative body art. The gallery now shows installations of visual and sound art, its main focus however shifted from body art to artistic interpretations of technology, and bio art.

Kersnikova 4, (438 03 02)
Bus 2, 6, 7, 8, 9, 11, 14, 19, 20, 23, 25, 27: Bavarski dvor
Mo-Thur 10 am to 5 pm,
Fri 10 am to 3 pm
www.kapelica.org

❸ Galerija Gregor Podnar — After seven years as the artistic director of Škuc Gallery, in 2003 Gregor Podnar started the first Slovenian commercial gallery also participating in major international art fairs. The gallery was founded in the city of Kranj, moved to Ljubljana and opened an additional space in Berlin in 2007. It represents Slovenian and international artists from, as Gregor Pod-

nar puts it, peripheries, be they in Slovenia, Hungary or Scandinavia. Among others, he exhibits IRWIN, Tobias Putrih, Dan Perjovschi, Yuri Leiderman, Vadim Fiškin, Nika Špan, Attila Csörgö and Alexander Gutke.

Kolodvorska 6, (430 49 29)
Bus 2, 9, 12, 23, 25, 27K: Kolodvor
Tue-Fri noon to 6 pm
www.gregorpodnar.com

Moderna galerija (Museum of Modern Art) and Museum of Contemporary Art — This is a national museum, although it has the word »gallery« in its name. It houses a collection of 20th century Slovenian art (paintings, sculptures, prints and drawings, photography, video and electronic media) and art from the former Yugoslavia. The current director Zdenka Badovinac has, since the end of the '90s, started the very exciting Arteast 2000+ Collection, which is based on the dialogue between works by key Western and Eastern European contemporary artists (www.2000p.org). The offshoot space of this institution, the Mala galerija (Little Gallery), serves as an interesting shop-window like venue in the city centre for more experimental and smaller exhibitions. The old museum building at Tomšičeva street was under extensive construction for a long period and re-open its doors in 2009. The opening of a new building of the Museum of Contemporary Art by Groleger Arhitekti (Groleger Architects) in the industrial complex Metelkova (near the main train station) is planned for the second half of 2010.

❹ *Moderna galerija*
Tomšičeva 14, (241 68 00)
Bus 1, 2, 3, 6, 11, 14, 19, 20, 23, 27: Konzorcij
Tue-Sun 10 am to 6 pm
www.mg-lj.si

❺ *Mala galerija*
Slovenska cesta 35, (251 41 01)
Bus 1, 2, 3, 6, 11, 14, 19, 20, 23, 27: Ajdovščina or Pošta
Tue-Sat 10 am to 6 pm,
Sun 10 am to 1 pm
www.mg-lj.si

❻ *Museum of Contemporary Art*
Metelkova 22
Bus 2, 9, 12, 23, 25, 27K: Friškovec

P74 and Kapsula — The non-profit space P74 was founded by artist and curator Tadej Pogačar. Located on the outskirts of Ljubljana, it promotes diverse programs of contemporary art and culture and supports young and innovative artists and curators. Since 2006, P74 has awarded the OHO award for young artists, and furthermore has an open call for the realization of artist

books. A year ago the centre opened a new small space called Kapsula (Capsule) in an underground passage in the city centre where you can also buy books published by P74.

❼ *P74: Prušnikova 74, (516 15 81)*
Bus 1, 8, 25: Podgora
Tue-Fri 4 pm to 8 pm
www.zavod-parasite.si

❽ *Kapsula: Ajdovščina 1, (232 29 69)*
Bus 1, 2, 3, 6, 11, 14, 19, 20: Ajdovščina
Mon-Fri 11 am to 3 pm
www.kapsula.si

❾ **Galerija Alkatraz** — This gallery emerged in the context of the alternative cultural centre Metelkova City, which is located on an ex-Yugoslavian army complex. In the past, Alkatraz Gallery presented mostly works from Metelkova ateliers, but under the leadership of Jadranka Ljubičić, who has been running the gallery since 2000, it has evolved a very full and interesting visual art program showing works not only by Metelkova artists but also by other local and foreign artists. Note the unusual opening times!

Masarykova 24, (434 03 45)
Bus 2, 9, 12, 23, 25, 27K: Friškovec
Mon-Tue 5 pm to 8 pm
Wed-Fri 9 pm to noon
www.kudmreza.org/alkatraz

❿ **Galerija Ganes Pratt** — This gallery is a fairly new commercial initiative and one of the few places in Ljubljana that promotes emerging artists from the younger Slovenian generation, several of whom have graduated from the Venice art academy. The gallery was opened three years ago by Primož Nemec and represents artists like Saso Vrabič, Janez Janša, Viktor Bernik, Jasmina Cibic and Ištvan Išt Huzjan.

Gregorčičeva 3, (251 16 33)
Bus 1, 2, 3, 6, 11, 19, 20, 27: Drama
bus 2, 3, 11, 20, 27: Križanke
Mon-Fri 10am to 1 pm, 2 pm to 6 pm
Sat 10am to 2 pm
www.ganes.si

⓫ **Galerija Vžigalica** — Vžigalica Gallery works as a platform under the guidance of the City Museum of Ljubljana focusing on visual and inter-media art. The projects are selected on the basis of an open call, so the program tends to be quite diverse.

Trg francoske revolucije 7,
(241 25 90)
Bus 2, 3, 11, 20, 27: Križanke
Tue-Sun 10 am to 6 pm
www.mestnimuzej.si

⓬ **T5 Project Space** — Located in a former tobacco factory, T5 Project Space works as a platform that promotes industrial design. The program consists of exhibitions of international designers as well as upcoming local talent, a

lecture series and occasional second-hand sale events.

Tobačna 5, Objekt 6, (241 76 30)
Bus 1, 6: Tobačna
Opening hours depend on events
www.t-5.si

⓭ AML: Arhitekturni muzej Ljubljana (Architecture Museum Ljubljana) — This museum in the Fužine castle is slowly waking up from its long winter sleep, maybe because the local architectural scene has been getting more and more influential in the last couple of years. The museum houses the permanent exhibition *The architect Jože Plečnik 1872–1957*. The initiative came by the way of the renowned architect Boris Podrecca, a Slovene from Trieste living in Vienna. The Museum also hosts changing exhibitions, talks, and lectures on contemporary Slovenian and European architecture and design and runs the Plečnikova hiša (Plečnik House) in the city of Trnovo (see below).

Grad Fužine, Pot na Fužine 2,
(540 97 98)
Bus 20, 22: Fužine
Mon-Fri 9 am to 3 pm,
Sat 10 am to 6 pm
Sun 10 am to 3 pm
Full price admission € 3
www.aml.si

⓮ Plečnikova hiša (Plečnik House) — The most renowned Slovenian architect Jože Plečnik, who left a great mark on the character of contemporary Ljubljana (otherwise he built mostly in Prague and some buildings in Vienna), lived in this quite intimate house for a large portion of his life and it contains an archive of his sketches, original furniture, models, his library and photo archive, his studio, etc. Note that visits are possible only in the form of a guided tour including no more than seven people.

Trnovo: Karunova 4, (280 16 00)
Bus 2, 3, 11, 20, 27: Križanke
Mon, Tue-Thur 10 am to 6 pm,
Fri 10 am to 3 pm, Sat 9 am to 3 pm
Mon and Fri only for groups
by appointment
Full price admission € 4
www.aml.si

ART EVENTS

Grafični bienale (Biennial of Graphic Arts) / Mednarodni grafični likovni center (International Centre of Graphic Arts) — This event, which has been held without interruption since 1955, is one of the oldest print biennials in the world. »It understands printing and the reproducible image as important artistic and civilizing tools that reflect and shape artistic, political, economic, and ideological systems.« In the last years the exhibitions have spread into the whole city, also into private apartments and galleries. Its home institution, the International Centre of Graphic Arts, is located in a castle in the Tivoli Park. It supports graphic design with printing studios, publications and exhibitions.

Biennial office:
MGLC: Mednarodni grafični likovni center
(International Centre of Graphic Arts)
Grad Tivoli, Pod turnom 3, (241 38 00)
Bus 1, 2, 3, 6, 11, 14, 19, 20, 23, 27:
Konzorcij
Full price admission to MGLC € 3.40
www.mglc-lj.si

Mednarodni festival sodobnih umetnosti – Mesto žensk (International Festival of Contemporary Arts – City of Women) — Ljubljana is without doubt a city of festivals: City of Women runs in October and is an international festival of contemporary art devoted to promoting high-quality innovative creations by female artists, theoreticians and activists from all over the world. The festival has been running since 1994 and presents exhibitions, performances, concerts, workshops, lectures, etc. at several locations in town.

Festival office:
Društvo za promocijo žensk v kulturi Mesto žensk (Association for the Promotion of Women in Culture – City of Women)
Metelkova 6, (438 15 85)
October
www.cityofwomen.org

Mednarodni gledališki festival Ex Ponto (International Theatre Festival Ex Ponto) — Since its origin in 1993, this festival has evolved from multidisciplinary to contemporary theatre, with project expansions into the visual arts and a concert or two. Damir Domitrović Kos has remained its »spiritus agens« from its start up to the present day. Held in several locations.

Festival office:
Kulturno društvo B-51 (KD B-51)
Prešernova cesta 7, (426 94 05)
September
www.exponto.net

Exodos – festival sodobnih odrskih umetnosti (Exodos – Festival of Contemporary Performing Arts) — Another major festival devoted to contemporary Slovenian and international performing arts, mainly dance and contemporary theatre. Held every year in November in several locations.

Festival office:
Zavod Exodos Ljubljana Metelkova 6, (431 03 44) November
www.exodos.si

Gibanica – Slovenski plesni festival (Moving Cake – Slovenian Dance Festival) — This festival of Slovenian contemporary dance is organized by the same institution as the Exodos Festival and presents current productions. A great place to catch the spirit of the Slovenian dance scene, which is, like the contemporary visual arts scene, constantly underfed and still somehow flourishes. It is held biennially in February at several locations.

Festival office:
Gibanica c/o Exodos
Metelkova 6, (431 03 44)
February
www.exodos.si

Trnfest – Mednarodni poletni festival (International Summer Festival) — This open-air festival lasts for one month and hosts concerts, theatre, films, a children's program and exhibitions, all events with free admission. A pain in the neck with locals since conversations can go well into the night and disturb their sleep, this is the place where you can meet locals having slow summer drinks and enjoying a cultural event. Often crowded, up until two or three years ago it was practically the only thing happening in Ljubljana in high summer apart from a very official Ljubljana festival. You might also check the location during the year when it serves as an indoor venue for diverse cultural events. The festival takes place every evening (late afternoon for the children's program) in August.

KUD France Prešeren Trnovo
Karunova 14, (283 22 88)
Bus 9, 19: Ziherlova,
bus 2, 3, 11, 20, 27:
Križanke
August
www.kud-fp.si

ALTERNATIVE SIGHTSEEING

15 Mestni muzej Ljubljana (City Museum of Ljubljana) — The City Museum of Ljubljana, daringly renovated by the local architectural office Ofis arhitekti, is showing a new permanent exhibition called *The Faces of Ljubljana.* Perfect to learn about the history of the city with a big pinch of salt. There you can see, for example, the Fiat 750 from the 1950s and '60s, nicknamed the »Fičko«. Practically all Slovenians born before Slovenia's independence rode in a Fičko at least once. Or there are the typical kitschy dolls with gored skirts that decorated almost every bedroom in Slovenia. Guided tours in English every Sunday at 1 pm. Perfect with children.

Gosposka 15, (241 25 00)
Bus 1, 2, 3, 6, 11, 19, 20, 27: Drama
Tue-Sun 10 am to 6 pm
Full price admission € 4
www.mestnimuzej.si

16 Tržnica (Market) — Although you can find it in probably every guide and it is not hard to find, Ljubljana's city food market is simply a must and still worth mentioning with a special advisory not to miss the covered underground fish market is located directly next to the river. The arcaded part of the market was designed by Slovenia's most well known architect, Jože Plečnik, in the 1940s. A meeting place every Saturday from morning until around 2 pm when the people of Ljubljana creep out of their apartments to buy their vegetables, fish etc. Some stands have imported vegetables, while others are local and on Saturdays also bring products from the coast. On Saturdays there is an organic market at the area closer to the Tromostovje (Triple Bridges) of Plečnik.

Vodnikov trg
Bus 1, 2, 3, 6, 11, 14, 19, 20, 23, 27:
Konzorcij, bus 2, 20: Krekov trg
Daily, except Sunday,
from early morning until 2 pm

Krakovo District — Walking around this small and unusual area between the city centre and the Trnovo district you can hardly believe you are in the heart of the country's capital city. It was traditionally the area where people grew vegetables and brought them to the market to sell. While there are only one or two old ladies left who still do this as a profession, the narrow and long houses are still surrounded by gardens. Pri Škofu restaurant is in this area and the Sax pub is also very close by (see »restaurants«).

Bus 2, 3, 11, 20, 27: Križanke

17 Knjižnica pod krošnjami (Library under the trees) — In cooperation with a group of Slovenian publishing houses, this is literally what it says – on summer weekends in Tivoli Park you can go for a stroll and make a pleasant book stop. The organizers say it is »without added concrete and sun instead of a bulb« and you can get something for everyone here, the newest Slovenian books, professional literature, a number of foreign magazines, some children's books, poetry, manuals and guidebooks, and there is also an English section. The event takes place in summer, from May 25 to September 30 (not if it rains), every Friday, Saturday and Sunday.

Tivoli park, (Tina Popovič: 040 546 817)
Bus 1, 2, 3, 6, 11, 14, 19, 20, 23, 27: Konzorcij
www.knjiznicapodkrosnjami.si

⓲ Špica — Located at the »peak« of the Ljubljanica since the river here splits into two. A nice place for a stroll from the city centre in summer or winter, although much more popular in summer, also for a drink in one of the boathouse bars. The area is about to get renovated and a new walking bridge is supposed to be added. To find it just follow the river south for about 10 to 15 minutes from the old town.

Bus 2, 3, 11, 20, 27: Gornji trg

⓳ Park Tivoli/Rožnika Hill — Tivoli Park and the adjacent Rožnik Hill are very popular for walks with the people of Ljubljana, especially on pleasant weekend days. In Tivoli Park you can find the MGLC – International Centre of Graphic Arts, which is the home institution of the Biennial of Graphic Arts (see »art events«) and the Čolnarna bar (see »kids«), while on top of Rožnik Hill (it takes about a half an hour to get up, depending on where you start) there is the charming tavern named after the hill, Gostilna Rožnik, which serves traditional Slovenian food.

Gostilna Rožnik:
Cankarjev vrh 1, (251 34 29)
Daily 10 am to 9 pm
www.gostilna-roznik.com

To the park: Bus 1, 2, 3, 6, 11, 14, 19, 20, 23, 27: Konzorcij

DAYTRIPS

Kras/Škocjanske jame/ Postojnska jama (Karst/Škocjan Caves Park/ Postojna cave) — Caves are common in the Karst region, because it is made of limestone, which is water soluble, and thousands of years of erosion have created amazing natural caves and cave systems. Among the bigger cave systems is the Postojnska jama (Postojna cave), which is advisable for a visit with children because the visit is done on a small drive through train. For those who like to discover on foot try the Škocjanske jame (Škocjan Caves Park). Štanjel is a small village and one of the oldest settlements in the Karst region. It rewards visitors with a picturesque view and a beautiful garden built between the wars by the village born architect Maks Fabiani.

Following the curvy Karst road and you'll come across the small village of Goče. Narrow streets in the culturally protected village hide many wine cellars, of which only a small portion are in active use today. Also in Goče is the Cejkotova domačija (Cejkotova House) where, if you reserve in advance, you can let yourself go to the »downtempo« of the landlord and get spoiled by superb food which comes with selected local wines. The landlord also gives a great tour of the tiny village and by the end of your stay he might turn into a singer for a song or two. For the Karst region follow the Ljubljana–Koper highway in the direction of the seaside and exit at Postojna or Divača.

www.vodnik.kras-carso.com
www.turizem-kras.si

Škocjanske jame (Škocjan Caves Park):
Divača: Škocjan 2, (0570 82 110).
Follow the Ljubljana–Koper highway, after approx. 1 hour, exit at Divača
Open daily
(check guided tours in winter in advance!)
Full price admission € 14
www.park-skocjanske-jame.si

Postojnska jama (Postojna cave),
(0570 00 163)
Follow the Ljubljana–Koper highway, after half an hour exit at Postojna and follow the signs for the cave, it is not far from the highway
Open daily
(check guided tours in winter in advance)
Full price admission € 20
www.postojna-cave.com

Izola — Slovenia has a short coastline of only 46.6 km but it presents it very proudly. Izola is a small town with an endearing old centre that used to be an island and makes a nice walk. If you want to eat in Izola, the restaurant Gostilna Sonja is highly recommendable; their specialty is tagliatelle with scampi and fish soup (main dishes from € 13: tagliatelle with scampi costs € 20, but one portion is enough for two).

By car: Follow the Ljubljana–Koper highway, and after the highway ends, continue on the regional road. Izola is the first town after Koper.
By bus: On weekdays there are five buses a day from Ljubljana to the coastal region including Izola. On weekends, however, they are more sporadic (all bus timetables from Ljubljana on the website:
www.ap-ljubljana.si/eng)

Gostilna Sonja (Pub Sonja):
Morova ulica 4, (05 640 35 00)
Thur-Tue noon to 9.30 pm
(Kitchen closed on Wednesday)
www.izola.eu

SHOPPING

⓴ Rustika — Chocolate lovers, you are about to enter heaven! This started out as a small business idea thought out by two chocolate and ice cream enthusiasts using only the best ingredients and chocolate with known origin. From chocolate with chilli candied ginger or almonds to your very normal milk chocolate, pralines and very, very good cakes. If your travels happen to include an anthropological visit to BTC City, one of the biggest shopping centres (that used to be warehouses) in Europe on the outskirts of Ljubljana, don't miss the Rustika shop there, since they only there do they serve the best ice cream you can find.

Trubarjeva 44, (0599 35 730)
Bus 5: Ilirska, bus 2, 13, 20: Zmajski most
Mon-Fri 8 am to 9 pm,
Sat 9 am to 2 pm

BTC City, Citypark
Šmartinska 152, (430 17 94)
Bus 27: BTC Kolosej
Mon-Sat 9 am to 8 pm

21 Knjigarna Behemot (Behemot Bookshop) — This cute independent bookshop that specializes in books in English opened in 2005 and as the owner

himself states, the bookshop is about »people that love books and about books that love people«. Behemot offers books from a variety of fields: art, film, architecture, philosophy, and also fiction.

Židovska steza 3, (251 13 92)
Bus 1, 2, 3, 6, 11, 19, 20, 27: Drama
Mon-Fri 10 am to 8 pm, Sat 10 am to 3 pm
www.behemot.si

22 Trgovina Ika (Ika Shop) — A shop offering diverse handmade products by Slovenian designers and selling handi-

crafts, from ceramic ware to jewellery to textiles. A lot of tschotkes, very kitschy, but also some wonderful useless useful things. Nothing for minimalists. Located close to the city food market Tržnica (see »alternative sightseeing«).

City center, Metodov trg 13, (232 17 43)
Bus 2, 20: Krekov trg
Mon-Fri 10 am to 7 pm, Sat 10 am to 2 pm
www.trgovina-ika.si

Rustika Souvenirs — Not to be mistaken for the chocolate shop that goes by the same name, they offer some nice, more or less traditional, handcrafted souvenirs. The shop has one branch in the Ljubljana castle and another near the Tromostovje (Triple Bridges).

23 *Ljubljana Castle, Grajska planota 1, (031 38 32 47)*
Bus 2, 20: Krekov trg,
or funicular to the castle
Daily from 10 am to 7 pm

24 *Stritarjeva 9, (031 45 95 09)*
Bus Krekov trg 2, 20: Krekov trg,
bus 1, 2, 3, 6, 11, 14, 19, 20, 23, 27: Konzorcij
Mon-Fri 9 am to 8 pm,
Sat 10 am to 2 pm and 3 pm to 7 pm,
Sun 10 am to 2 pm

CAFÉS

25 BI-KO-FE — A place for the young at heart. Coffee during the day, beer or wine in the evening, this place is quite often crowded, especially in summer a lot of people sit or even stand outside with their cool evening beer. One of the rare bars in Ljubljana with selected music and an occasional DJ on weekends.

Židovska steza 2, (251 12 49)
Bus 1, 2, 3, 6, 11, 19, 20, 27: Drama
Mon-Fri 7 am to 1 am,
Sat-Sun 10 am to 1 am

❷❻ **Kavarna Zvezda** — A nice selection of cakes and ice cream in the city centre. Called the »star« after the Zvezda Park (Star Park) where it is located. They also took over the coffee shop in the Hotel Slon next to the old post office at the beginning of the Čopova street in the pedestrian zone.

Kongresni trg 4, (421 90 90)
Bus 1, 2, 3, 6, 11, 14, 19, 20, 23: Konzorcij
Mon-Sat 7 am to 11 pm, Sun 10 am to 8 pm

RESTAURANTS

❷❼ **Špajza** — A restaurant in the old town that has immediately received renown for its special ambiance, fish dishes and wine. All the seafood is fresh and arrives daily from Croatia. If you want to make an impression, have a nice dinner for two or show off to your friends, you will definitely get spoiled at Špajza. Reservations are highly recommended. Main dishes from € 10.

Gornji trg 28, (425 30 94)
Bus 2, 3, 11, 20, 27: Gornji trg
Mon-Sat 12 pm to 11 pm,
Sun 12 pm to 10 pm
American Express, Diners, Visa, Mastercard

❷❽ **PEN Club** — This legendary restaurant at the top of old wooden steps in the headquarters of the national journalists' association is a gourmet place with old school waiters and is an experience of its own that is definitely worth the while. In the evenings you might literally meet a group of more or less »amused« writers. A pleasant summer garden with live jazz in summer. Main dishes from € 10.

Tomšičeva 12, (25 14 60)
Bus 1, 2, 3, 6, 11, 14, 19, 20, 23, 27: Konzorcij
Mon-Fri noon to 11 pm
American Express, Diners, Visa, Mastercard

❷❾ **Pri Škofu** — Located in the endearing Krakovo district (see »alternative sightseeing«). Here you can eat very tasty food in a cosy ambiance, some say it feels like your grandmother is cooking and your friends are serving. They have no written menu, so be prepared to listen well to the waiters when they list all the possibilities and specialties. The food is a mixture of traditional Slovenian flavoured with a modern touch and a bit of international to top it off. It is even nicer to sit outside in warmer times of the year. It is a good idea to reserve in advance. Main dishes from € 8.

Rečna cesta 8, (426 45 08)
Bus 2, 3, 11, 20, 27: Križanke
Mon-Fri 8 am to midnight,
Sat-Sun noon to midnight,
closed on holidays
American Express, Diners, Visa, Mastercard

❸⓿ **Thai Inn Pub** — The offer of »exotic« international foods in Ljubljana's restaurants is still on the lower part of the scale and you should definitely not visit any Indian restaurant you find! But finally we have got a very decent Thai bistro where a green curry tastes like a green curry. The choice of foods is a bit limited but what they do have they state is fresh and it definitely tastes good and is spicy enough. Every dish costs € 6.

Rimska 17, (421 03 77)
Bus 1, 2, 3, 6, 11, 19, 20, 27: Drama
Mon-Fri 7 am to 12 am, Sat 8 am to 12 am
Mastercard, Visa, Diners

31 Bazilika — If you are thinking organic, here is where you can buy your midday sandwich or salad. They go by the rule fresh-seasonal-organic. They also sell some products that are quite expensive but make nice gifts. Sandwiches from € 2.50.

Miklošičeva 22, (031 26 17 85)
Bus 2, 6, 7, 8, 9, 11, 14, 19, 20, 23, 25,27: Bavarski dvor
Mon-Fri 7 am to 7 pm
www.bazilika.si

32 Falafel — There is only one falafel »joint« in Ljubljana, and we're very lucky it's a good one! Falafel from € 2.60.

Trubarjeva 40, (041 752 977)
Bus 5: Ilirska; bus 13: Zmajski most
Mon-Sat 10 am to 12am, Sun 1 pm to10 pm
alja-shaar.com/falafel.htm

PARTY

33 Sax pub — You cannot miss this place, a semi-old house with graffiti sprayed walls. A very cosy bar and one of the only places in Ljubljana with selected music, in Sax pub it is oriented towards jazz, but not exclusively. The live music has been important since the bar opened in 1988 (!) and has had a steady slot on Thursday evenings since 1999. Also a nice place for a summer coffee outside.

Eipprova 7
Bus Križanke 2, 3, 11, 20, 27: Križanke
Tue-Sat noon to 12am,
Sun 5 pm to 12 am
www.myspace.com/sax_pub

34 Metelkova — These former military barracks near the main railway station have been occupied since the beginning of the '90s and have developed into a hub of Ljubljana's independent cultural scene while still holding a more or less autonomous position. Here you can party at night in several clubs (Klub Gromka, Menza, Gala hala, Channel Zero) and listen to free jazz, hiphop, electronica or hard core. Don't miss the theatre shows and visit an exhibition in the Galerija Alkatraz (see »art«), or just

stay overnight in the Celica Hostel, Metelkova's former prison (see »sleep«).

Masarykova 24
Bus 2, 9, 12, 23, 25, 27K: Friškovec
www.metelkova.org

35 K4 — This legendary club was founded in 1989 and since then has been the symbol of young urban culture and musical development in Slovenia. The club presents the newest and most experimental musical genres. Its reputation was earned by the enthusiastic work of its program managers as well as by all the young people who put their creative energies into presenting experimental, non-commercial, alternative and modern musical cultural events. Club K4 is the place for students, intellectuals and innovators of all generations.

Kersnikova 4, (43 80 261)
Bus 2, 6, 7, 8, 9, 11, 14, 19, 20, 23, 25, 27: Bavarski dvor
Daily 9 pm to 4 am, closed in summer!
www.klubk4.org

36 Etno klub Zlati zob (Ethno-Club Golden Tooth) — This ethno club is owned by members of the gipsy band Šukar, which also gives you an idea of its orientation. Snacks like burek or meza (cut cheese and salami) are served. You might get surprised by a concert from a band from the Slovenian Prekmurje region or the best brass band from the Guča festival. (Guča is a small village in Serbia where thousands of people come for this festival from all over Europe: www.guca.rs). In spring and summer, you can sit outside as they are also open in the morning (from around 10 am).

Zaloška 69, (040 56 31 00)
Bus 2, 9, 11, 20, 25: Tržnica Moste
Mon-Thur 5 pm to 1 am
Fri-Sat 5 pm to 3 am
www.myspace.com/etnoklubzlatizob

37 Orto bar — A rock club with a touch of a legend, the last place you might end up at night in Ljubljana because of its long opening hours. Frequent concerts on the upper floor!

Grablovičeva 1, (232 16 74)
Bus 2, 9, 12, 23, 25, 27K: Friškovec
Mon-Wed 9 pm to 4 am
Thur-Sat 9 pm to 4.30 am
www.orto-bar.com

SLEEP

38 Grand Hotel Union Executive — This hotel near the city centre was built in October 1905 in Art Nouveau style. Designed by the architect Josip Vancaš, it was then one of the most modern hotels in Europe, equipped with an elevator, central heating and telephone, which was truly exceptional. If you want to follow the Queen of England, this is your hotel. Double rooms from € 209.

Miklošičeva 1, (308 11 70)
Bus 2, 9, 12, 23, 25, 27K: Kolodvor
bus 1, 2, 3, 6, 11, 14, 19, 20, 23, 27: Konzorcij
www.gh-union.si

39 City Hotel — A hotel with design ambitions in the medium price range in the city centre. Its special offers include free bike rental and a play-space for children. Double rooms from € 84.

Dalmatinova ulica 15, (239 00 00)
Bus 2, 9, 12, 23, 25, 27K: Kolodvor
www.cityhotel.si

40 Antiq Hotel — If you want to stay in the old town, and if you like bombastic antique-like decoration, the little Antiq Hotel might be the right address for you. Double rooms from € 77.

Gornji trg 3, (421 35 60)
Bus 2, 3, 11, 20, 27: Gornji trg
www.antiqhotel.si

41 Hostel and Hotel Park — What used to be a »single's home« – a building with rooms for accommodating single men, became the Hotel Park after renovation and also includes a hostel (dorm rooms and lower prices). The rooms are ordinary but what is exceptional is that each of the 12 floors has a great view. It is located very close to the Metelkova complex (see »party«). Double rooms in the Hostel from € 58. Double rooms in the Hotel from € 90.

Tabor 9, (300 25 00)
Bus 5: Ilirska
www.hotelpark.si

42 Hostel Celica 42 — Celica offers the most unique sleeping experience in town – in a former military prison cell. Twenty cells were transformed by dif-

ferent artists and architects into rooms for guests. The Celica is similar to a boutique hotel despite shared bathrooms, and has youth hostel prices. Located in the Metelkova complex (see »party«). Double rooms from € 56.

Metelkova 8, (230 97 00)
Bus 2, 9, 12, 23, 25, 27K: Friškovec
www.hostelcelica.com

KIDS

43 Sezam — An association for parents and children providing very dependable and experienced babysitter contacts. On the premises you can also find

157 *Ljubljana*

a comfortable space to change or breastfeed your baby. Mind the very limited opening times when ordering babysitters!

Novi trg 1 (251 12 18)
Bus 1, 2, 3, 6, 11, 19, 20, 27: Drama
Mon-Thur 8 am to 3.30 pm,
Fri 8 am to 3 pm
www.zdruzenje-sezam.si

44 Frockarije — Creative workshops for kids from 5 to 12 years old where each month has a different mentor and theme. Kids might be making objects out of recycled material, sometimes instruments or they might be having fun exploring movement. Free of charge, material provided.

Novi trg 2, Atrium of ZRC, (470 64 75)
Bus 1, 2, 3, 6, 11, 19, 20, 27: Drama
From Mar to Dec; every Tuesday at 5 pm
azil.zrc-sazu.si

45 Café SEM — The coffee house of the Slovenski etnografski muzej (Slovenian Etnographic museum) has a toy basket and also a nice lawn for outside play.

Metelkova 2, (300 87 00)
Bus 2, 9, 12, 23, 25, 27K: Friškovec
Tue-Sun 10 am to 10 pm
www.etno-muzej.si

46 Oton Župančič Library — Hidden in an under passage, the public library has a comfortable play space on the 2nd floor and a baby changing space in the basement.

Kersnikova 2, (600 13 00)
Bus 2, 6, 7, 8, 9, 11, 14, 19, 20, 23, 25, 27: Bavarski dvor
Mon-Fri 8 am to 8 pm, Sat 8 am to 1 pm, first Tue of the month:10 am to 8 pm
www.koz.si

47 Kinodvor – Kinobalon and Sezamov kotiček — Kinodvor offers a program for children and youth on Saturdays at 3 pm, and on Sundays at 5 pm. Every Sunday from 11 am to 1 pm you can enjoy your breakfast and see a film in the Kinodvor cinema, while the Sezam animators have fun with your kids. Note: a children's film here and there might be synchronised, otherwise all films in Slovenian cinemas are subtitled, so check what the original language is.

Kolodvorska 13, (239 22 17)
Bus 2, 9, 12, 23, 25, 27K: Kolodvor
www.kinodvor.org

GOOD TO KNOW

48 Tourist Information

Adamič-Lundrovo nabrežje 2, (306 12 15)
Bus 1, 2, 3, 6, 11, 14, 19, 20, 23, 27: Konzorcij, bus 2, 20: Krekov trg
1 October to 31 May: daily 8 am to 7 pm
1 June to 30 September: daily 8 am to 9 pm
www.visitljubljana.si

INTERNET

49 Kiberpipa — This place is operating a cultural centre, computer laboratory and a internet café with free Wifi. It is near the Kaplica Gallery and the Bazilika and the Club K4.

Kersnikova 6, (438 03 05)
Bus 2, 6, 7, 8, 9, 11, 14, 19, 20, 23, 25, 27: Bavarski dvor
Mo-Fr 10 am to 10 pm
www.kiberpipa.org

MEDIA

www.ljubljana-life.com — An English guide in the web about what's going on in Ljubljana.

www.slovenia-life.com/ljubljana — A guide in print every 2-3 months with reviews and tips.

www.sloveniatimes.com — A monthly newspaper/guide in print in English available at the Tourist Information and in hotels containing culture, business, and politics.

www.radiostudent.si — Radio Student is not really broadcasting in English but is nevertheless interesting for its diversity. It is one of the oldest and biggest European non-commercial radio stations. 89,3 MHz

TRANSPORT

From the airport — There is a bus service connecting the airport with the city. It takes about half an hour and costs € 5 one-way. Taxis are available for approximately € 39 in front of the terminal.

Taxis — Taxis are cheapest when you call them in advance. Costs range from € 0.73 per kilometre to around € 1. Taxi Intertours (031 311 311), Taxi Laguna (080 1117), Taxi Metro (080 1190)

Public transport — Ljubljana only has buses, no tram or metro. Currently the system is one bus ride for 1 token or € 1 (so if you need to change buses, you need to pay 2 tokens or 2 x € 1). The tokens, »žeton« in Slovenian, can be bought at most of the kiosks and currently cost € 0.80. You always enter a bus at the driver's door and throw in a token or € 1.

Car — The inner city centre around the old town, Čopova, Wolfova Street and the Triple Bridges is closed to traffic. Blue zones mean parking for 1/2 hour, white zones parking up to 2 hours. Outside the city centre parking is mostly free but difficult to find. There are several garages in town.

#

Important	Numbers
Telephone country and city code	*+386 1*
Telephone information	*1188*
Police	*113*
Fire Brigade	*112*
First aid	*112*
24h-Pharmacy	*Lekarna pri polikliniki, Prisojna ulica 7 (23 06 230), bus 9, 25: Poliklinika, bus 2, 9, 12, 23, 25, 27K: Friškovec*

City in	Numbers
Inhabitants	*276,000*
Average income	*€ 1.391*
Cup of coffee	*€ 1.50*
Bottle of beer	*€ 2.50*
Cigarettes	*€ 2 – 3*
Most talked about artists	*Marjetica Potrč, Marko Peljhan, IRWIN, Tadej Pogačar*
Collectors of contemporary art	*5*
Biggest art scandal	*1983: the band* Laibach *was forbidden to perform by the goverment*

Short Art History
LJUBLJANA

1966 – 1971
The OHO Group, the most important representative of the Slovenian 60's avant-garde, is active and dealing with their own versions of Reism (a non-anthropocentric view of the world), Arte Povera, process art, performance, body art, land art and conceptualism. The tandem of Srečo and Nuša Dragan emerges from the OHO and presents the work *Belo mleko belih prsi* (White Milk of White Breasts) in 1969, also known as the first Ex-Yugoslavian video.

1978
Škuc Gallery is founded. In the '80s it becomes an important meeting place for artists and intellectuals, some even say a melting pot for Slovenia's independence.

1992
The groups from Neue Slowenische Kunst found NSK State.

First half of the '90s
Marko Peljhan starts the Makrolab project, an autonomous communication, research and living unit, and a space capable of sustaining the concentrated work of four people in isolated/insulated conditions for up to 120 days. In 1994 Vuk Ćosić, the pioneer of the net.art movement, starts to work.

2005
The untimely death of Igor Zabel, probably the most important »exporter« of Slovenian contemporary art and a connector for the Slovenian art scene with the rest of the world. He was a curator, writer and theoretician active from the beginning of the '90s.

After 2009
Slovenia gets its first museum for contemporary art and collecting contemporary art becomes a national sport.

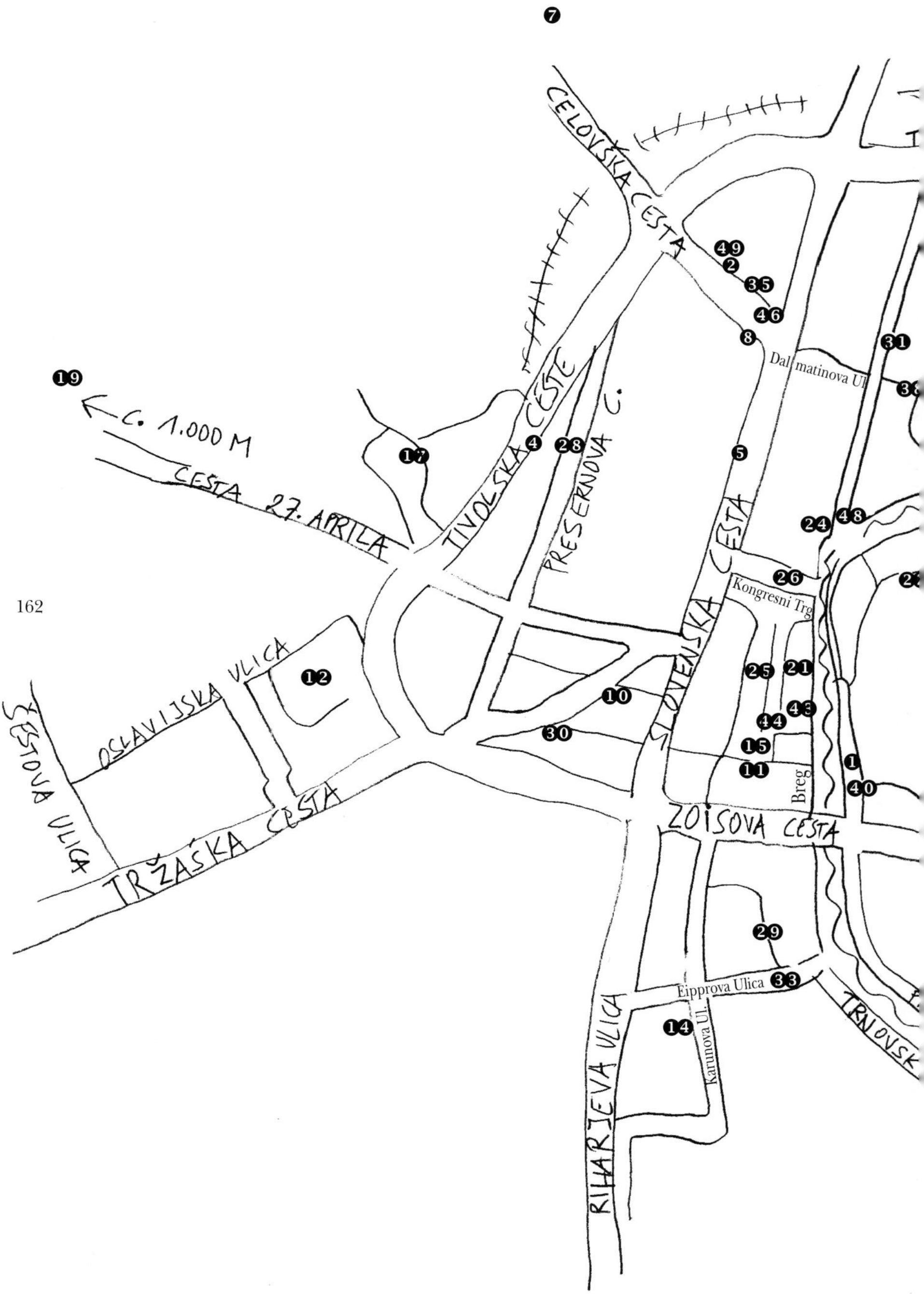
CELOVŠKA CESTA
TIVOLSKA CESTE
PRESERNOVA C.
← c. 1.000 M
CESTA 27. APRILA
SLOVENSKA CESTA
Dalmatinova Ul.
Kongresni Trg
Breg
ZOISOVA CESTA
OSLAVIJSKA ULICA
ŠESTOVA ULICA
TRŽAŠKA CESTA
Eipprova Ulica
Karunova Ul.
RIHARJEVA ULICA

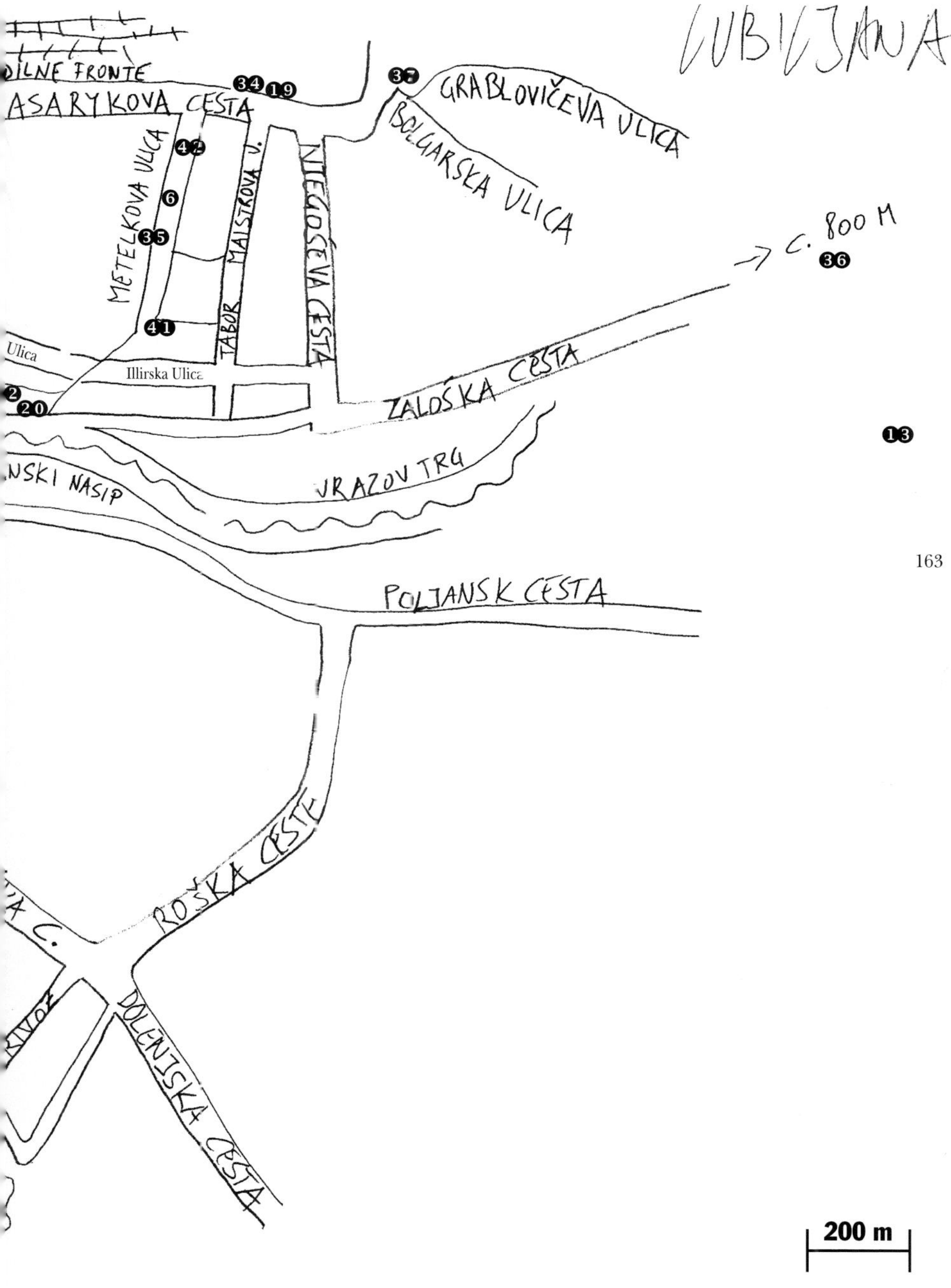
LJUBLJANA
ILNE FRONTE
ASARYKOVA CESTA
34
19
37
GRABLOVIČEVA ULICA
BOLGARSKA ULICA
METELKOVA ULICA
42
6
35
41
MAISTROVA U.
NJEGOŠEVA CESTA
TABOR
Ulica
Illirska Ulica
2
20
ZALOŠKA CESTA
C. 800 M
36
13
VRAZOV TRG
NSKI NASIP
POLJANSK CESTA
ROŠKA CESTE
A C.
RIVOZ
DOLENJSKA CESTA
200 m

Prague

Charles bridge with St. Nikolas church in the background

With kind regards from Švejk

Czech artists manage to do a lot with a little and keep it fun with irony and typical black humour.

166

—

By Mimi Fronczak Rogers

As the twentieth anniversary of the 1989 revolution rolls around, it's dispiriting that two decades of Czech art still suffer from an entrenched provincialism – and it's no longer possible to blame this isolation solely on forty years of Communism. The rivalries and squabbles inherent in a cultural scene where everyone knows everyone prevent a broader outlook from taking root. And then there's the burden of the grand cultural heritage of the Czechs: »Czech artists have to live with the burden of their grand cultural heritage, which makes them less free« says the Slovak artist Boris Ondreička.

Yet it was only a century ago that Czech culture readily embraced new ideas from abroad. In the first decade of the 20th century, the S.V.U. or Mánes Spolek výtvarných umělců (Mánes Association of Fine Artists) staged a series of important shows – Auguste Rodin, the Nabis, French Impressionists – that put Prague on the European art map. There was a lively exchange between Prague and other art centres, especially Paris, which kept fresh impulses flowing to the Bohemian metropolis. Czech art historian and collector Vincenc Kramář was one of the first anywhere to recognize Picasso's genius and bring his works to Prague, where his Analytical Cubism not only received a warm welcome but was quickly adopted by Czech artists and spawned the uniquely Czech phenomenon of Cubist architecture and design.

Now, Prague can once again claim multiple big shows and fairs of international contemporary art – the Prague Biennial, the art fair Art Prague and the annual event Tina B (an acronym for »this is not another biennial«), which grew out of a frustration with the unprofessional bickering between the organizers of the other events. Tina B aims to challenge the public's conception of major art events through actions like placing billboards with texts by artists in public spaces throughout the city. While these shows haven't turned Prague into a must-go art city, there is a glut of biennials, they have managed to exposed local audiences to loads of contemporary art from abroad.

Of course, chronically meagre funding and state support stalls progress. Even before the worldwide economic crisis, art institutions were struggling to stage major exhibitions of international art, usually »package shows« picked up from other institutions. The insurance alone is prohibitive. It means that anyone wanting to see important international shows has to head to Vienna or Berlin. And perhaps this is the biggest change since 1989, people can now freely cross borders for art's sake.

But Czech culture has a talent for doing a lot with a little. A significant number of Czech artists are developing subversive strategies to address the country's socio-political realities, recalling the

There was a lively exchange between Prague and other art centres, especially Paris

Letná Park

Monument to the Victims of Communism
by Olbram Zoubek

View from Shooter's Island to Prague Castle over Museum Kampa

Holešovice Port

Metro station námestí míru

Sculpture by David Černý inside of Lucerna Passage

best of the pre-revolution underground art scene. Artists like Kateřina Šedá are making art that takes a conceptual approach to the social space. Her Chalupecký Prize–winning project *It Doesn't Matter* was a social action that was realized in the intimate sphere of her own family's daily life. It was prompted by her grandmother's circumstances; after she retired from her job as the head of a stockroom she retreated into a life of absolute idleness. Her response to nearly every question was »to je jedno« (it doesn't matter) a common Czech phrase which, taken to this extreme, became a declaration of her utter indifference to life. Šedá literally drew her grandmother out of her torpor, putting her »back to work« making drawings of all the items from the stockroom. The intangible yet transformative project resulted in nothing less than the reawakening of her grandmother's connection to society. Groups like Guma Guar, Rafani and Ztohoven are also making strong and direct artistic statements. Ztohoven's high jinx of hacking into an early-morning weather report and superimposing footage of a mushroom cloud rising from the north Bohemian mountains won the art collective a prestigious national art award even as the group was facing trial for scaremongering.

Another positive aspect of Czech culture is its ability to laugh at itself. The Czech art world was stirred up by David Černý's sculpture *Entropa*, unveiled in Brussels to mark the Czech takeover of the revolving EU presidency in 2009. Černý was commissioned by the Czech government to create a sculpture collaboratively with one artist from every EU member state. Instead, he and two friends created the piece themselves, a fact that was revealed only when the work was already in place. The hoax included the creation of fake artists names, CVs, even websites. It was conceptual art as dreamed up by Švejk.

A positive aspect of Czech culture is its ability to laugh at itself

Entropa, with its »grotesque exaggeration and mystification,« which Černý cites as typical characteristics of Czech art, sends up popular Czech misconceptions and stereotypes about the rest of Europe. Černý was showing uncharacteristic optimism that Europe could laugh along with him. This art prankster's sculpture – probably the only remarkable EU-funded artwork to date – has held a mirror up to the Czech Republic and all of Europe and sparked heated debate, as good art has always done. —

Each year a little better

The U.S.-born artist and curator *Barbara Benish*, who lives in the Czech Republic, on the hard reality of the art market machine in the post-Communist '90s, the conformity of some young emerging artists today, and the hope for change.

By *Mimi Fronczak Rogers*

As an American-born artist with Czech roots, you travelled to Prague and forged connections with the unofficial, pre-1989 art scene and then settled here in the early '90s. What have been the biggest changes you've witnessed in this period?

BARBARA BENISH: Well, there are the obvious changes that have affected the entire region. It was an exciting and fascinating period for that middle generation of artists who had grown up under Bolshevism, and were suddenly »let out of the cage«. Art thrived. But artists were eventually faced with the hard reality of surviving in a very competitive and international market. There are lots of young, savvy artists who have entered that art market machine who don't much remember what happened before 1989, and are cranking out work that looks like the »flavour-of-the-month« and is totally unoriginal. That's the downside of it. They've lost their roots and a connection to the older generation of Czech artists. Traditionally, each generation of art passed on something to the next, like a teacher to a student. That continuum was interrupted here to some extent with the incredible changes in 1989.

In the summer of 1989, the Dialogue: Prague / Los Angeles *project you co-curated with Zdenka Gabalová in Prague broke down cultural barriers months before the start of the revolution on November 17th. How did people react to the show?*

The exhibtion the Lidový dům (House for People) in Prague was unique since it was the first time since the Cold War began that contemporary American art came to Prague with the artists themselves participating in the exchange. Hundreds of people came to Prague from all around the country, pitching in money for gas and car-pooling to attend our opening night. Grannies were pulling our posters off the walls around town, telling us they never thought they would live to see the day when the American flag was posted in their country again without prosecution.

How have the artists who were active in the underground scene before 1989 adjusted?

My guess would be that about 20 to 30 percent survived the changes. Their every breathing moment in the '80s was filled with trying to bring about change. It takes a strong individual to be able to leave that kind of passion behind and suddenly try to survive on selling a painting to a rich collector visiting from New York. So unfortunately there are many good Czech and Slovak artists from the older generation who are still not known in the West, because they don't have any »marketing skills«.

The cash is here, but it's only been 20 years since anyone has legally had it

Which Czech artists have succeeded abroad?

Ivan Kafka from the middle generation and Kateřina Štenclová, younger artists like Jiří Černický, David Černý, Milena Dopitová or Veronika Bromová. They were already the best here in the Czech Republic.

Barbara Benish was raised in the U.S. and moved to the Czech Republic in 1993, after completing a year as a Fulbright scholar in Prague. She has had numerous exhibitions in Europe and the U.S., and her work is represented in public and private art collections around the world. Benish has additionally curated and organized a dozen shows, including the groundbreaking project *Dialogue: Prague/Los Angeles* in 1989. She is also director of Galerie Califia.

Have the major institutions like the National Gallery and the Prague City Gallery genuinely transformed themselves?

I think Olga Malá and Karel Srp, the head curators at the Prague City Gallery have done a fantastic job of blending the best young and middle-generation Czech art with incoming foreign impulses, despite having to deal with a difficult budget. The National Gallery is another story.

What continues to hinder the development of a normally functioning art market? Classic Modernist Czech art sells moderately well, but what needs to happen for contemporary Czech art to find its market?

Taste and time. The cash is here, but it's only been 20 years since anyone has legally had it. So this nouveau-riche generation has to buy all their toys – cars, computers, houses – before a more mature sense of acquisition sets in. But it will happen. Each year gets a little better.

Who is collecting Czech art?

Foreigners visiting here, Czech émigrés returning to Prague, new business investors. There is a large international community in Prague that is a vibrant combination of locals and foreigners, the moneyed circle. They look at one another's collections and then want to get the same artists for their collection, and then it starts. We just need to be patient. —

Prague

By Mimi Fronczak Rogers

View on Prague Castle

ART

❶ **Dům U Zlatého prstenu (House at the Golden Ring)** — This is where the Prague City Gallery houses its permanent collection of 20th-century art in addition to rotating short-term exhibitions. Recently reopened after reconstruction, the house (two unified medieval buildings) combines original architectural features with 21st-century touches. The newly installed permanent display focuses on the development of Czech art after 1989, offering a fresh take on contemporary art history. There is also an onsite literary café.

Týnská 6, (224 827 002)
Metro A, tram 17, 18: Staroměstská
Tue-Sun 10 am to 8 pm
Full price admission 120 Kč
www.ghmp.cz

❷ **Museum Kampa** — One of the most respected art institutions in town, the Kampa Museum is located in a former mill on the riverfront with a gorgeous terrace café. Its exceptional collection of Modern art was built up over decades by financier Jan Mládek and his wife, art patron Meda Mládek, who lived in exile before the Velvet Revolution. Sculpture by Otto Gutfreund and works by František Kupka are the high points and mingle with Modern art from Central Europe. It puts on strong temporary shows in its Stables gallery.

U Sovových mlýnů 2,
Kampa Island,
(257 286 147)
Metro A: Malostranská,
tram 6, 9, 22, 23: Újezd
Mon-Sun 10 am to 6 pm
Full price admission 120 Kč;
free first Wednesday of the month
www.museumkampa.cz

❸ **Dům u erné Matky Boží (House at the Black Madonna)** — This temple to Cubist art, operated by the National Gallery, is located in a building designed by Josef Gočár – perhaps the finest example of Cubist architecture in Prague. Its Cubist café is one of the most stylish places to sip coffee in town. A street-level shop sells reproduction pieces from this seminal design movement.

Ovocný trh 19, (224 211 746)
Metro B, tram 5, 14, 26: Náměstí Republiky
Tue-Sun 10 am to 6 pm
Full price admission 100 Kč;
free first Wednesday of the month
from 3 pm to 8 pm
www.ngprague.cz

❹ **Galerie Rudolfinum** — The Kunsthalle-style gallery inside this 19th-century Rudolfinum concert building has so far been the only place in Prague to regularly exhibit travelling shows by international names. In between these shows it presents retrospectives of Czech artists from the middle generation as well as overlooked Modernists,

peppered with engaging shows of contemporary Chinese art, a specialty of the gallery's director Petr Nedoma.

Alšovo nábřeží 12, (227 059 346)
Metro A, tram 17, 18: Staroměstská
Tue-Sun 11 am to 6 pm
Full price admission 120 Kč
www.galerierudolfinum.cz

❺ Dům U Kamenného zvonu (House at the Stone Bell) — This space, run by the Prague City Gallery in a Gothic sandstone building on the Old Town Square, is known for staging retrospectives of Czech Modernist artists as well as for exhibiting contemporary artists such as Veronika Bromová. It is also home to the Zvon biennial.

Staroměstské náměstí 13,
(224 827 526)
Metro A, tram 17, 18: Staroměstská
Tue-Sun 10 am to 8 pm
Full price admission 120 Kč
www.citygalleryprague.cz

❻ Staroměstská radnice (Old Town Hall) — Old Town Hall contains two different exhibition spaces. The one on the ground floor shows mostly photography exhibitions, while the one on the second floor is operated by the Prague City Gallery and specializes in introducing the public to the youngest wave of Czech artists, sometimes fresh from the art academy, by giving them their first big solo show.

Staroměstské náměstí 1,
(224 810 036 or 224 482 751)
Metro A, tram 17, 18: Staroměstská
Tue-Sun 10 am to 6 pm
Full price admission 40 Kč
www.citygalleryprague.cz

❼ DOX: Centrum současného umění (Centre for Contemporary Art) — Five years in the making, this new independent centre for contemporary art opened in the autumn of 2008 in a complex that combines stunning renovated industrial spaces with newly constructed spaces. Its powerful debut, featuring installations by several artists, including José María Cano's *Welcome to Capitalism!*, illustrated DOX's mission

to present current trends in contemporary art, emphasizing global issues, and to spark dialogue among artists and disciplines. Its program of panel discussions and artist talks takes place Mondays at 6 pm in its café, which in warm weather opens onto a large terrace.

Osadní 34, (224 930 927)
Tram 5, 12, 15: Ortenovo náměstí
Mon 10 am to 6 pm, Wed-Fri 11 am to 7 pm,
Sat-Sun 10 am to 6 pm
Full price admission 120 Kč
www.doxprague.cz

❽ Karlín Studios — Housed in a two-story former factory building with large expanses of floor space and lots of natural light, Karlín Studios operates its own public gallery in addition to providing space for the private gallery Entrance, which gives young artists their start. It also contains studio space for a select group of more than 25 of the country's leading contemporary artists, including Josef Bolf, Štěpánka Šimlová and Evžen Šimera, and holds open houses inviting the public into the artists' studios. Recently, Divus, the publisher of the art magazine *Umělec* (Artist), moved its offices into the complex.

Křižíkova 34, (251 511 804)
Metro B: Křižíkova,
tram 8, 24: Karlínské náměstí
Tue-Sun noon to 6 pm
www.karlinstudios.cz

❾ TranzitDisplay — This independent art spaces began life as Galerie Display in a graffiti-splashed storefront in 2001, but has relocated under the name TranzitDisplay to more refined quarters together with tranzit, a long-term initiative by Kontakt. The Arts und Civil society Program of Erste Group. Its risk-taking program emphasizes conceptual art from abroad and cross-border cooperation, connecting Prague audiences with young European artists. It is co-directed by prominent curator Vít Havránek.

Dittrichova 9, (604 722 562)
Metro B: Karlovo náměstí, tram 3, 4, 10, 14, 16: Palackého náměstí, 18, 24: Moráň
Tue-Sun noon to 6 pm
www.tranzitdisplay.cz

❿ Futura — After its opening in 2003, Futura rose to the top ranks of the Prague gallery circuit with remarkable speed and finesse. Blending

white-cube and warren-like cellar spaces, plus a labyrinthine series of nooks for video works and a project room for experimental installations, Futura is worth the trip to Smíchov to see a blend of young and established Czech artists and bright stars of European contemporary art. Don't miss David Černý's provocative installation in the courtyard.

Holečkova 49, (251 511 804)
Tram 4, 7, 9, 10: Bertramka,
bus 176: Holečkova
Wed-Sun 11 am to 6 pm
www.futuraprojekt.cz

⓫ Galerie Václava Špály — The Václav Špála Gallery's golden era was the second half of the '60s, when its curator was the theoretician and critic Jindřich

Chalupecký, but its standards sank drastically in recent years and its closure in 2006 was the coup de grace. It has recently reopened under the guidance of well-known critic Lenka Lindaurová and artists Pavel Humhal and Vladimír Skrepl with a daring and intelligent program and has returned to a newer tradition, which began after the Velvet Revolution, of hosting a solo show for the past year's Chalupecký Prize laureate.

Národní třída 30, (222 356 213)
Metro B, tram 6, 9, 18, 21, 22, 23:
Národní třída
Tue-Sun noon to 8 pm,
Thur noon to 10 pm
Full price admission 60 Kč,
free Thurs 6 pm to 10 pm
www.spalovka.cz

⓬ **Hunt Kastner Artworks** — This private gallery was established by American art professionals Camille Hunt and Kacha Kastner, both longtime residents of Prague, with the aim of nurturing the careers of a stable of Czech contemporary artists, including Josef Bolf, Štěpánka Šimlová and Daniel Pitín, and to help develop the contemporary art market. The gallery has been active on the international art fair circuit, presenting its artists in places like Basel, Miami and Vienna.

Kamenická 22, (233 376 259)
Metro C: Vltavská, tram 1, 8, 15, 25, 26:
Kamenická
Tue-Fri 1 pm to 6 pm,
Sat 2 pm to 6 pm,
closed in August
www.huntkastner.com

⓭ **Jiří Švestka Gallery** — Since 1995, returned émigré Jiří Švestka has been specialising in internationally recognised Czech artists like Krištof Kintera and Markéta Othová and showing international names like Ioana Nemes. Located in a former photography atelier, it is one of the few Czech galleries to be active on the international art fair scene, disseminating information about Czech art beyond its borders.

Biskupský dvůr 6, (222 311 092)
Metro B: Náměstí Republiky,
tram 3, 8, 24, 26: Bílá labuť
Tue-Fri noon to 6 pm,
Sat 11 am to 6 pm
www.jirisvestka.com

⓮ **Galerie Zdeněk Sklenář** — Along the banks of the Vltava River, the classy Zdeněk Sklenář Gallery showcases the latest works of the still-active senior generation of artists such as Karel Malich and Zdeněk Sýkora, but also presents younger artists like Federico Díaz. The gallery publishes gorgeous monographs and editions of graphics, and has also brought the art of Czech Modernist František Kupka to China, Cambodia and Thailand. The gallery staff is enthusiastic and happy to discuss the works with visitors.

Smetanovo nábřeží 4, (224 218 528)
Metro B: Národní třída,
tram 6, 9, 17, 18, 21, 22, 23:
Národní divadlo
Wed-Sat 1 pm to 6 pm
www.zdeneksklenar.cz

⓯ **Leica Gallery Prague** — This highly respected photography gallery, especially notable for supporting documentary work, recently reopened in a new location in New Town. There is an excellent onsite photography bookshop and a café serving international fare. When it was without a permanent home after losing its space at Prague Castle, it cleverly invited photographers, most notably Sebastiao Salgado, to exhibit their work on a renovated train that took art to people throughout the country.

Školská 28, (722 924 039)
Tram 3, 9, 14, 24: Vodičkova
Mon-Sun 11 am to 9 pm
Full price admission 50 Kč
www.lgp.cz

⓰ **Langhans Gallerie Praha** — This beautifully renovated building used to contain the Jan Langhans Atelier, where the elite of interwar Prague went to have their portraits made. The gallery puts on an excellent program of photography exhibitions by established and emerging, local and international photographers.

Vodičkova 37, (222 929 333)
Metro A, B: Můstek,
tram 3, 9, 14, 24: Vodičkova
Tue-Fri noon to 6 pm,
Sat 11 am to 4 pm
Full price admission 60 Kč
www.langhansgalerie.cz

ART EVENTS

Prague Biennial — The Prague Biennial, which started in 2003, was the brainchild of Giancarlo Politi, the publisher and editor of *Flash Art*, and Helena Kontová, the journal's top editor and a Czech émigrée. They originally worked in cooperation with their old friend Milan Knížák, the director of the National Gallery, but after an acrimonious split the latter decided to start his own biennial event. Concept: Young curators represent a selection of young, mostly unknown, mainly European, artists, in each case united by a special theme.

Thámova 8 Karlín Hall, (224 254 435)
Metro B: Křižíkova, tram 8, 24:
Karlínské náměstí
May/July
www.praguebiennale.org

Tina B — The anti-biennial (its name a crafty acronym for »This Is Not Another Biennial«), Tina B is an annual contemporary art festival started in 2006 and held in the autumn. It hasn't yet solidified its identity or anchored in one particular space, bouncing from the pristine halls of the National Gallery's Veletržní palác to an alternative space in a run-down building across the street from Veletržní. In addition to highlighting emerging artists from diverse geographical locations, Tina B has moved art out of traditional exhibition spaces with an art street party, a citywide artists' billboard project, and even a recreation of a meeting of Communist leadership, which took place in a factory the day after the Russian-led invasion in August 1968.

Biennial office:
Janovského 23, (774 155 591)
Metro C: Holešovice
Autumn
www.tina-b.com

Art Prague – veletrh současného umění (Art Prague contemporary art fair) — A beacon of the cause to rebuild a tradition of art collecting in this country, the Art Prague art fair is usually held in May or June at the Mánes Gallery and various other venues, and is growing bigger by the year. More than 40 galleries from the Czech Republic are joined by a sprinkling from France, Germany, Italy and elsewhere. Roundtable and panel discussions are well attended, and especially popular is its Nocturno event, when the fair venues stay open late at night, allowing people who work during the day to see the exhibits. An outgrowth of the art fair is the Association of Gallerists of the Czech Republic, established in 2006 with the twin goals of educating the art-buying public and supporting the careers of contemporary artists.

Art fair office:
Řetězová 7, (602 277 210)
Tram 17, 18: Karlovy lázně
May/June
www.artprague.cz

Prague Photo veletrh fotografie (photography fair) — In 2008, the organisers of Art Prague (Iva Nesvadbová and Milan Jaroš) started a separate fair focusing on contemporary and Modern photography. It is held every April in the Mánes Gallery spaces and showcases the work of around 80 artists and more than a dozen galleries focusing on photography, also including the publishers of photography books and magazines.

Art fair office:
Římská 32, (602 277 210)
Tram 11: Italská
April
www.praguefoto.cz

ALTERNATIVE SIGHTSEEING

⓱ Žižkovská televizní věž (Žižkov TV Tower) — Known popularly as Husák's Finger, for the last Communist president, or by the more vulgar nickname the »Prague Penis«, this space-age transmission tower was started in Communist times but completed only in 1992. Considered an eyesore by many, it is a soaring Prague landmark that can't be ignored. You can take an express lift up to the observation deck for stunning views of Prague and well beyond on a

clear day, and there is also a restaurant where you can have a drink or a meal 66 metres above the city (standard Czech fare, but with prices corresponding to the altitude). The original retro-futurist décor is well preserved. David Černý's giant baby sculptures appear to be crawling up the outside of the tower.

Mahlerovy sady 1, (242 418 778)
Metro A, tram 11: Jiřího z Poděbrad
Daily 10 am to 11.30 pm
www.tower.cz

⓲ Vyšehrad (High Castle) — A favourite place for Prague natives to escape urban stress while staying well within city limits, the hilltop fortress Vyšehrad is a peaceful green space infused with ancient legends about the first Bohemian rulers, the Přemyslids. It is held dear by Czechs as a mystical place connected with the birth of the Czech nation. The cemetery next to the church of St. Peter and Paul is the final resting place of many great personalities including Mucha, Smetana and Dvořák (no politicians, please). Vyšehrad (it means high castle) affords lovely views and also has a Romanesque rotunda, an open-air theatre and a children's playground, among other attractions. Below Vyšehrad there is an enclave of Cubist buildings.

V pevnosti 159/5b, (241 410 348)
Metro C: Vyšehrad
November-March : daily 9.30 am to 5 pm,
April-October: daily 9.30 am to 6 pm
www.praha-vysehrad.cz

⓳ Letenské sady (Letná Park) — The giant metronome on a hill overlooking the river marks the spot where an enormous statue of Stalin once stood, and it leads the way to the wonderful Letná Park, where you'll find the oldest still-functioning carousel in Europe. The area behind the metronome (by the sculptor Vratislav Karel Novák, erected in 1991) is famous with skateboarders around Europe, and the large outdoor beer garden (line up at the kiosk for drinks) is a great spot to drink in the view of Prague and people-watch. Next to the beer garden is the Letenský zámeček restaurant in a little castle-like building.

Letenské sady
Tram 1, 25, 26:
Letenské náměstí;
tram 5, 8, 12, 14, 17:
nábřeží Kapitána Jaroše

Muellerova Villa (Müller Villa) — The clean geometric planes and stark facade of this famous villa built by Adolf Loos in 1928–30 still seem contemporary today. Now operated by the Prague Municipal Museum, this house in the lovely Střešovice neighbourhood was Loos' most important building in the Czech lands and the house the architect himself considered his most beautiful. He declared that it best embodied his »Raumplan« concept. After a painstaking reconstruction, the villa was opened to the public in 2000 and now can be toured by appointment (an online reservation form is on the website).

Nad Hradním vodojemem 14, (224 312 012)
Tram 1, 18: Ořechovka
Viewing by appointment
www.mullerovavila.cz

Kutná Hora — Around 70 km outside of Prague, Kutná Hora rose to fame in the Middle Ages and was the second most important city in the Bohemian kingdom because of its vast silver deposits, which were mined and minted here. St. Barbara's Cathedral was constructed over the course of two centuries and is topped by a great sail-like roof. A trip to Kutná Hora isn't complete without a visit to the »Bone Church« in the village of Sedlec, 1.6 km from Kutná Hora, where human bones – from victims of plague and war – have been artistically arranged into bizarre sculptures.

Buses to Kutná Hora run from
Florenc bus station
Metro B and C: Florenc
Trains run from the main railway.
Check timetables at www.idos.cz
A local bus runs between Kutná Hora
(Masarykova Street) and Sedlec.
Get a ticket at a newsstand before boarding
www.kostnice.cz

SHOPPING

❷⓪ Bohemian Retro — For a long time you couldn't find many vintage shops in former Eastern-bloc countries, because everyone wanted to buy from stores like Zara and H&M. But it seems people are starting to grow tired of this global style and are scouting out places like this shop, which specializes in Bohemian vintage from the '20s to the '80s. Full of cool stuff at great prices.

Čajkovského 22, (607 914 992)
Tram 5, 9, 26: Lipanská
Tue-Fri 2 pm to 7 pm
www.bohemianretro.com

❷① Shakespeare and Sons — A English-language bookseller, with two locations. The Krymská Street location, a bit removed from the city centre, sells new and used books, offers a great selection of art and design books and has a café/bar that hosts literary readings and live music. The centrally located Malá Strana shop sells new books in English and German also about design, art and architecture.

Krymská 12, (271 740 839)
Tram 4, 22, 23: Krymská
Mon-Sun 10 am to 12 am

U Lužického semináře 10,
(257 531 894)
Metro A: Malostranská
Mon-Sun 11 am to 7 pm
www.shakes.cz

㉒ Dvorní vinotéka (Dvorní wineshop) — Prague is full of shops where you can buy a bottle or two of Czech tipple to bring back home, and most ordinary groceries even have a liquor section, but the Dvorní wineshop offers a couple of harder-to-find specialties and you can also ask the staff here for recommendations of excellent Moravian wine. Slivovice, a kind of plum brandy, is best when homemade and from Moravia, but Žufánek is a top-quality commercial brand that can be found here. Among other Czech specialties is the herbal liquor Becherovka (available everywhere), which is made from a closely guarded secret recipe in the spa town of Karlovy Vary (Carlsbad). It is an acquired taste for some, but there are those who swear by it. Many visitors to Prague are eager to sample the fabled »green fairy«, but Czech absinthe has little relation to the historical drink of the Belle Époque and can be extremely bitter.

Uhelní trh 9, (224 239 600)
Metro A, B: Můstek
www.dvornivinoteka.cz

CAFÉS

㉓ Café Louvre — Franz Kafka, Max Brod, Albert Einstein and the brothers

Karel and Josef Čapek used to frequent this café. The deep pink and cream walls, replete with stucco detailing, together with the waitstaff bustling about in long white aprons and bowties, create a gracious atmosphere that recalls the golden era of Bohemian café society. Downstairs is the Galerie Fotografie Louvre, which reopened in 2008 with a program of high-quality photography shows.

Národní třída 20, (224 930 949)
Metro B, tram 6, 9, 18, 21, 22, 23: Národní třída
Mon-Fri 8 am to 11.30 pm,
Sat-Sun 9 am to 11.30 pm
www.cafelouvre.cz

㉔ Café Slavia — This legendary literary and theatrical haunt, with its huge green-dialed clock and Viktor Oliva's painting *The Absinthe Drinker*, is still one of the premier meeting places in the city centre. Unbeatable views of Prague Castle across the river and great people-watching plus moderately priced food and drink, and Wi-Fi access. Just steps away is the Zdeněk Sklenář Gallery and down the street is the Václav Špála Gallery (see »art«). Across the street is Nová Scéna, an annex to the National Theatre designed by Karel Prager and completed in 1983 – memorably described as looking like »frozen piss«.

This is where the world-renowned Laterna Magica performances are held.

Národní třída at Smetanovo nábřeží,
(224 218 493)
Tram 6, 9, 17, 18, 21, 22, 23:
Národní divadlo
Mon-Sun 8 am to 11 pm
www.cafeslavia.cz

㉕ Historie cukrárny MYŠÁK (Historic confectionery MYŠÁK) — After a painstaking reconstruction, this famous First Republic sweet shop and café is open once again, serving delicious cakes and coffee drinks in a space that beautifully recreates its glory days, elaborately decorated with the original stucco, mosaics, marble staircase and woodwork.

Vodičkova 31, (731 653 813)
Metro A, B: Můstek, tram 3, 9, 14, 24:
Václavské náměstí
Mon-Fr 8 am to 8 pm,
Sat 9 am to 8 pm

RESTAURANTS

㉖ La Degustation Bohême Bourgeoise — Perhaps the most interesting restaurant on the Prague dining scene, an evening spent here is less a meal than an event, tripping delightfully from course to course – seven in all plus seven amuses-bouches. Chef Oldřich Sahajdák draws inspiration from 19th-century Bohemian cuisine and enlivens it with modern molecular gastronomy. A full meal here can last three hours, but you can opt for an abbreviated after-theatre menu. Prix fixe lunch menus with two courses start at around 600 Kč; seven-course dinners range upward from around 1,800 Kč.

Haštalská 18, (222 311 894)
Tram 5, 8, 14: Dlouhá třída
Mon-Sat 5 pm to 12 am
Visa, Mastercard, American Express, JCB
www.ladegustation.cz

㉗ Angel — Chef Sofia Smith has been active on the Prague dining scene for several years, having run a popular series of monthly dining events at other restaurants and, before that, the Angel Café and catering business. At the end of 2007 she opened this sophisticated bastion of fusion cuisine, marrying Asian and Continental traditions with deft balance. Main dishes start at 325 Kč.

V Kolkovně 7, (773 222 422)
Metro A, tram 17, 18: Staroměstská
Mon-Sat 11.30 am to 2.30 pm,
6.30 pm to 10 pm,
Sun 11 am to 4 pm
Visa, Mastercard, American Express
www.angelrestaurant.cz

㉘ Lehká hlava (Light Head) — Set in a 15th-century building on a tiny Old Town street, this is probably the best place in the city for vegetarian fare, with lots of vegan options. The cheerful and eclectically decorated restaurant and teahouse is non-smoking and child-friendly. Main dishes start at 130 Kč.

Boršov 2, (222 220 665)
Metro A: Staroměstská,
tram 17, 18: Karlovy Lázně
Mon-Fri 11.30 am to 11.30 pm,
Sat-Sun noon to 11.30 pm
Visa, Mastercard, JCB
www.lehkahlava.cz

㉙ Akropolis — This complex is one of the leading Prague concert venues, and its connected restaurant is a popular meeting place for a meal or drinks. Akropolis' ongoing *United Colours of Akropolis* and *EuroConnections* cycles bring important world and ethnic acts to Prague. The interior design of the concert hall and restaurant is by well-known artist František Skála. Vegetarian main dishes start at 85 Kč.

Kubelíkova 27, (296 330 911,
Metro A: Jiřího z Poděbrad,
tram 5, 9, 26: Lipanská

Café: Mon-Fri 10 am to 12 am,
Sat-Sun 4 pm to 12 am
(box office is in the café)

Restaurant: Mon-Sun 11 am to 1 am;
performances usually start at 7.30 pm
www.palacakropolis.cz

❸❶ **Jan Paukert** — Beautifully constructed chlebíčky, little open-faced sandwiches with ruffles of deli meats, cheeses, sprigs of herbs and fanned pickle garnishes, are the star at this newly reopened delicatessen, where they are said to have been first created around 1916. Along with Paukert's array of dainty sandwiches, one of the best bargains in town are hot breakfasts and lunches, with vegetarian options, cold salads and pastries. Ideal for a quick bite between stops at the many neighbourhood galleries. Sandwiches start at 17 Kč.

Národní třída 17,
(224 222 615)
Metro B, tram 6, 9, 18, 21, 22, 23:
Národní třída
Mon-Fri 8 am to 8 pm,
Sat-Sun 10 am to 8 pm
www.janpaukert.cz

PARTY

❸❶ **Roxy** — This legendary club right in the heart of Old Town served as a ballroom in former times and its shabby-chic interior is full of atmosphere. The Roxy has a rich and varied program of dance music, theatrical performances, film screenings, and parties and pulls in concerts by such acts as Skinny Puppy, Arrested Development, Transglobal Underground and Maximo Park. Inside the same complex, up the stairs, is the alternative gallery NoD.

Dlouhá 33, (224 826 296)
Tram 5, 8, 14: Dlouhá třída
Mon-Thur 8 pm to 2 am,
Fri-Sat 8 pm to 4 am
www.klubroxy.cz

❸❷ **Chapeau Rouge** — This Old Town haunt, whose history dates back to the First Republic, has, in its current incarnation, a bar at street level with a slightly seedy vibe and two floors below deck, a downstairs dance club and a Live Underground space one more flight down. Decorated by the noted Czech street artist Cheet, this space is where live acts perform everything from hip hop to hardcore. The bar, with drinks that are low-priced for the location, attracts a lively mix of people and can get quite crowded.

Jakubská 2, (222 316 328)
Metro B: Náměstí Republiky
Mon-Thur noon to 3 am, Fri noon to 4 am,
Sat-Sun 4 pm to 4 am
www.chapeaurouge.cz

❸❸ **Mecca** — A bit outside the city centre, in the trendy industrial neighbourhood of Holešovice, this large club is where the cream of Prague nightlife comes to dance. The club brings in excellent DJs like David Morales who play the music loud enough for you to feel the beat. Drink prices tend to be somewhat lower than at clubs in the centre, justifying the taxi fare after the dancing is done.

U průhonu 3, (283 870 522)
Tram 5, 12, 15: U průhonu
Wed, Fri, Sat 10 pm to 6 am
www.mecca.cz

34 Radost FX — Hot club with a disco, lounge, good vegetarian restaurant and café. This is where »tout le monde« gathers to celebrate parties and dance to soul, house and R&B. On the second Friday of each month is the gay-friendly Lollypop night, with fashion shows, entertainment and DJs into the wee hours.

Bělehradská 120, (224 254 776)
Metro C, tram 4, 6, 10, 11, 16, 22, 23: I.P. Pavlova, Daily 11 am to 4 am
www.radostfx.cz

35 Divadlo Archa (Archa Theatre) — Archa is the address for experimental theatre, dance and music as well as intimate concert performances by big names like Philip Glass, Meredith Monk or even King Crimson. This is where Václav Havel's first play in twenty years, *Leaving*, premiered in Prague.

Na Poříčí 26, (221 716 333)
Metro B: Náměstí Republiky,
tram 3, 8, 24, 26: Bílá labuť
Box office open Mon-Fri 10 am to 6 pm and 2 hours before curtain
www.archatheatre.cz

36 La Fabrika — This experimental space in the Holešovice neighbourhood retains the industrial feel of its former life as a factory. It has a large bar whose spacious interior of warm exposed brick and wood is punctuated by industrial touches like slender cast-iron columns and heavy-duty ventilation ducts. It is a great place to see dance, jazz or concerts, or even to sit in on the filming of the noted Czech photographer Jan Saudek's talk show.

Komunardů 30
Tram 1, 3, 5, 12, 15, 25: Dělnická
Bar and ticket office open from 6.30 pm
www.lafabrika.cz

37 Kino Aero — In the gritty Žižkov district, this arthouse cinema is highly popular with locals. Its slightly shabby interior has great atmosphere, and the foyer bar is a neighbourhood magnet (you can bring your drinks to your seats in the cinema). The Aero hosts festivals, retrospectives, a children's series and a once monthly »blind date«: You show up not knowing what film is playing and pay a sum of your choosing only after the film, depending on how much you liked it. If you've already seen the movie and leave within the first 15 minutes, tell the bartender and you'll get a free beer.

Biskupcova 31,
(608 330 088)
Tram 1, 9, 16: Ohrada, 9, 10, 16, 19: Biskupcova
Screenings daily at 6 and 8.30 pm

(except Sun), with late showings on Fri and Sat
www.kinoaero.cz

38 Jazz Lounge »U staré paní« (»At the Old Lady's«) — Prague is a jazz city, and the club »At the Old Lady's«, located in a charming cellar space on one of Old Town's romantic cobble-stoned streets, is a wonderful place to catch ensembles like the Robert Balzar Trio and other regulars on the lively Czech jazz scene. The club serves light international fare as well as snacks all night long. The place can fill up quickly, so arrive early to ensure getting a table.

Michalská 9, (603 551 680)
Metro A, B: Můstek
Mon-Sun 7 pm to 2 am,
shows start at 9 pm
www.jazzlounge.cz

39 Tretters — This is a great place to get an expertly made cocktail in Old Town. The '30s-era décor and grand bar are a classy stage set for Tretters' talented mixologists – and the beautiful people who come here to imbibe their creations. Live jazz on Tuesdays.

V kolkovně 3, (224 811 165)
Metro A, tram 17, 18: Staroměstská
Mon-Sun 7 pm to 3 am
www.tretters.cz

40 Lucerna Music Bar — Located in the Lucerna complex, the »grande dame« of Prague arcades built by the grandfather of Václav Havel, this concert and dance hall has an eclectic roster of acts, from European rock to American jazz. On Friday and Saturday nights you can dance the night away to a DJ playing the sounds of the '80s and '90s. Inside the arcade you'll also see David Černý's suspended sculpture of the Czech patron St. Wenceslas mounted on the belly of his upside-down dead horse.

Vodičkova 36, (224 217 108)
Metro A, B: Můstek, tram 3, 9, 14, 24: Václavské náměstí
Mon-Sun 8 pm to 3 am, shows usually start at 9 pm (box office opens at 7 pm)
www.musicbar.cz

SLEEP

41 Hotel Hoffmeister — Location and luxury, coupled with artistic legacy, are what makes this family-operated »romantic« hotel worth the splurge. Kitschy on a high level! Situated in the shadow of Prague Castle, this small hotel has every imaginable modern comfort and is decorated with paintings, collages and caricatures by Adolf Hoffmeister (1902–1973), the owner's father. A double room starts at € 290.

Pod Bruskou 7, (251 017 111)
Metro A, tram 12, 18, 20, 22, 23: Malostranská
www.hoffmeister.cz

42 Dům U Tří Čápů (House At the Three Storks) — The contemporary interior of this small intimate hotel (with 20 rooms) near the Prague castle is designed by the architectural studio Eva Jiřičná Architects in London. Exceptional is the composition of modern design and the old Renaissance elements in the rooms and the huge Gothic ceiling in the entrance hall. The hotel restaurant Wallenstein (main vegetarian dishes start at 140 Kč.) – also newly designed – is well-known since the '30s when it was frequented by a number of personalities of Czech cultural and political life. Double rooms from € 180.

Tomášská 20/16, (257 210 779)
Metro A: Malostranská,
tram 12, 22: Malostranské náměstí
www.utricapu.cz

43 Hotel Josef — This hotel in Prague's former Jewish Quarter garnered several prizes for its designer, Prague-born Eva Jiřičná of London Architects. Her hallmarks are a stunning combination of glass and light and a flair for pared-down elegance. The centrepiece of the lobby is a sculptural steel-and-glass spiral staircase and floor-to-ceiling windows that seem to bring the outdoors inside. Double rooms from € 129.

Rybná 20, (221 700 111)
Metro B: Náměstí Republiky,
tram 5, 8, 14: Dlouhá třída
www.hoteljosef.com

44 Botel Admiral — Anchored on the left bank of the Vltava River since 1971, this floating hotel, decorated with lots of dark wood panelling and polished brass, provides a unique experience. There are lovely views from the boat's deck, and an upscale restaurant offers Czech and international cuisine. A double room costs € 105 in season, with off-season rates about two-thirds that price.

Hořejší nábřeží, (257 321 302)
Tram 12, 14, 20: Na Knížecí
www.admiral-botel.cz

45 The Castle Steps — A series of five buildings, three on Nerudova – part of the traditional coronation route to the Castle – and two on Úvoz, house an array of single rooms, studios, two-room apartments and two bedroom apartments furnished with antiques and oil paintings and bearing poetic botanical names like Dahlia, Hyacinth and Sycamore. Guests get free Internet access and can burn photos on Cd or use the printer in the morning, when free coffee and vegan breakfasts are served. A great value for the location. The Josef Sudek Gallery, the photographer's flat from 1959–76, is also on Úvoz Street. Double rooms begin at € 63 in the summer season and € 47 off season.

Reception: Nerudova 7,
(257 216 337)
Tram 12, 20, 22, 23:
Malostranské náměstí
www.castlesteps.com

46 Czech Inn — Off the beaten path, the Czech Inn, located in a restored 19th-century building in the leafy residential neighbourhood of Vinohrady, is Prague's first designer hostel. It has quickly caught on with savvy travellers seeking inexpensive lodging with contemporary flair. There is an onsite café and bar and free Wi-Fi access. The excellent Shakespeare and Sons bookshop

and bar is nearby. Prices start at around € 10 per person in a dorm-style room, € 34 for a private room and € 56 for an en suite apartment.

Francouzská 76, (267 267 600)
Tram 4, 22, 23: Krymská
www.czech-inn.com

KIDS

47 Muddum — This community art centre offers a rich program of children's workshops, from ceramics to juggling lessons in the nearby Letná Park. Every first and third Saturday of the month, you can drop off the kids from 10 am to 2 pm and hit the Holešovice art district. By appointment, Muddum (which means »Mud House«) will prepare a claymation workshop for a minimum of three children. The friendly staff speaks English, Czech and French.

Kostelní 24, (777 876 541)
Metro C: Vltavská, tram 1, 3, 5, 8, 12, 14, 17, 25, 26: Strossmayerovo náměstí
Children's art workshops held Sat 10 am to 2 pm twice monthly
www.muddum.cz

48 Agentura Prague Family — Offers babysitting services in Prague hotels. Babysitters all speak English, with other languages available on request. 150 Kč per hour, with a three-hour minimum; you pay the taxi fare or drive the babysitter home if you return after 11 pm.

Senovážné náměstí,
(224 224 044 or 777 624 380)
Tram 3, 9, 14, 24: Jindřišská
www.praguefamily.cz

GOOD TO KNOW

Tourist Informations

Old Town Hall: Metro A: Staroměstská
Rytířská 31: Metro A: Můstek
Main railway station: Metro C: Hlavní nádraží, tram 5, 9, 26: Hlavní nádraží
Malá Strana Tower: Tram 12, 20, 22, 23: Malostranské náměstí
(12 444 or 221 714 444)
Open Mon-Fri 9 am to 6 pm
www.pis.cz

INTERNET

Internet Café Spika
A café in the centre with friendly stuff and about 18 computers, drinks and other refreshments.

Dlazdena 4, (224 211 521)
Metro B: Náměstí Republiky
daily 8am-12pm
netcafe.spika.cz

MEDIA

www.praguepost.com — Published since 1992, this weekly English-language newspaper comes out on Wednesdays and has a pull-out section with reviews and listings for the week's art exhibitions, restaurants, concerts and other cultural happenings.

www.prague.tv & **www.expats.cz** — These two community web sites have discussion forums for English speakers plus listings of cultural and community events along with restaurant and other reviews.

www.divus.cz — The *Umělec* (Artist) magazine is available at some central newsstands and at select art galleries. This quarterly art magazine publishes separate Czech and English editions. It focuses on contemporary Czech art and culture but its coverage has a broader international perspective.

TRANSPORT

From the airport — Ruzyně Airport is located about 15 kilometres from the city centre. A taxi from the airport to the centre should cost about 500 to 600 Kč using one of the radio taxi services mentioned below. A very inexpensive option is the Airport Express bus, which costs 50 Kč and connects with the main railway station (Hlavní nádraží) which connects you with the Metro C line. A midrange option is the Čedaz shuttle, costing 480 Kč for up to four people.

Taxis — Dishonest Prague cabbies are the stuff of local folklore. Taxi drivers hailed on the street have a deservedly lousy reputation among travellers and locals alike. Prague's mayor Pavel Bém found this out for himself when he disguised himself as an Italian tourist and got taken for a ride – overcharged 500 percent for a 3-kilometre trip to Prague Castle. The city initiated a network of about 50 »Taxi Fair Place points« in central Prague, where riders are guaranteed a maximum charge of 40 Kč to board and 28 Kč per kilometre and 6 Kč for waiting time. Ask for a receipt (»účtenka« in Czech). Locals usually call ahead to one of the trustworthy radio taxi services. English is spoken by dispatchers at AAA Radiotaxi (140 14 or 222 333 222) and Profi Taxi (844 700 800 or 261 314 151).

Public transport — Metro and tram tickets cost 26 Kč for 90 minutes of travel, with transfers allowed, or 18 Kč for 20 minutes of tram or bus travel with no transfers, or 30 minutes of metro travel up to a maximum of five stations (excluding the boarding station). A good bargain are one-, three- and five-day passes, costing 100, 330 and 500 Kč, respectively; the three- and five-day passes allow an accompanying child between 6 and 15 to ride for free.

Car — Street parking has become increasingly restrictive, in the centre and in some of the outlying districts. While there is some metered parking in the centre (orange zones for 2 hours, green zones for up to 6 hours), the blue zones are reserved for residents and businesses with parking permits. There are underground garages next to the National Theatre in Divadelní Street, at several big hotels (the Renaissance, Marriott and Intercontinental, for example) and near Hlavní nádraží, the main train station (Opletalova Street and Wilsonova Street). A good option are the Park and Ride lots, located at the following metro stations: Skalka (A, or green, line); Zličín, Nové Butovice, Radlická, Opatov, Rajská zahrada and Černý Most (B, or yellow, line); Nádraží Holešovice (C, or red, line). The lots are guarded and cost only 10 Kč for the whole day, from 4 am to 1 am, or 100 Kč to leave the car overnight. Look for the P+R signs.

#

Important Numbers

Telephone country and city code	*+42 0*
Telephone information	*1180*
Emergency	*112*
Police	*156 or 158*
Ambulance	*155*
Fire brigade	*150*
24h-Pharmacy	*Palackého 5, (224 946 982), metro A, B: Můstek (exit Jungmannovo náměstí), tram 3, 9, 14, 24: Vodičkova*

City in numbers

1 Euro	*ca. 27.3 Kč (Czech koruna)*
Inhabitants	*1.2 million*
Average income	*€ 944*
Cup of coffee	*25 Kč (ca.€ 1)*
Bottle of beer	*25 Kč (ca. € 1)*
Cigarettes	*65 Kč (ca. € 2.60)*
Most talked about artists	*Milena Dopitova, Jiří Kovanda*
Collectors of contemporary art	*10*
Biggest art scandal	*David Černý's sculpture of EU-stereotypes* Entropa *in Brussels 2009*

Short Art History
PRAGUE

Around 1908
Picasso's work finds a warm reception when art historian and collector Vincenc Kramář (1877–1960) befriends Picasso and brings his works to Prague. They have a profound effect on the development of Czech art, helping to spawn the uniquely Czech phenomenon of architectural Cubism.

1958 *Brussels World Expo*, the first post-war world exposition, is an enormous success for Czechoslovakia. The country's pavilion wins the Grand Prix and many other awards. *Expo 58* ushers in the »Brussels style«, a modern look of organic abstraction and pastel colours.

1987 The *Tvrdohlaví* exhibition breaks the long-standing hegemony of the official Union of Fine Artists, becoming the first show initiated outside the Union to win approval from the authorities. Petr Nikl, one of the group's eight members, calls it the defining moment of »cultural perestroika«".

1989 *Dialogue: Prague/Los Angeles*, the groundbreaking initiative by American artist Barbara Benish and Czech Zdeňka Gabalová in the Lidový dům (House for people) in Prague, brings together works by 16 California and 12 Czech artists in the summer of 1989 and opens the scene to the world, two months before the revolution begins.

2002 The August flood submerges several art galleries and lays waste to many artists' studios and storage locations. The long-term effects on the art world are far-reaching.

2003 The Prague Biennale becomes the city's first international biennial. An internal split triggers a counter-biennial, now the ITCA, and the »anti-biennial«, Tina B.

2009 *Entropa*, David Černý's »model kit« sculpture of the Europe Union becomes an international cause célébre when it is unveiled in Brussels to mark the Czech takeover of the revolving EU presidency, not only for its unflattering stereotypes of some countries but mainly when it emerges that Černý fabricated the 26 other artists he supposedly collaborated with.

Charles bridge

196

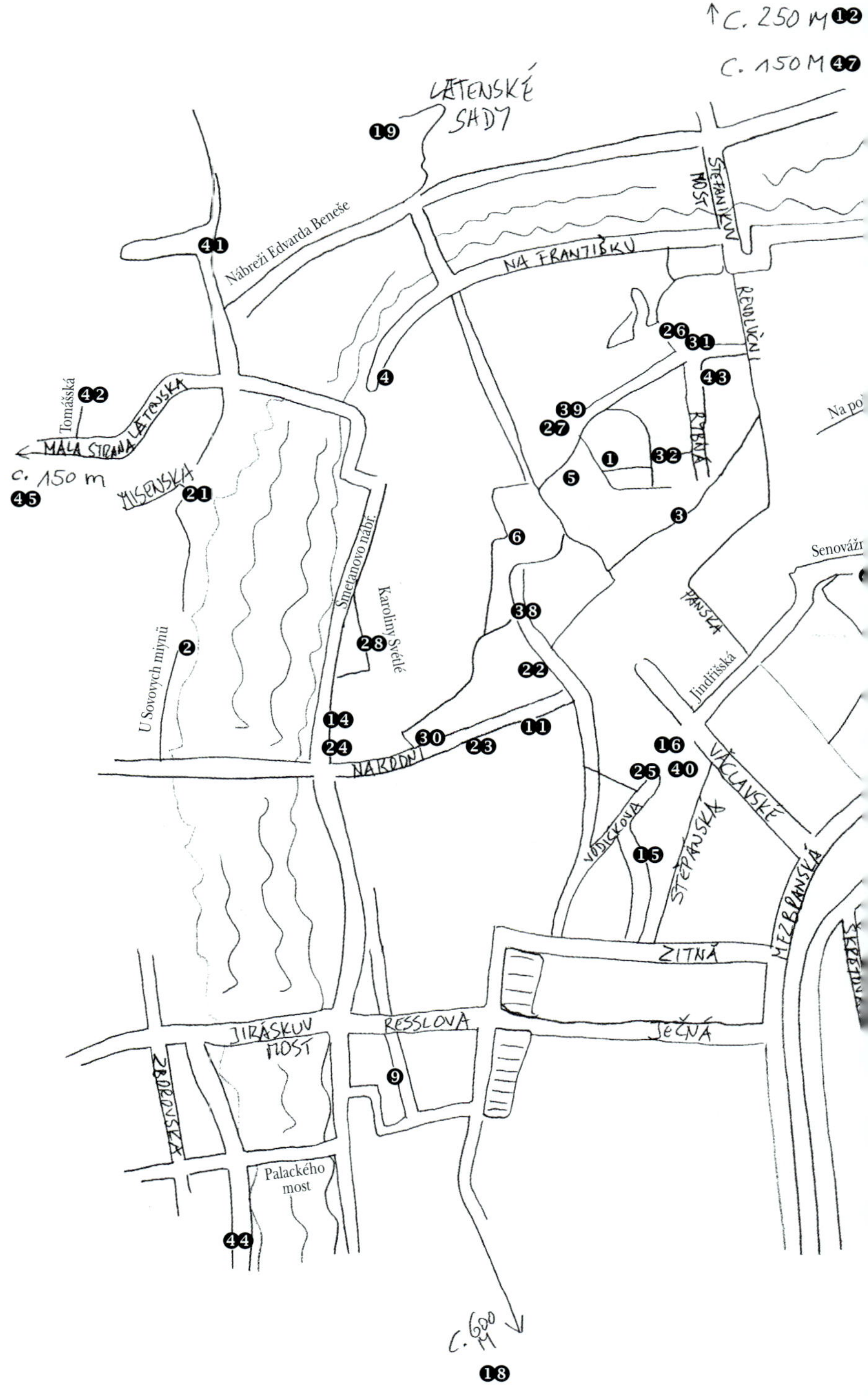
↑ C. 250 M 12
C. 150 M 47
LETENSKÉ SADY
19
Nábřeži Edvarda Beneše
41
ŠTEFÁNIKŮV MOST
NA FRANTIŠKU
REVOLUČNÍ
26
31
43
4
Tomášská
42
LETENSKÁ
MALÁ STRANA
c. 150 m
45
TRŽIŠTĚ
VLAŠSKÁ
39
27
RYBNÁ
1
32
5
3
Na poříčí
Senovážné
21
6
Smetanovo nábř.
Karoliny Světlé
38
PANSKÁ
U Sovových mlýnů
2
28
22
Jindřišská
14
24
30
23
11
16
25
40
NÁRODNÍ
VÁCLAVSKÉ
VODIČKOVA
ŠTĚPÁNSKÁ
15
MEZIBRANSKÁ
ŽITNÁ
KREMENCOVA
JIRÁSKŮV MOST
RESSLOVA
JEČNÁ
ZBOROVSKÁ
9
Palackého most
44
C. 600 M
18

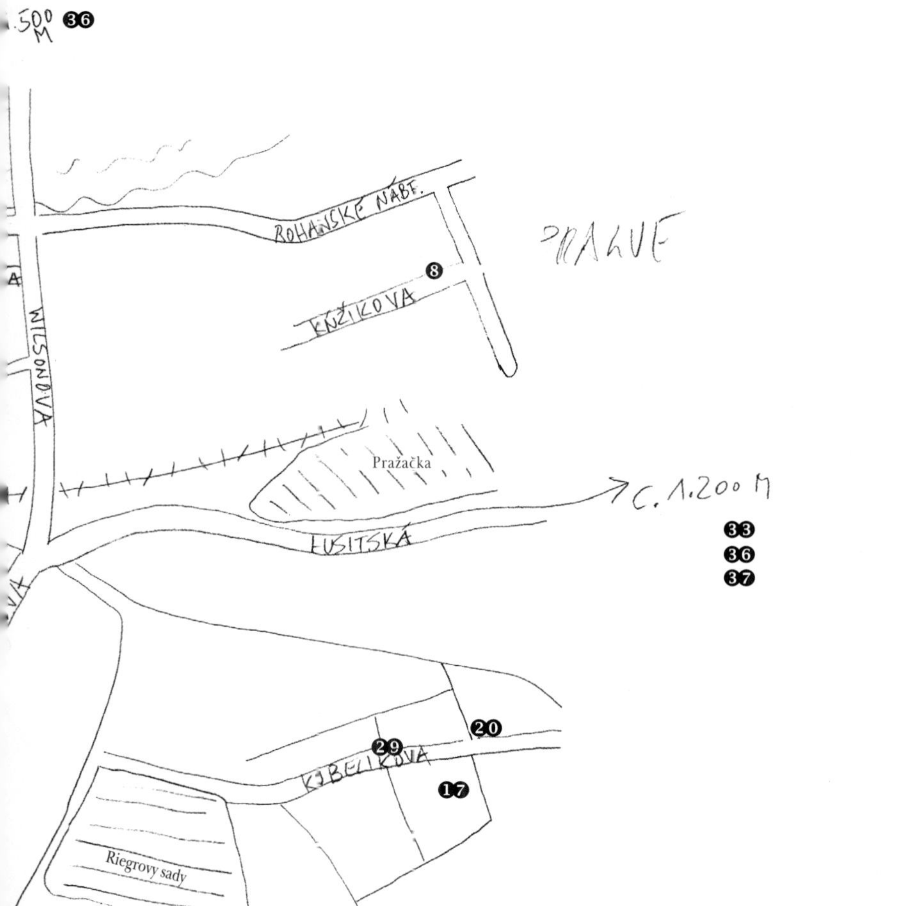

.500 M
36
ROHANSKÉ NÁBŘ.
PRAGUE
8
WILSONOVA
Pražačka
C. 1.200 M
33
36
37
20
29
17
Riegrovy sady
VINOHRADSKÁ
SLOVENSKA
21
FRANCOUZSKA
KRYNSK
200 m

Sarajevo

A Weekend in Sarajevo

Art and architecture, culture, great food, and strong spirits – all surrounded by mountains.

By Silvija Dervišefendić

What is the best time to visit Sarajevo? Many people will say August, during the Sarajevo Film Festival, while others will choose the fall season, when MESS, an international theatre festival, and the Jazz Festival take place. The rest might select wintertime and enjoy the opportunities for winter sports. After all, Sarajevo, which is surrounded by lovely mountains, was the host of the 1984 Olympic winter games.

Whether you reach the city overland by bus or train, of if you land at Butmir International Airport, you will notice the remnants of the past war and the nearly four year siege between 1992 and 1996: some of the reconstructed houses still have bullet holes and scorch marks on their facades. The first interesting experience you might get is on your way to the city centre. The taxi drivers in Sarajevo are known to gossip a lot, and they always have anecdotes that they like to share. On the main road into the city you can see how Sarajevo looks today, with post-war urbanization and the so called »symbols of transition«: shopping centres almost every kilometre, new uniform buildings that oppose previous Modern architecture with an uncreative use of glass and concrete, while downtown the Ottoman period architecture joins together with the Austro-Hungarian. The progress of Austro-Hungarian city planning strengthened the atmosphere of modern Europeanism in Sarajevo. Parallel to the Vienna Secession movement, local architects such as Ludwig Huber, Josip Vancaš, Josip Pospišil and Rudolf Tönnies used Secession elements in their works; geometric forms are especially visible on many buildings.

Today Sarajevo seems to have conquered its war trauma. There is a strong sense that people have decided to move on and avoid perpetuating the image of Sarajevo as the »city of the siege«. Its rich tradition is intermingled with the lively ferment of new ideas, a place of warm and welcoming people. When a visitor asks a local for directions or information, instead of a short answer he/she will get a pleasant chat or even a drink invitation.

Sarajevo natives always say that you can't be hungry or thirsty in this city. In the centre, the choice of restaurants, grills, and typical Bosnian restaurants called »aščinica«, »buregdžinica« and »ćevabdžinica«, where Bosnian dishes are served, is ample for every age, taste, and budget. National cuisine includes a variety of dishes with meat and vegetables, including Sarma (cabbage rolls stuffed with meat), Bosanski lonac (goulash with two kinds of meat and vegetables) or Klepe (Bosnian ravioli). You can find these Bosnian delicacies at famous places in the old town, which is called Baščaršija, a former trade and business centre from the Sarajevo Ottoman period. The most popular spirit is rakija, made of various fruits. Be advised: don't try competing with locals in drinking

Sarajevo natives say that you can't be hungry or thirsty in this city

View of Novi Grad

A cemetry above the city

Holiday Inn Hotel by Ivan Štraus

View of the city centre

Inside the Holiday Inn Hotel

because you'll probably lose. A city walk will lead you to Ferhadija, a pedestrian street in the centre of the city that has different shops, cafes and restaurants. One of the street passages leads to Stakleni grad (Glass City), where two alternative galleries are located, Duplex and Galerija 10m2. The Duplex is dedicated to exhibiting and promoting artistic projects in a variety of media. Twice a year, it presents an exhibition of young Bosnian artists in addition to public interventions and discussions related to other artistic activities. Next to it stands the Galerija 10m2, started by French artists Pierre Courtin and Claire Dupont in a vacant store in 2004. These two art spaces gather innovative young local and international artists, creating a productive alternative scene in Sarajevo. A cultural crisis seems to have been present for many years in this city. It not only brings the quality of cultural events and their production into question, but also how conscious Sarajevo natives are of the significance of culture. The unconventional and popular artist's group Zvono (The bell), formed in 1982 and named after the café where they hang out, organize happenings, actions, performances and unconventional exhibitions opposing the academic influence and limitations of institutionally accepted art. However, the history of urban- and sub-culture in Sarajevo started long ago with punk culture, fanzines and alternative clubs like KUK and AG. Celebrated bands like SCH, who changed their sound from post new wave to noise rock, reflected the time and rebellion against the system through their individual activities and their presence in public affairs. At the end of the '90s, Barake (Barracks), which no longer exists, was a new alternative place for exhibitions, concerts and various unconventional social events.

The major project of the Centar za savremenu umjetnost Sarajevo (Centre for Contemporary Arts or SCCA), founded in 1996 as one of the last in the network of twenty Soros Centres for Contemporary Art in Central and Eastern Europe, is to establish an unitary organization that can create a database, form a library, and promote and ensure participation of Bosnian visual artists in international art currents. On another note, the primary intention of the Ars Aevi Museum of Contemporary Art is to set up Sarajevo as a centre for international dialogue and cultural exchange. After a city cultural tour, spending a weekend in the surrounding mountains is a perfect choice and a great escape from city pollution in the wintertime. In only a half hour trip from Sarajevo, you'll find yourself in open countryside, drinking mulled wine or rakija, enjoying the fresh air and eating some Bosnian specialties. If you decide to stay overnight, you'll find suitable accommodation at hotels in Bjelašnica (2,067 meters) and Jahorina (1,913 meters). This would be the perfect end to a short trip to this unique European city. —

»Zetra«, part of the Olympic Complex built in 1984

A cultural crisis seems to have been present for many years

Post-war blues

From the time the Bosnian filmmaker *Namik Kabil* returned to Sarajevo from Los Angeles, he has had success both in screenwriting and film directing. In his works, he manages to capture the specific atmosphere of Sarajevo, the mentality of its inhabitants, and their deep inner conflicts.

By Asja Mandic

Since you are very observant, what would you say is the specific atmosphere in Sarajevo art and culture?

NAMIK KABIL: Sarajevo is certainly very specific. It's full of the post-war blues, which I find very inspiring though it's not always easy to live with such blues on an everyday basis. The challenge for local artists is the fact that there is not really a very well organized and thought-out politics of culture, which forces people to develop their own systems. This, in fact, has produced a lot of original and authentic artwork in the last ten, fifteen years. I guess this is the main colour of the Sarajevo's atmosphere, many individual energies trying to develop their own micro-systems.

From the perspective of someone like you, who has been exposed to shows at MoMA New York or the MOCA in Los Angeles, does the Sarajevo art scene offer gratifying experiences in terms of art exhibitions?

Bosnia is in transition and there is a lack of funds to organize expensive exhibitions. Still, there is a lot to explore in this country in terms of the human spirit because, despite of the lack of funds, Sarajevo has developed a special type of culture, the so called »festival culture« which is represented by major festivals such as the Sarajevo Film Festival, the theatre festival MESS and the Jazz Festival.

Sarajevo has a size that I find very manageable because you can get in a situation to meet almost anyone you want to. I do get along with a lot of artists in Sarajevo, such as the photographer Damir Šagolj, film director Faruk Lončarević and writer Peđa Kojević and I find these contacts very vibrant and professionally helpful.

What was it that made you decide to leave the centre of the film industry and come to Sarajevo? Is this socio-political and cultural context inspiring?

My decision to come back to Sarajevo was inspired by two aspects that are, of course, interwoven. It was both a personal and professional decision. If I had to rationalize such a choice I would say that you can only do minimalism in a place that you are familiar with, and they call me »minimalist«, though it wasn't a conscious artistic choice. Actually, it was the way things unfolded naturally for me. Certainly I am happy to be back because this is the place where I made a breakthrough in my career and made movies like the documentaries *Interrogation*, and *Believers* as well as the feature film *Nightguards*.

It is valid to have war as an inspiration as long as it comes out of you naturally

You do not work with issues related to the recent war or not in a direct way, as do most of the local artists and film directors. Do you think they achieve visibility and success internationally by exploiting war-related topics?

The war has defined me for sure. I guess you cannot choose an inspiration, not in an ontological way, and you can only deal with things that are chosen for you on a more subconscious level. It is valid to have war as an inspiration as long as it comes out of you naturally. Once you start constructing the war as an inspiration because you think the audience will find it interesting, either a domestic or foreign audience, you will probably get into the slippery political position of potential self-victimization. It hasn't happened even once in history that a people or entire nations got trapped in such a way.

Namik Kabil was born in 1968 in Tuzla. Before the war in Bosnia and Herzegovina he was a medical student. The war changed his professional direction and he ended up in Los Angeles where he studied cinema. In 2002 he returned to Sarajevo where he currently works as a screenwriter and director. His documentary *Interrogation* was named the best documentary film by the Sarajevo Film Festival and the feature film *Nightguards* premiered at the 65th Venice Film Festival in 2008.

Film is the only art form that is being supported by the Ministries of Culture in this country. Do you feel film directors are privileged in comparison to local artists?

Since the international success of the film *No Man's Land* in 2001, which won the Oscar for best foreign film, Bosnian filmmakers have gotten more attention from the government in terms of formal support, which you could call a privilege. At the same time, I have the impression that artists from other fields expect the film professionals to fight for their rights, as well. This is a bit unrealistic, since nobody fought for filmmaker's rights in Bosnia but the filmmakers themselves. —

Sarajevo

by Silvija Dervišefendić

Skenderija annex

ART

❶ Umjetnička galerija Bosne i Hercegovine (National Gallery of Bosnia and Herzegovina) — One of the most significant galleries in Sarajevo with a great collection of Bosnian Modern and contemporary art. The new permanent exhibition *Retrospectrum* takes the colour spectrum as a point of departure to present a survey of Bosnian art from the past two centuries.

Zelenih beretki 8, (266 550)
Trolley bus 101, 103, 104: Drvenija
Tue-Sat noon to 8 pm

❷ Ars Aevi Museum of Contemporary Art — The museum collection was a contribution by over 140 renowned international artists (including Michelangelo Pistoletto, Joseph Kosuth and Marina Abramović), whose works are waiting for their permanent home, designed by the master of museum architecture, Renzo Piano. Even though the Ars Aevi does not have its own exhibition space, it holds exhibitions in various galleries as well as unconventional spaces in Sarajevo and abroad, including the first Bosnia and Herzegovina pavilion at the Venice Biennale. The Ars Aevi collection is now stored in the »exhibition depot«, located in the Skenderija Youth Hall, and can be visited if scheduled in advance.

Terezije bb (Centar Skenderija)
(216 919)
Trolleybus 101, 103, 104:
Skenderija
Mo-Fri 9 am to 4 pm
www.arsaevi.ba

❸ SCCA: Centar Za Savremenu Umjetnost Sarajevo (Sarajevo Centre for Contemporary Art) — At a new address, the Centre for Contemporary Art continues to promote the regional contemporary art scene. Director Dunja Blažević gathers

young teams of artists and art historians mostly on a voluntary basis. SCCA founded the Young Visual Artists Award in Bosnia and Herzegovina, ZVONO, in 2006. A multi-media laboratory for production, Pro.ba, is an important segment of the SCCA.

Obala Kulina bana 22, (665 304)
Tram 1, 2, 3, 4, 5: Katedrala
Mon-Fri 10 am to 4 pm
www.scca.ba

❹ Galerija 10m2 — The size is the name. This gallery in the centre of Sarajevo was designed from the outset to be a place

for experimenting, testing and discovery, to be exploited by each guest artist as he or she pleases. 10m2 is an art laboratory with a very high level of art activity (exhibitions, artist's talks, presentations etc.), which, by gathering young Bosnian visual artists together, creates a unique alternative art scene.

Ferhadija 17, (063 952 197)
Tram 1, 2, 3, 4, 5: Katedrala
Mon-Sat 2 pm to 7 pm

❺ **Duplex** — Next to the Gallery 10m2 stands the 150 m2 venue where activities are split on two different levels: one is dedicated to production, the other to exhibitions. This is a friendly and stimulating environment where the general public can see and learn about art through a high-profile program of exhibitions, workshops, performances, film and video screenings and other artistic events. The owner of Duplex, as well as of Gallery 10m2, is Pierre Courtin, an energetic French guy who also used to be an artist.

Ferhadija 15, (063 952 197)
Tram 1, 2, 3, 4, 5: Katedrala
Mon-Sat 2 pm to 7 pm

❻ **Charlama** — A small alternative gallery, ran by Association KULT Zona, specifically by Bosnian artist Jusuf Hadžifejzović, that periodically offers exhibitions that are the perfect opportunity to get drunk with artists and talk about art and culture in the city. Charlama has several meanings; it refers to a certain kind of wild dance, performance, play, as well as to a good trick, deception but not in negative sense – a jest.

Terezije bb, Centar Skenderija
Trolleybus 101, 103, 104: Skenderija
Mon-Sat 12 pm to 8 pm

ART EVENTS

Sarajevo Film Festival — Founded in 1995, the Sarajevo Film Festival is the most important (and so to say legendary) film festival in the Balkans, attracting thousand of film fans from all over the world every August. International and local films in different categories are shown and awarded. It was founded in 1995 during the siege of Sarajevo, and brings not only local but also well-known international celebrities to Sarajevo every year.

Festival office:
Zelenih beretki 12/1, (221 516 or 209 411)
August
www.sff.ba

Internacionalni festival Sarajevo »Sarajevska zima« (International Festival Sarajevo – »Sarajevo Winter«) — Founded in 1984, the long-running Sarajevo Winter Festival (from mid February to the beginning of March) offers a wide program of films, performing and visual arts, music, literature and intercultural workshops at different locations all around the city. Because it even took place during the war, the festival has become a symbol of creative freedom and still has a big impact on city life.

Festival office:
M. Tita 9 a, (207 945), February-March
www.sarajevskazima.ba

ALTERNATIVE SIGHTSEEING

Tanzelarija — The non-governmental »Organization for the Promotion of Contemporary Dance in Bosnia and Herzegovina« has a few major activities such as Firedance, a dance therapy program, Papričice u pokretu, a program for young dancers and movers and Danceplants. In 2008, Tanzelarija organized the first International Contemporary Dance Festival – ZVRK in Sarajevo.

Tina Ujevića 15, (061 517 356)
Tram 1, 2, 3, 4, 5: Narodna banka/Čeka
www.tanzelarija.org

❼ Svrzina kuća (Svrzo's House) — Built in 18th century, this house represents a typical Bosnian home from the Ottoman period. The unique architectural style shows the home life of one Bosnian family, reflecting the strict rules of behaviour for female and male members on the family. To visit, you need to be in a good shape because it requires strenuous uphill walking.

Glodina 8, (252 213)
Tram 1, 2, 3, 4, 5: Baščaršija
Winter Season (October-March):
Mon-Fri 10 am to 4 pm, Sat 10 am to 3 pm
Summer Season (April-September):
Mon-Fri 10 am to 6 pm, Sat 10 am to 3 pm
Full price admission 2 BAM

DAYTRIPS

Lukomir — This little village of stone houses lies at almost 1,500 meters in elevation. You can stay overnight at a renovated former elementary school that now serves as a space for workshops and seminars with furnished rooms for sleeping with kitchens and bathrooms. The village is under snow almost nine months of the year and is a well-hidden place in the Bjelašnica mountains. It was a place where Franciscan friars escaped from the Ottoman army and they dubbed it their »Harbor of Peace«. It takes half an hour by car to get there: Drive from Sarajevo in the direction of Šabići (Bjelašnica mountains), after the turnoff at Šabići, it is another 17 kilometres to Lukomir.

www.bhtourism.ba/eng/lukomir.wbsp

Barice — This is a popular resort only half an hour from Sarajevo. From Barice you can hike to Bukovik, a mountain close to Sarajevo and the mountain path leads to the Skakavac

Waterfall (Grasshopper Waterfall), a tourist attraction, which is 98 meters high and in a beautiful natural landscape.

Minibus 64 to Barice, Park stop, Koševo ulica, Sat-Sun 8 am, 9 am, 10 am, 3 pm, 4 pm, 5 pm

Olympic mountains: Bjelašnica, Igman, Jahorina — The Winter Olympics of 1984 took place in the so called »Olympic mountains«: Bjelašnica, Jahorina, Igman. In summer you can enjoy the beautiful natural surroundings and go hiking, while in winter skiing is highly recommended. Bjelasnica offers fewer trails for skiing, but is perfect for advanced winter-sport fans. Jahorina has a very learner-friendly environment and the biggest choice of trails. Its ideal geographical position more or less guarantees four months of good ski snow. The high season is mid December to late February. Mount Igman is the smallest of all. If you plan on travelling with children, you'll appreciate their kid-friendly slopes and trails. Mountain apartments, chalets and hotels can be found on area websites. A ski pass for one-day costs approx. 37 BAM at Jahorina, a very reasonable price when compared to other European ski resorts.

Bjelašnica and Igman: Bus from the National Museum, Franje Račkog street Dec- Feb, Sat-Sun, 9 am to Bjelašnica, 3.30 pm from Bjelašnica, March Sat-Sun, 9 am to Bjelašnica, 4.30 pm from Bjelašnica. A return ticket costs 7 BAM.

Car: From Sarajevo via East Sarajevo there are signs marked for the Hotel Marsal about 6 km east of the airport. There is only one right turn to be made at the large quarry and that road leads directly to the ski centre. Approx. 45 minutes.
www.bjelasnica.ba

Jahorina: The Bus from Sarajevo–Jahorina leaves from the Dobrinja bus station at 8 am and leaves from Jahorina at 3.30 pm. Return tickets cost 10 BAM.

Car: E 761 Road, 20 min in the direction of Pale, from there another 20 minutes up the mountain (28 km from Sarajevo)
www.jahorina.org

SHOPPING

❽ **BHcrafts** — »Shopping with purpose« is their favourite line. BHcrafts is a local NGO founded under the auspices of the Norway NPA humanitarian organization in the late '90s. If you are looking for a warm, colourful, practical, stylish gift, you've found your oasis. Everything is handmade, from woollen

clothes and handbags to other fashionable goodies. These specifically Bosnian, authentic products are created by different groups of women who live on the margins of society. All the products are oriented towards preserving and promoting the cultural heritage of Bosnia and Herzegovina.

Ćulhan 1, Ćulhan 11, (551 535)
Tram 1, 2, 3, 4, 5: Baščaršija
Mon-Fri 8 am to 8 pm, Sat 9 am to 7 pm,
Sun 10 am to 4 pm
www.bhcrafts.org

❾ **Butik Badem** — If you are looking for a tea and spice market or a place where you can find oriental sweets such as Turkish delight (with dozens of flavours), tahan halva or candied and spiced nuts, this is the perfect place for you. Located in the centre of the old town Baščaršija, it is a frequent stopover for many who like to snack while taking a walk in the busiest pedestrian city quarter.

Abadžiluk 12, (533 135)
Tram 1, 2, 3, 4, 5: Baščaršija
Mon-Sun 8 am to 11 pm

❿ **Buybook Book Club** — A bookstore plus literary/social club. If you want to participate in local intellectual discussions, you should become a Buybook Book Club member and enjoy discounted drinks and books. Buybook is one of the best-supplied bookstores in town with a nice English section and a selection of books about art and design.

Radićeva 4, (716 450)
Tram 1, 2, 3, 4, 5: Narodna banka/Čeka
Mon-Sat 9 am to 10 pm

CAFÉS

⓫ **Zlatna ribica** — Everyone falls in love with the interior, which is impossible to describe or determine. Different artistic styles can be recognized, from neo-Secession or Art Nouveau to very creative uses for old furniture with old sewing machines as tables. Using the restroom is mandatory; it's like being in someone's bathroom overloaded with different cosmetic products, make-up and a homey decor.

Kaptol 5, (253 607)
Tram 1, 2, 3, 4, 5: Narodna banka/Čeka
Mon-Sun 10 am to 12 am

⓬ **Torte i to** — This café/pastry shop, a Croatian franchise, offers a large number of cakes, the most popular being cheesecake. The restroom is equipped for mothers with babies. The café is a nice place to read magazines or books and where children can play with toys. It is the only place in Sarajevo with an exclusively non-smoking area. Has Wi-Fi.

Grbavička 6, (717 176)
Trolley bus 101, 103, 104: Kovačići
Mon-Sun 8 am to 11 pm
www.torte-i-to.ba

⓭ **So.ba** — A student place during the day, perfect for coffee and conversation, it changes on weekend nights, when there are a variety of DJs playing music. Formerly at the Academy of Fine Arts, now located at the Faculty of Architecture, so.ba also promotes urban culture by organizing various cultural events.

Patriotske lige 30, (278 491)
Trolley bus 102, 105: Ciglane

Mon-Fri, 8 am to 10 pm
www.soba.ba

RESTAURANTS

⓮ **Kibe** — Finding this restaurant is a small adventure, so it's easier to take a taxi to make sure you arrive. One of the most popular restaurants in the city, it offers an exquisite menu: sautéed veal, lamb on a skewer, meatballs in sour cream, sautéed veal scaloppini and other Bosnian specialties. In the evening one can enjoy a meal with traditional Bosnian songs performed live. Kibe has a recognizable culinary tradition that continuously stimulates newcomers and guarantees return visits. Main dishes from 15 BAM.

Vrbanjuša 164, (441 936)
Tram 1, 2, 3, 4, 5: Baščaršija
Mon-Sat 10 am to 11 pm
Visa, Mastercard
www.restorankibe.ba

⓯ **Dveri** — Near the BHcrafts shop (see »shopping«) on the left side of the street (your nose will guide you in the right direction) is a restaurant with amazing regional specialties. It is a place of incredible culinary pleasures, with an impressive array of tastes and smells. The friendly environment and excellent

service are good reasons to become a regular here. Dogs and other pets allowed. Main dishes from 10 BAM.

Prote Bakovića 12, (537 020)
Tram 1, 2, 3, 4, 5: Baščaršija
Mon-Sun 10 am to 11 pm
www.dveri.co.ba

⓰ **Vegehana** — The only vegetarian restaurant in town, kind of a mix of vegan and Indian food. A new menu every week. While you're drinking natural fruit juices or eating carrot cake, you can soak up the spiritual atmosphere by relaxing in one of the beanbags scattered around. For an affordable price you get not only delicious food and the smiling faces, your cholesterol also stays low. Main dishes from 10 BAM.

Kemal-begova 4, (215 699)
Tram 1, 2, 3, 4, 5:
Predsjedništvo
Mon-Sat 11 am to 10.30 pm
www.vegehana.com

⓱ **Delikatesna Radnja** — With its classy hip decor, this is one of the fancy overpriced places in the city that invites you to enjoy a diverse menu of international cuisine. The food is quite delicious, the wine list and dishes will ensure a fulfilling experience both memorable and rare. Next to the restaurant is a café bar with Wi-Fi. Main dishes from 9 BAM.

Obala Kulina bana 10, (208 855)
Tram 1, 2, 3, 4, 5: Čobanija
Mon-Sat 8 am to 11 pm,

Sun 10.30 am to 12 am
Visa, Mastercard, Diners Club
www.delikatesnaradnja.ba

PARTY

⓲ Pravda — Stylish lounge bar and restaurant with a great wine list and a variety of cocktails. Real party place with DJs on weekends.

Radićeva 4c, (558 215)
Tram 1, 2, 3, 4, 5:
Narodna banka/Čeka
Mon-Sun 8 am to 12 am

⓳ Underground — Kind of a rock club, where you can meet a variety of people, from students, painters, writers to businessmen, bankers and economists. It is located in the basement of the School of Applied Arts. Since it is always overcrowded, it is best to come early. Entertainment and low drink prices are guaranteed until the early morning hours.

Gimnazijska 11, (440 520)
Tram 1, 2, 3, 4, 5:
Drvenija
Mon-Sun 8 pm to after midnight

⓴ Mash — This lounge balances its trendy atmosphere, swanky modern lighting, and black leather couches with affordable drinks, (mostly) friendly waiters and great DJs.

Branilaca Sarajeva 20/1
Tram 1, 2, 3, 4, 5:
Čobanija
Mon-Sun 9 am to midnight

SLEEP

㉑ Hotel Europe — Hotel Europe Sarajevo has recently been renovated, after it was completely destroyed during the war. It is one of the most exclusive hotels in the city, in an exceptional location. It was the first modern hotel in Sarajevo, designed by Karl Paržik and built in 1882 by Gligorije Jeftanović (the street, where the hotel is situated, was named after him). Before the war it was a popular place for hanging out and mingling with friends, now the new cafe pastry shop and restaurant have an exclusive selection of cakes and an overall international spirit. The hotel provides 160 luxury rooms, 10 apartments, four of them presidential, four fully equipped congress halls and a rich wellness centre: fitness, swimming pool, sun rooms, saunas, Turkish bath, massages rooms and beauty treatments. Comfortable beds and couches, and attractive retro style decor. Double rooms from € 120.

Vladislava Škarića 5, (580 500)
Tram 1, 2, 3, 4, 5:
Principov most/Latinska ćuprija
www.hoteleurope.ba

㉒ Hotel Gaj — A small, pleasant place in the centre of the city, the oldest (former) pizzeria in the city expanded its offerings by adding hotel accommodation. Rooms are equipped with phones, cable TV and a mini bar. Professional service and favourable prices make the stay even more enjoyable. Double rooms from € 100.

Skenderija 14, (445 200)
Trolley bus 101, 103, 104: Skenderija
www.hotel-gaj.co.ba

23 Hotel Hecco Deluxe — This hotel is located in the most vibrant part of the city, directly on the pedestrian street Ferhadija. It is situated on the top of one of the highest buildings, which is also known for its historically preserved Modern architecture. There are beautiful views from the rooms, as well as from the restaurant and gallery. Double rooms from € 90.

Ferhadija 2, (558 995)
Tram 1, 2, 3, 4, 5: Katedrala
www.heccodeluxe.com

24 Pansion Čobanija — Situated on the left riverbank, this three-star bed and breakfast offers 10 comfortable and modern rooms with phones, free cable Internet, satellite TV and air-conditioning. Service is good and continental breakfast is a nice treat. Double rooms from € 60.

Čobanija 29, (441 749)
Trolley bus 101, 103, 104: Čobanija
www.pansion-cobanija.com

KIDS

Kids festival — A major event for the youngest generation, each year brings more than 40,000 children from all parts of the country to Sarajevo. The festival engages youngsters with a film program, workshops, exhibitions, concerts, street actions, etc.

Halilbašića 52, (232 644)
May
www.kidsfest.ba

Zoo Pionirska Dolina — A small Zoo and Luna Park for kids. Today this green oasis is home to a number of domestic species. Because of its appearance and environment, it looks like a wildlife sanctuary dedicated to eco-tourism. There are some kiosks located in the park selling drinks and food, mostly sandwiches and hamburgers.

Nahorevska 103, (668 166)
Trolley bus 102: Jezero
Mon-Sun 7 am to10 pm
Admission fee 0.50 – 1.00 BAM

GOOD TO KNOW

㉕ Tourist Information
Zelenih beretki 22, (22 07 21)
Tram 1, 2, 3, 4, 5: Drvenija
www.sarajevo-tourism.com

INTERNET

㉖ Internet club Click
Kundurdžiluk 1, (236 914) 27
Tram 1, 2, 3, 4, 5: Baščaršija

TRANSPORTATION

From the airport — The only transportation from the Butmir International Airport is by taxi. Taxi trip from the airport to the city centre costs around 22 to 26 BAM.

Taxis — There are about 1,200 taxis and more than 50 taxi stands in the city. The standard of the cars and the friendliness of the drivers is diverse. The standard starting rate for taxis is 1 BAM and 1 BAM is charged for every kilometre. Sarajevo Taxi, (1515, 660 970, 660 666) Žuti Taxi (663 555), Crveni Taxi (760 600, 760 601, 760 602), Sami i Emir Taxi (1516, 667 681), Kale Taxi (570 901)

Public transport — Public transportation consists of trams, trolleybuses and buses. Tickets are available from the driver (1.80 BAM) or at most of the newspaper stands (1.60 BAM) where you can also buy a daily ticket (5.30 BAM). Be sure to punch the purchased ticket in the designated machines to avoid any unpleasant confrontations with the controllers who check the tickets.

Car — Avoid to move around by car. There are designated parking spaces in the city, but they are usually very crowded. Have your headlights on all the time, speed limits in cities 40–60 km/h.

#

Important | Numbers

Telephone country and city code	*+387 33*
Telephone information	*1182*
Police	*122*
Fire Brigade	*123*
Emergency	*124*
24h-Pharmacy	*Apoteka Baščaršija, Obala Kulina bana 40, (272 300), Tram 1, 2, 3, 4, 5: Baščaršija*

City in | Numbers

1 Euro	*1.96 BAM (BiH Convertible Mark)*
Inhabitants	*300,000*
Average income	*€547*
Cup of coffee	*2 BAM (ca. €1)*
Bottle of beer	*3BAM (ca. €1.50)*
Cigarettes	*3 BAM (ca. €1.50)*
Most talked about contemporary artist	*Maja Bajević, Braco Dimitrijević, Jusuf Hadžifejzović, Šejla Kamerić*
Collectors of contemporary art	*0*
Biggest art scandal	*No ministry of culture on the state level yet*

Short Art History SARAJEVO

1987 and 1989 The *Yugoslav Documenta*, an art show of contemporary Yugoslav artists, is the first art exhibition on such a large scale in Sarajevo. The exhibition takes place in the Kulturno Sportski Centar Skenderija (Skenderija Sports and Cultural Centre) since there is no proper art venue for such an event. The third *Documenta* is planned to be international in scope, but is never realized because the war breaks out in 1992.

1993 *Svjedoci postojanja* (Witnesses of Existence), is an exhibition which gathers together the series of individual art interventions by Sarajevo artists (Nusret Pašić, Zoran Bogdanović, Petar Waldegg, Mustafa Skopljak, Edin Numankadić, Sanjin Jukić, Ante Jurić and Radoslav Tadić) from the time during the massive attack on the city and its inhabitants (1992–1993). Their work, exhibited in the burned-out Kino Sutjeska (Sutjeska cinema), shows life and cultural resistance in the besieged city.

1997 *Meeting Point*, the first annual exhibition by the SCCA, (Soros Centre for Contemporary Arts Sarajevo), is organized as a series of site-specific interventions in the public space Ćulhan, the point of departure for many young Bosnian artists who have since received international recognition and success. The work with SCCA launches their careers.

1999 *Ars Aevi Collection* is the first show organized by the Ars Aevi Museum of Contemporary Art in Sarajevo, in cooperation with artists and museums all over the world who participate in the creation of this collection to express solidarity with the inhabitants of the destroyed city of Sarajevo. This is the first time that the Sarajevo public sees works by so many significant international artists.

2001 Since the Ars Aevi Museum of Contemporary Art is still waiting for its permanent home, six exhibitions of the artists from its collection (Michelangelo Pistoletto, Richard Nonas, IRWIN, Daniel Buren, Joseph Kosuth, Joseph Beuys) are organized in different galleries and alternative spaces in Sarajevo.

2009 Stagnation. Sarajevo still does not have adequate art venues for large-scale exhibitions, and there are no plans for building new galleries or expanding the existing ones.

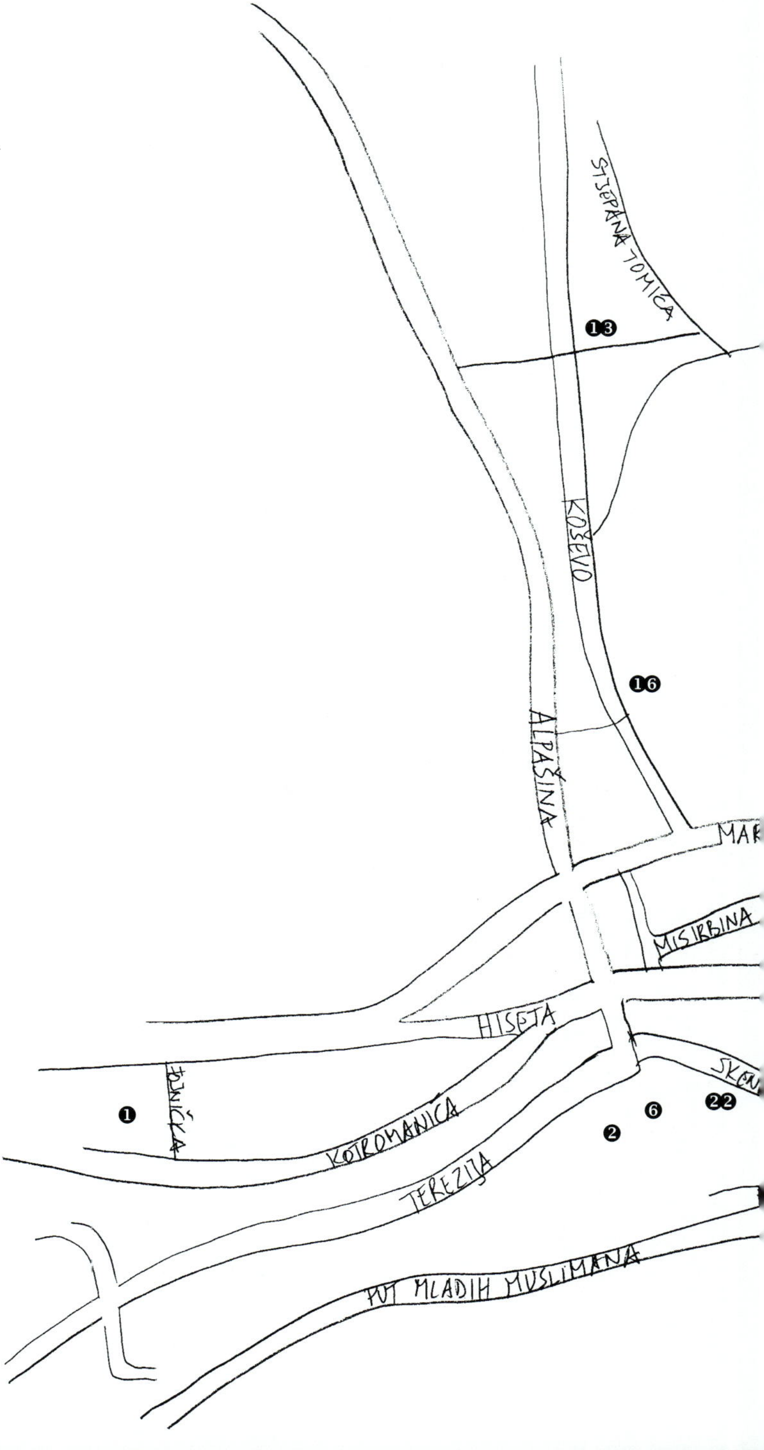
STJEPANA TOMIĆA
13
KOŠEVO
16
ALIPAŠINA
MAR
MISIRBINA
HISETA
SKEN
22
6
1
2
KOTROMANICA
TEREZIJA
PUT MLADIH MUSLIMANA

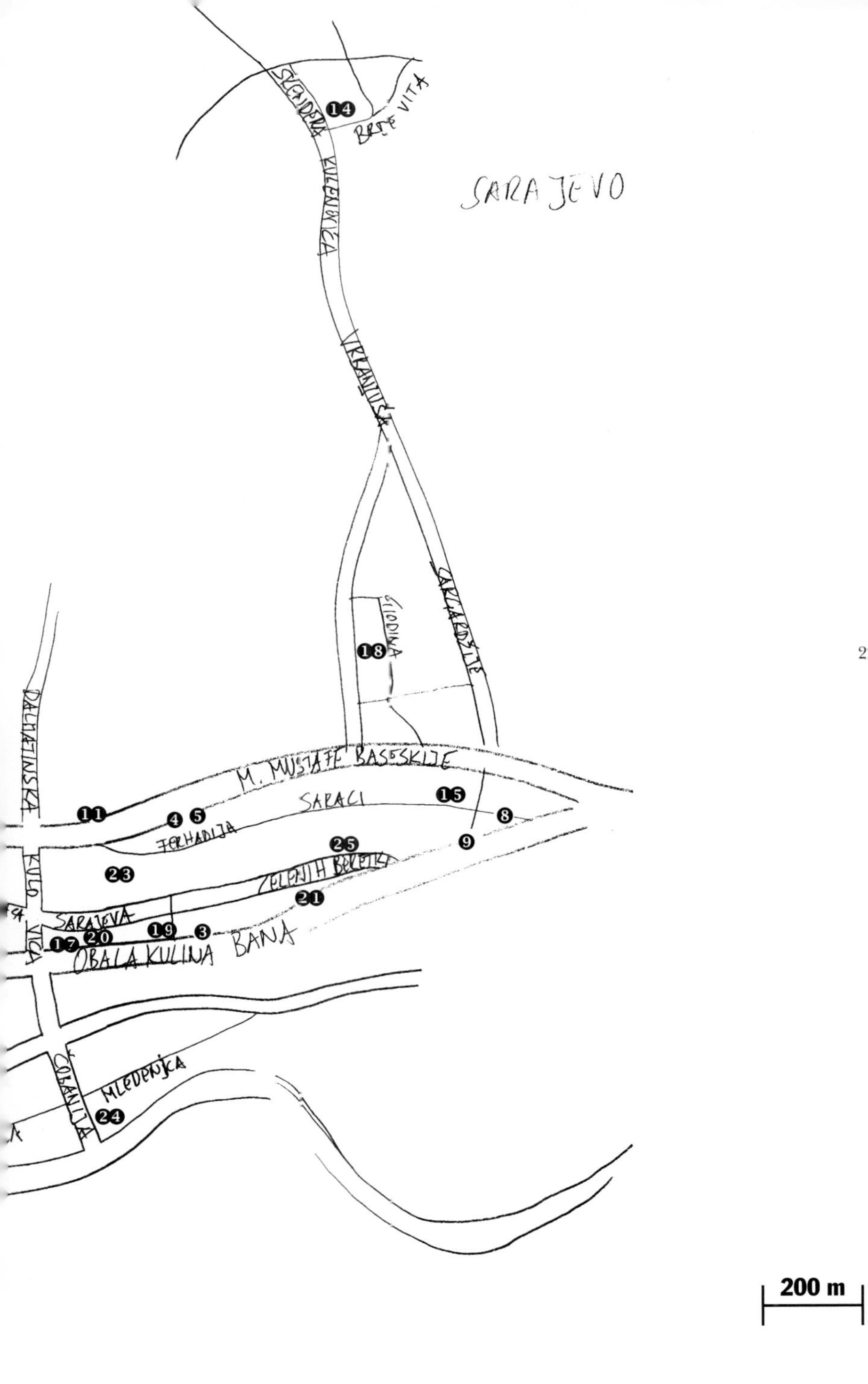
SARAJEVO
M. MUSTAFE BAŠESKIJE
SARACI
FERHADIJA
ZELENIH BERETKI
SARAJEVA
OBALA KULINA BANA
DALMATINSKA
ČOBANIJA
VRBANJUŠA
200 m

So

Fountain in front of the National Theatre

fia

European = Better

Sofia, a city that is a conglomeration of architecture, styles, religions and people, has a small contemporary art scene. It is fighting for survival, and succeeding.

—

By Antje Mayer

»In Communist times the only demand made on art was that it should be entertaining and beautiful«, says Bulgarian curator Iara Boubnova. »These days, I'm afraid, the people and government in Bulgaria haven't had a change of heart.« We are sitting in one of the many new smart dining and drinking places in Sofia, the Opera, which is designed in a typically Mediterranean »Beautiful Homes« style. On the menu: crossover cuisine, but certainly not Bulgarian. »The word ›European‹ is a synonym for ›better‹ in Bulgarian«, Iara Boubnova explains, pointing outside to where new apartment blocks are going up in a faceless, international style on every empty building site in the margins of a city that is a conglomeration of styles, peoples and religions. Accommodation for globalised IKEA people. They look modern at first glance, but when you look again the first bits of plaster are falling off, even though the buildings are not yet finished. Quite commonly, the inhabitants have no heating in these new buildings because the owner has given no thought to conduits for distance heating, or even to asphalt streets or a local infrastructure. Nouveau-riche citizens, as well as foreigners who have realised their dream of a one-family home, especially retired Japanese and Brits, live in virtually »prohibited areas« in the beautiful foothills of the Vitosa Mountains at the gates of Sofia, not in the chaotically proliferating city centre and its unwelcoming margins.

Russian by birth, Iara Boubnova, who moved from Moscow to Sofia in the '80s, is a sharp-tongued critic of social conditions in Bulgaria, and acts as a sort of spokeswoman for Bulgaria in the West. This art historian is one of the advertising pillars for contemporary art and is part of a generation of Bulgarian art publicists and cultural producers who rose up against the ancient art doctrine of entertainment and beauty with alternative projects, performances and actions This was just before Communism collapsed, rather late compared to other Communist countries.

Left over from that time of resistance are a few stubborn people with whom she founded the Institut za savremenno izkystvo – Sofia (Institute of Contemporary Art – Sofia) in 1993, including artists like Mariela Gemisheva, Alla Georgieva, Pravdoliub Ivanov, Nedko Solakov and the curator Maria Vassileva. Only a few younger members have joined the group since it was founded, mostly because they preferred to go looking for a break-through somewhere in the rest of Europe.

Those who stayed behind organise readings, debates and performances on contemporary art in constantly changing venues, especially in illegal private clubs and cafés, which are born and buried again at irregular intervals in Sofia. The events are announced on the Internet or by word of mouth. At present, con-

In 1996 all of Bulgaria sank into economic anarchy and the inflation rate reached 1,000 percent

National Palace of Culture

Hotel Rodina, 16th floor

The National Assembly of Bulgaria

temporary art has a fixed venue, at best, in the Sofia Art Gallery. Curator Iara Boubnova is especially proud that in the past, especially in 1996, when all of Bulgaria sank into economic anarchy and the inflation rate reached 1,000 per cent, she accepted no »unclean money« for her Institute of Contemporary Art project. »In those days we were in the midst of a trauma of change from Communism to capitalism, which we simply couldn't digest, because we were right in the middle of it.« This »trauma«, which many of the artists we met in Sofia talked about, manifested itself – just ten years ago – quite simply as hunger. »Our grandparents had to go begging, and sometimes we had no idea where to buy our bread.« Iara remembers it well.

It irritates her that it has not been possible up to this point to bring a qualitatively valuable international art exhibition – one that deserves the name – to Sofia. »Nobody would lend us a big Picasso exhibition, just to name one example. We are third class citizens, the poorest country in the EU, and we are neither interesting as a political, nor as an economic, partner. We can't offer an interesting counter offer, and we can't find anybody here, certainly not in the government, who is willing to insure such an exhibition« says Boubnova angrily.

The artists in Sofia are drawing some hope from the Scottish-Bulgarian team of Chris Byrne and Iliyana Nedkova, who opened »the first commercial gallery of an international kind« in Bulgaria in autumn 2007. »We think it was a very optimistic time to be opening a gallery in Sofia« says Chris Byrne. »We had practically no competition because other galleries in Sofia have been acting like shops until now, selling old masters, icons or academic art. Since the accession to the EU in 2007 we've had fewer problems with customs, and the economic situation of the country is also becoming more stable, bit by bit. We see the fact that there has been no art market until now as a challenge to create one.« —

Nobody would lend us a big Picasso exhibition

Our artists were too comfortable under Communism

Maria Vassileva is one of the most prominent personalities in Sofia's art scene. One of her personal triumphs is the development of a collection of contemporary Bulgarian art within the »Sofia City Art Gallery«.

By Antje Mayer

The Bulgarian women artists I've met until now have all painted a rather gloomy picture of the art scene in Sofia. Is the situation there really that bad for contemporary art?

MARIA VASSILEVA: There are hundreds of galleries in Sofia but, until now, only two of them could be taken seriously as far as contemporary art is concerned. In all Bulgaria there are just a few people who collect contemporary works systematically, among them artist Nedko Solakov, our international star. We therefore have no market for art. Our efforts to establish a museum for contemporary art failed. Naturally enough, our artists then go abroad, because that is where they find better opportunities.

It is more than seventeen years now since the fall of the Iron Curtain. In the Czech Republic, Slovakia, Hungary, and even in Romania, contemporary art has been able to establish itself; there are galleries there now, and even a few collectors. Why hasn't Bulgaria been able to do the same?

There are historical reasons. In contrast to the countries you've mentioned, we have no tradition of conceptual or performance art from the '60s, where the roots of contemporary art are found. Our tradition for contemporary art started very late, in fact only at the end of the '80s, and then it jumped straight from zero to one hundred. Our artists were too comfortable under Communism, even though that may sound a bit cynical. They lived as privileged members of The Union of Bulgarian Artists, in peaceful coexistence with the state. Why should they have rebelled, considering the »relative freedoms« they had? As an artist one could even travel, one had a regular income and was treated with greater tolerance by the regime. Because of its privileged status, the art profession still has a rather bad reputation in many parts of the Bulgarian population. The stuff that was produced in the Union in those days, especially painting, is still deemed to be the »state of true art« in formal circles in Bulgaria today.

As I have personally witnessed, contemporary art is taking place in Sofia!

You can find events scattered around Sofia in various places, including here at the Sofia City Art Gallery, where I work as a curator. However, it's a museum that covers art from the 19th century to the present day and within that I have built up the contemporary art sector over the past few years by myself and with enormous effort. Our collection of contemporary art, the only public collection of its kind in the country, includes just 80 works, which artists have donated, and even a small archive, which was inspired, by the way, by the artist database of basis wien. One positive thing is that, in spite of everything, we still have quite outstanding artists in Bulgaria who live up to international standards. I would say that 10 of them are really at the top.

Contemporary art survives thanks to the initiative of certain individuals in official institutions

So how do the artists in Sofia manage to survive?

Almost all of them have other jobs as well. Local NGOs, such as the Institute of Contemporary Art – Sofia, Interspace – New Media Art Center, or the Center for Culture and Debate – The Red House are almost the only organisations that give substantial aid toward keeping contemporary art alive. Contemporary art survives thanks to the initiative and motivation of certain individuals in official institutions. —

Maria Vassileva, (born 1961 in Sofia) is an art critic, curator and art historian. She is chief curator of the Sofia City Art Gallery and founding member of the Institute of Contemporary Art – Sofia.

Sofia

By Maria Vassileva

At Vaska Emanouilova Gallery

ART

SCAG: Sofiiska gradska hydojestvena galeria (Sofia City Art Gallery) — Located in the very heart of Sofia, this gallery houses a large collection of works by modern Bulgarian artists. Its contemporary art department was founded in 2004 and has been regularly hosting contemporary art-related events. Do not miss the Vaska Emanouilova Gallery (VEG) – a recently opened SCAG branch. Secluded behind a beautiful city park, the gallery is home to a

permanent exhibition featuring works by the Bulgarian sculptress Vaska Emanouilova and is also a venue for frequent contemporary art-related events. Young curator Vladiya Mihaylova will show you works by the most promising young Bulgarian artists and elaborate in detail about the contemporary art scene.

❶ *SCAG*
Gen. Gurko Str. 1, (987 21 81)
Tram 2, 10, 12, 18: Garibaldi Sq.
Tue-Sat 10 am to 7 pm, Sun 11 am to 6 pm
www.sghg.bg

❷ *VEG*
Yanko Sakazov Blvd. 15, (944 11 75)
Tram 20, 22: Vassil Levski Blvd.
Tue-Sat 10 am to 7 pm, Sun 11 am to 6 pm
www.veg.cult.bg

❸ **ICA: Institytat za savremenno izkystvo – Sofia (Institute of Contemporary Art – Sofia)** — The Institute of Contemporary Art Sofia, which was founded in 1995, is one of the most leading institutions promoting contemporary art in the capital city. Its director Iara Boubnova is an internationally known curator. The artists, who are members of the institute, namely Nedko Solakov, Luchezar Boyadjiev, Pravdoliub Ivanov or Stefan Nikolaev, have also received international recognition. After changing a number of addresses, the ICA opened its new exhibition space in 2009 in the vicinity of the University of Sofia, the National Academy of Fine Arts and the National Library.

Chataldja Str. 28, (846 64 33)
Trolley bus 1, 4: Slivnitza Blvd.
Mon-Fri 3 pm to 7 pm or by appointment
www.ica.cult.bg

❹ **ARC Projects** — If you would like to buy contemporary art works by Bulgarian or Eastern European artists, you should definitely go to this gallery. It opened its doors in the autumn of 2007 and happens to be the only commercial gallery for contemporary art in Sofia. Iliana Nedkova and her husband Chris Byrne are the ambitious owners of this beautiful venue. The gallery is located in Sofia's main shopping district, on the fourth floor of a distinctive blue colour-building on the Vitosha Blvd., right across from the National Palace of Culture, and above the Emporio Armani store.

Vitosha blvd. 90, 4th floor, (952 39 02)
Tram 1, 7: National Palace of Culture
Wed-Sat 3 pm to 8 pm or by appointment
www.arcprojects.org

❺ Studio Plastelin — This is an alternative space for young artists located in the old city centre, where you can see new faces. Do not expect art of very high quality, as the studio is a place for experimentation, yet this is what lends specific charm to the place.

Tzar Simeon Str. 48
Tram 20, 22: Mladejki teatar
Mon-Fri 6 pm to 9 pm
atelie-plastelin.blogspot.com

❻ Zentar za kyltyra I debat – Chervenata kasta (Centre for Culture and Debate – The Red House) — A cosy centre for culture with a restaurant and an attached hostel. A good place to see current, alternative, socially critical works representing a variety of artistic genres, i.e. theatre, literature, dance and music.

Ljuben Karavelov Str. 15, (988 81 88)
Tram 2, 10, 12, 18: Vassil Levski Blvd.
Mon-Sun 10 am to 6 pm
www.redhouse-sofia.org

❼ Natzionalna galleria za chyjdestranno izkystvo (National Gallery for Foreign Art) — – This gallery is housed in a beautiful building located right next to two major Sofia landmarks, namely the Alexander Nevski Cathedral and the National Assembly. The collection was built in the late '70s and the early '80s thanks to the initiative and power of Ms. Liudmila Zhivkova, daughter of ex-Communist leader Todor Zhivkov. The permanent exhibition represents a weird, yet curious mixture of Modern European art and the art of distant lands. The gallery hosts many temporary exhibitions.

Aleksander Nevski Sq. 1,
(988 4922)
Trolley bus 1, 4: Vassil Levski Blvd.
Wed-Mon 11 am to 6.30 pm
Full price admission 4 BGN,
free entrance on Mondays
www.foreignartmuseum.bg

ART EVENTS

Mejdynaroden Sofia Film Fest (Sofia International Film Fetival) — It may be little known in »the West« but the biggest film festival in South Eastern Europe is growing fast in scope, acclaim and popularity. It takes place in March every year, having started in 1997 as a rock festival with some music videos. However under the leadership of Stefan Kitanov it has grown to its current size. The film festival isn't all about celluloid. A carnival atmosphere surrounds the screenings and there can hardly be a better time to be in Sofia.

Festival office:
Bulgaria Sq. 1, (952 6467)
March
www.cinema.bg/sff

Sofia Jazz Peak — Sofia Jazz Peak has been standing in the centre of Sofia's musical life since the spring of 2003. The festival is organized by Cantus Firmus and Jazz FM Radio. Since 2006 it has had two editions – spring and autumn. The festival's concept is based on an open definition of jazz, paving the way for contemporary jazz, world music and soul artists, many of whom have hit Bulgarian stages since it all began. Sofia Jazz Peak quickly became the most important high scale jazz festival in South Eastern Europe.

Panayot Volov Str. 3, (400 14 23)
Spring
www.sofiajazzpeak.org

Sofia Dance Week — An international festival for contemporary dance which takes place in autumn every year. The organizers have the ambition to promote contemporary dance theatre in Bulgaria and bring about a change in public perception.

Festival Office: Patriarh Evtimii Bul. 22,
(981 23 47 or 988 10 09)
Autumn
www.sofiadanceweek.com

ALTERNATIVE SIGHTSEEING

❽ Boyanska tzarkva (Boyana church) — This church is a UNESCO World Heritage site and one of the few complete and perfectly preserved medieval monuments with murals from the 11th century. There is a nice garden and this is a good chance to see a perfect example of the so called »Bulgarian Renaissance«.

Boyansko Ezero Str. 1-3, (959 0939)
Bus 64, 107; minibus 21: Boyanska tsarkva
Apr-Oct from 9.30 am to 5.30 pm,
Nov-Mar from 9 am to 5 pm
www.boyanachurch.org

❾ Natzionalen istoricheski myzei (National Historical Museum) — Besides the very rich collection (650,000 items from the Prehistoric period up to the present day including the Bulgarian pride and joy - the »Thracian gold«) this museum is located in one of the residencies of ex-Communist leader Todor Zhivkov – an interesting example of totalitarian architecture. The best way to get there is by taxi.

Vitoshko lale str. 16, (955 42 80)
Nov-Mar 9.00 am to 5.30 pm
Apr-Oct 9.30 am to 6.00 pm
Full price admission 10 BGN
www.historymuseum.org

⓾ Bania bashi djamia (Banya Bashi Mosque) — Many of the city's main attractions are centrally located and easily explored on foot. Banya Bashi Mosque is the city's only surviving, functioning mosque, which serves the small legacy of centuries of Ottoman rule. The nearby Tsentralni Hali (Central Food Halls), Tsentralnata Banya (Central Baths) and the Synagogue offer a glimpse of early 20th-century architecture. You can hear the muezzin from the minaret five times a day. The Zhenski Pazar (Women's Market) is also worth a visit.

Bul. Maria Luiza
Tram 1, 7: Zentralni Hali

DAYTRIPS

Priroden park Vitosha (Vitosha Nature Park) — The beautiful landscape of the Vitosha mountains, only a quick drive or lift trip away, is popular for skiing and snowboarding in the winter and hiking in the summer. The mountain resort is situated in the immediate vicinity of Sofia, on the eastern sloped of Cherni Vrah (2,290 meters), the highest Vitosha peak. This is Bulgaria's highest ski resort, and only a 22 km distance from the centre of Sofia. The whole of the Vitosha mountain range, which starts where the Sofia suburbs end, has been designated a National park. You can go there by car, bus or by lift, really the best way to enjoy beautiful views and see Sofia from above.

Tram 18 from the city centre: Seminariata, then bus 123: Simeinovo lift (last stop)
www.park-vitosha.org

Rilski manastir (Rila monastery) — This Eastern Orthodox monastery, a UNESCO World heritage site, is »a must do trip« not only once in the life of a Bulgarian, but also for tourists. It is said to be the largest and most famous cultural, historical and architectural monument in Bulgaria. It occupies an area of 8,800m² and has a unique architecture with ancient wall-paintings and icons from the 14th century. The monastery is located 117 km south of Sofia in beautiful countryside in the deep green valley of the Rilska River. Take a picnic basket with you, enjoy your lunch within the spiritual walls, which whisper stories from former times. Maybe you get a spark of inner enlightenment.

You can reach the monastery by taking the E-79 road, follow the sign, then take a small asphalt-paved road, leading directly to the monastery.

Rila Monastery Reception,
(089 687 20 10)
Mon-Sun 9 am to 5 pm
www.rilamonastery.pmg-blg.com

SHOPPING

⓫ Totally Erected — Here people from different spheres of art, fashion, music and photography find a place to manifest themselves. The activity of the studio includes creation of a fashion brand of the same name, development of styling conceptions, as well as collaboration with different designers, photographers, make-up artists, hairdressers and musicians.

Han Krum Str. 48, apt. 9,
(986 38 55)
Tram 2, 12, 14, 18:
Slaveykov Sq.
Mon-Sat 10 am to 7 pm
www.totallyerected.net

⓬ Octopus Industries — A contemporary art and design label, producing limited edition design objects and street wear clothing. The mission of the owners is to promote and support young emerging designers, as well as to create an outstanding range of exciting products. Their ranges cover: badges, t-shirts, hooded tops, refrigerator magnets, cups, cards, books, coasters, bags, pillow cases, original limited edition prints.

Tzar Asen Str. 69, (088 720 21 66)
Tram 1, 7: National Palace of Culture
Tue-Sat 11 am to 7 pm
www.octopusindustries.org

⓭ Zona Urbana — This shop sells and designs the following products: bracelets made of real leather, cotton and silk, key chains made of fabric, leather and metal, toys, and even bags made of recycled materials: leather, metal and paper.

Han Krum street 4 B, 1 fl., (981 22 78)
Tram 2, 12, 14, 18: Slaveykov Sq.
Mon-Sat 10 am to 7 pm
www.zurbana.com

KIDS

⓮ Kokolandia Adventure Park — Located in Borissovata Garden, close to the city centre, this park offers different adventures including rope parapets, dangling rope ladders and metal ropes, a climbing wall, bungee jumps, and mini-golf.

Nezabravka Str., house of Baba Iaga,
(491 24 12)
Tram 18: Park-hotel Moskva
Apr-Oct 9 am to 9 pm daily
www.kokolandia.hit.bg

⓯ Sofiiska zoologicheska gradina (Zoological garden Sofia) — On an area of 230,000 m^2 you can see more than 1,000 animals representing 244 species housed in the biggest zoo in Bulgaria, located south of Sofia's city centre.

Srebarna Str. 1, (868 20 43)
Wintertime 9 am to 5 pm,
summertime 9 am to 7 pm daily
Full price admission 1 BGN
www.sofiazoo.eu

CAFÉS

⓰ Apartment — Why are there no such cosy spots in other cities? This is an »illegal« coffee shop in an apartment, still inhabited by the owner, especially nice for relaxing and arguing after an exhibition opening, or for the early morning after a late night out. The private apartment has been re-modelled to create an enormously comfortable coffee shop, with beautiful vintage wallpaper, sectional sofas and a fantastic selection of teas. Surfing on discreetly placed Macs is possible.

Neofit Rilski Str. 68, (886 655 093)
Tram 2, 12, 14, 18: Slaveykov Sq.
Mon-Sun 10 am to 2 am

⓱ Tea House — This place has a nice, calm and homey ambience that is hard to find in the busy city. The moment you get inside, your senses start to work in a different way or are at least offered a whole new variety of sensations. The exotic oriental scents that fill the air add to the comfort of the place. The menu, as you might guess, offers an exhaustive list of tea flavours to suit various moods. Soft drinks and alcohol are served as well. The food menu is equally interesting and strictly vegetarian. The best Bulgarian jazz musicians perform live here.

Georgi Benkovski Str. 11, (888 431 007)
Tram 20, 22: Mladejki Teatar
Mon-Sun 10 am to 11 pm

RESTAURANTS

⓲ Motto — This restaurant and bar with brick walls and a glass ceiling is recommended by everyone, probably because »all of Sofia« meets here. The place has a specific atmosphere due to the fact that the first private gallery in Sofia was opened here in the early 1900s. A variety of titbits, cool drinks and, most of all, the pleasure of seeing and being seen. A hip place that is always crowded. Incredible garden with venerable trees

right in the centre of the city. Wi-Fi available. Main dishes from 7.20 BGN.

Aksakov Str. 18, (987 27 23)
Trolley bus 9: Vassil Levski Blvd.
Mon-Sun 10 am to 12 am
Visa, American Express, Mastercard
www.motto-bg.com

⓳ Brasserie — Next to one of the most famous landmarks in Sofia, the open-air book market at Slaveykov Square, Brasserie transports you to a Manhattan eatery. Catering to a younger, trendy crowd, this bistro is popular for both

dinner and drinks. The food is the closest to fusion with an Asian twist that you can get in Sofia. It has a modernistic design and the garden is really great, although closed in winter. A bit pricier than the average Sofia dining establishment, but your few extra levs will be well spent. Plus it is close to the major downtown shopping areas. Main dishes from 10 BGN.

Raiko Daskalov Sq. 3, (980 63 98)
Tram 2, 12, 14, 18: Slaveykov Sq.
Mon-Sun 9 am to 11 pm
Visa, American Express, Mastercard

❷⓿ **Opera** — With its black panes, it looks so elegant from the outside that it gives off an air of inapproachability. It's on the ground floor of the National Opera and Ballet House and offers good international cuisine. After having dinner in this calm atmosphere you can go down the stairs and continue your night in the nightclub Mascara. Reservations are recommended. Main dishes from 6.20 BGN.

Rakovski Str. 113, (988 21 41)
Trolleybus 9: Alexander Nevski Cathedral
Mon-Sun 11 am to 12 am
Visa, American Express, Mastercard
www.opera-bg.info

❷❶ **Cactus** — Some artists' favourite restaurant with international cuisine at moderate prices. A pleasant alternative

to the hundreds of fancy places in the city, this restaurant creates great comfort with its pub style design. Main dishes from 8 BGN.

Hristo Belchev Str. 20, (986 74 31)
Tram 2, 12, 14, 18: Garibaldi Sq.
Mon-Sun 11 am to 11 pm
Visa, American Express, Mastercard
www.restaurant-cactus.com

22 Before & After Club — Another alternative to the lifestyle mainstream. A restaurant located in a stunning turn-of-the-century salon, where a high-society lady used to receive Sofia's artistic community. Sometimes tango evenings happen here, too. The place is fabulous, the food acceptable. Main dishes from 8 BGN.

Hristo Belchev Str. 12, (981 60 88)
Tram 1, 7: Solunska
Mon-Sun 10 am to 12 am
Visa, American Express, Mastercard
www.club-cabaret.net

PARTY

23 Hambara — This thoroughly nice and secluded pub, housed in a former corn warehouse featuring wooden furniture and candlelight, has reached cult status in Sofia. It is very difficult to find, and you are only let in after knocking and being given a look over. Regular discussions and lectures on contemporary art take place here. In the late hours, sometimes a combo will start to jam spontaneously.

Shesti Septemvri Str. 22
Tram 2, 12, 14, 18: Slaveykov Sq.
Mon-Sun 8 pm to 2 am

24 Swinging Hall — This live music club opened its doors back in 1995, when it only had one stage. Mainly jazz musicians performed here. Now there are two stages and every night you can listen to different musical genres: jazz, pop, rock, funk, etc. Sundays are reserved for jazz only. Jam sessions are a must.

Dragan Tsankov Blvd. 8, (896 840 180)
Tram 2, 12, 14, 18: Journalist Sq.
Mon-Sun 9 pm to late
Admission 5-10 BGN
www.swinginghall.com

25 Black Label Whisky Bar — A cool place to go after dinner. Housed in an historical building, the Central Military Club, whose foundations were laid in 1895, this club has always been an important cultural centre for the capital.

Its rich collection of drinks, decadent design, nice music and location, on the corner of Tzar Osvoboditel Blvd. and Rakovski Str., make it very attractive.

Tsar Osvoboditel Blvd. 7, (987 86 64)
Trolleybus 9: Alexander Nevski Sq.
Mon-Sun 6 pm to late

㉖ Blaze Club — The design isn't spectacular, but here DJs play the newest electronic sounds live – for the sake of music, rather than for the sake of loud volume. Close to the city centre, and within walking distance of the University of Sofia. Highly recommended.

Slavyanska Str. 36, (888 354 004)
Trolleybus 1, 2, 5, 8, 10: Gen. Gurko Str.
Mon-Sun 10 pm to 3 am

㉗ Mascara — This very popular fancy nightclub is under the restaurant Opera, in the huge basement of a landmark building. A favourite haunt for young people with sophisticated tastes who avoid chalga (popular music with oriental motives, vulgar texts and »breast implant« aesthetics).

Rakovski Str. 113, (988 21 41)
Trolleybus 9: Alexander Nevski Sq.
Mon-Sun 10 pm to 6 am
Admission 10 BGN

㉘ 4km. Party Center — The most hip club (with house and techno DJs, like the good old days) outside the centre, in the no-man's-land between Sofia and the airport, in an old military building with a huge dance floor and lounge bar. Since taxis are outstandingly inexpensive in Sofia, a trip out there is easily affordable.

Tsarigradsko Shose Blv. 111, (870 07 75)
Bus 1, 3, 5, 6, 84, 280, 313,
trolleybus 4, 5, 8, 11: 4-th Kilometer
Admission starts at 10 BGN
www.4-km.com

㉙ Yalta — One of the oldest, and therefore best tested, clubs for dancing until 6 in the morning. Here well-known international DJs can be heard. Caution – there's not always a program! But the bar on the ground floor is open every day. Its spacey design makes a heavenly ambiance for a drink (or two?).

Tsar Osvoboditel blvd 20, (980 12 97)
Trolleybus 1, 4: National Public Library
Mon-Sun 8 pm to 6 am
Admission 10 BGN
www.yaltaclub.com

SLEEP

㉚ Sheraton Sofia Hotel Balkan — One of the best and priciest hotels in Sofia,

considered to be one of the symbols of the city and also the epitome of luxury because of its huge chandeliers and all the Eastern glamour and sophistication you can imagine. Double rooms from € 320.

Sveta Nedelya Sq. 5, (981 65 41)
Tram 1, 7: Sveta Nedelya Sq
www.luxurycollection.com/sofia

❸❶ **Anel** — Within immediate reach of the city centre, this five-star hotel is made unique through its collection of contemporary Bulgarian art, comprised mostly of paintings and sculptures. The owner, Angel Simeonov, one of the most

prominent Bulgarian collectors, generously shares his collection with the hotel's visitors. Works of art are to be seen everywhere around the place – in the lobby, in the hallways, the restaurant, the breakfast room, the hotel suites, even in the fitness centre. Double rooms from € 290.

Todor Alexandrov Blvd. 14, (911 99 00)
Tram 9: Pirostska Str.
www.hotelanel.com

❸❷ **Arena Di Serdica** — This hotel is located in the heart of the city – just behind the National Art Gallery and across from the Goethe Institute, Sofia. Underneath the hotel the ruins of an ancient amphitheatre can be seen, dating from the 3rd century AD. A deluxe hotel within walking distance of business centres, banks, cultural and historical landmarks. Double rooms from € 145.

Budapeshta Str. 2-4, (810 77 88)
Tram 20, 22: Mladejki Teatar
www.arenadiserdica.com

❸❸ **Sveta Sofia** — This hotel is located in the oldest part of the city on Pirotska Str., a pedestrian street, which is also a main shopping area. It is close to the central open-air market and some of the city's most interesting buildings: Halite (a covered market), the Synagogue, the Mosque and the Central Mineral Baths. Double rooms from € 100.

Pirotska Str. 18, (981 26 34)
Tram 1, 7: Zentralni hali
www.svetasofia-alexanders.com

❸❹ **Hemus** — One of the prides of the Communist era, this three-star hotel was recently renovated featuring a total of 210 guestrooms. The Hemus hotel is conveniently located in the immediate vicinity of the National Palace of Culture. Although the hotel is not within the deluxe price range and its lobby may seem uninviting, it houses a casino and the best fish restaurant in town, SASA, whose location on the 18th floor offers a marvellous view of the city. Just across the hotel is one of the biggest shopping places in the city – City Centre Sofia. Double rooms from € 54.

Cherni Vruh Blvd. 31, (816 50 00)
Tram 6: Hotel Hemus
www.hemushotels.com

㉟ Slavyanska Beseda — Perhaps one of the worst hotels in the city, but also one of the oldest and worth a night for hardcore »Eastalgic« types. Cult bar on the first floor and extremely centrally located (close to all the other bars and pubs). Double rooms from € 52.

Slavianska Str. 3, (980 13 03)
Trolleybus 9: Satirichen teatar
www.slavyanska.com

Moria Flats — A perfect alternative to traditional hotel services. Clean, renovated flats, all equipped with cooking facilities located in residential buildings all over downtown Sofia for very reasonable prices. Moria flats can be 5 to 6 times less expensive than a hotel suite. Highly recommended. Flats from € 30.

Different locations in Sofia's city centre, (986 12 46)
www.moriahflats.com

㊱ The Rooms Hostel — Perhaps the cosiest and also the least expensive beds in the city, in an old, and unfortunately rather poorly renovated, urban villa. A hostel run by the daughter of an antique dealer, who has fitted all the rooms out with old junk. The antique shop is under the villa. Double rooms from € 20.

Pop Bogomil Str. 10, (898 260 316)
Trolleybus 9: Pop Bogomil Str.

GOOD TO KNOW

㊲ Tourist Information
pl. Sveta Nedelya 1, (933 58 45)
Tram 1, 7: Sveta Nedelya Sq.
Mon-Fri 9 am to 5 pm
www.bulgariantourism.com

INTERNET

㊳ Garibaldi
Graf Ignatiev Str. 6, (989 42 85)
Tram 2, 10, 12, 18: Garibaldi Sq.
Open 24 hours
www.garibaldicafe.net

㊴ Internet Café
45 Vitosha Blvd, (986 08 96)
Tram 1, 7: Solunska Str.
www.siteout.net

MEDIA

www.programata.bg — This magazine, in print and on the internet, provides all the information you might need – exhibitions, concerts, theatres, cinemas, cool places. It's the best way to know everything about art events and restaurants in Sofia. In English!

www.sofiaecho.com — The Sofia Echo provides news in English for and about foreigners in Bulgaria and South Eastern Europe. Priority areas of coverage: Business; Laws; Property; Travel and Tourism; Lifestyle; Eco; Sport. The Sofia Echo is distributed as a weekly newspaper in Sofia's finest hotels and entertainment venues and through a distribution network throughout Bulgaria and via computers and mobile devices on their website.

TRANSPORT

From the airport — There are two bus lines (84 from terminal 1, 284 from terminal 2) connecting Sofia Airport with the city centre in about half an hour. A single ticket costs 1 BGN, the price for a taxi is about 11 BGN to the centre.

Taxis — Taxi services are very cheap. Check the rate on the rear window – it should be about 60 stotinki per kilometre. There are »rip-off taxi drivers«, whose rates are several times higher than normal. Recommended taxi companies in Sofia are OK Supertrans (973 21 21), Taxi C Express (912 80), Yes & Yellow (911 19) and Radio SV Taxi (912 63).

Public transport — The centre of Sofia is rather small and almost everything is within walking distance. Walking is the best way to move around. Public transport is not very reliable, and although there is a quite well developed system it's difficult to find a map. In case you decide to use tram, bus or trolley bus, you can buy your ticket inside for 1 BGN.

Car — Traffic in the city is a mess. Forget about driving. If you decide to drive, remember that the whole city centre is a »blue zone«, you have to pay parking fees using a ticket (1 BGN/hour) or by phone (the telephone number is specified on the special street signs).

# #

Important Numbers

Telephone country and city code	*+359 2*
Telephone information	*11 800*
Police	*166 / 112*
Fire Brigade	*160 / 112*
Ambulance	*150 / 112*
Anti-corruption unit	*982 22 22*
24h-Pharmacy	*First Private Pharmacy, Tsar Assen I Str. 42, (46 54 35), tram 1, 7: Solunska Str.*

City in Numbers

1 Euro	*ca. 2 BGN (Bulgarian Lev)*
Inhabitants	*1.25 Mio*
Average income	*€ 268*
Cup of coffee	*1 BGN (ca. € 0.50)*
Bottle of beer	*1.3 BGN (ca. € 0.70)*
Cigarettes	*4 BGN (ca. € 2.00)*
Most talked about contemporary artist	*Nedko Solakov*
Collectors of contemporary art	*5*
Biggest art scandal	*The black cloth that covers (thanks to Bulgarian officials) the Bulgarian »toilet« within David Cerny's installation* Entropa *in Brussels.*

Short
Art History
SOFIA

1989 The group show *Earth and Sky*, curated by Diana Popova, takes place on the roof of the exhibition hall of the Sauza na balgarskite hydojnitzi (The Union of Bulgarian Artists) in Sofia. For the first time in Bulgarian art history there are installations, happenings, performances, etc.

1995 Institytat za savremenno izkystvo – Sofia (The Institute of Contemporary Art – Sofia) is founded, a driving force for the most important contemporary art events in Bulgaria.

1999 The group exhibition *Locally Interested* and a cycle of lectures curated by Iara Boubnova takes place at the Institute of Contemporary Art – Sofia, including the artists Douglas Gordon, Peter Kogler, Oleg Kulik, Pipilotti Rist, Nedko Solakov, Rirkrit Tiravanija and Uri Tzaig. This is the first exhibition where international stars are invited by a local curator.

2003 *Export-Import. Contemporary Art from Bulgaria*, curated by Maria Vassileva, Sofiiska gradska hydojestvena galeria (Sofia City Art Gallery), is the first big retrospective of contemporary Bulgarian art presented in a museum.

2006 The Sofia City Art Gallery establishes the Contemporary Art Fund. For the first time in Bulgaria, contemporary art becomes part of a museum collection.

Outskirts of Sofia

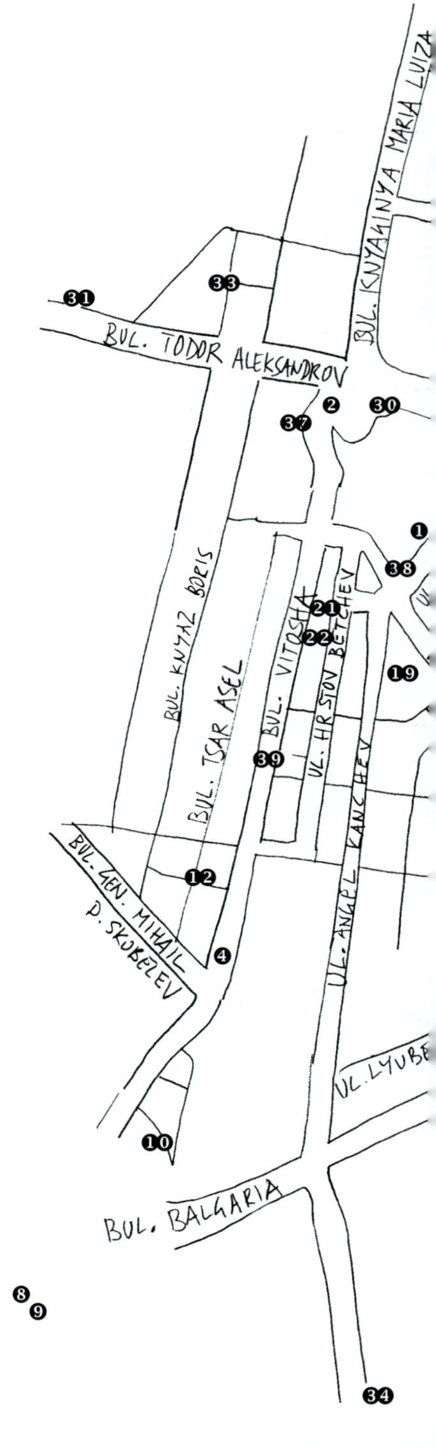
BUL. KNYAGINYA MARIA LUIZA
33
31
BUL. TODOR ALEKSANDROV
2
30
37
1
38
BUL. KNYAZ BORIS
BUL. TSAR ASEL
BUL. VITOSHA
UL. HRISTOV BETCHEV
21
22
19
39
UL. ANGEL KANCHEV
12
BUL. GEN. MIHAIL D. SKOBELEV
4
UL. LYUBE
10
BUL. BALGARIA
8
9
34

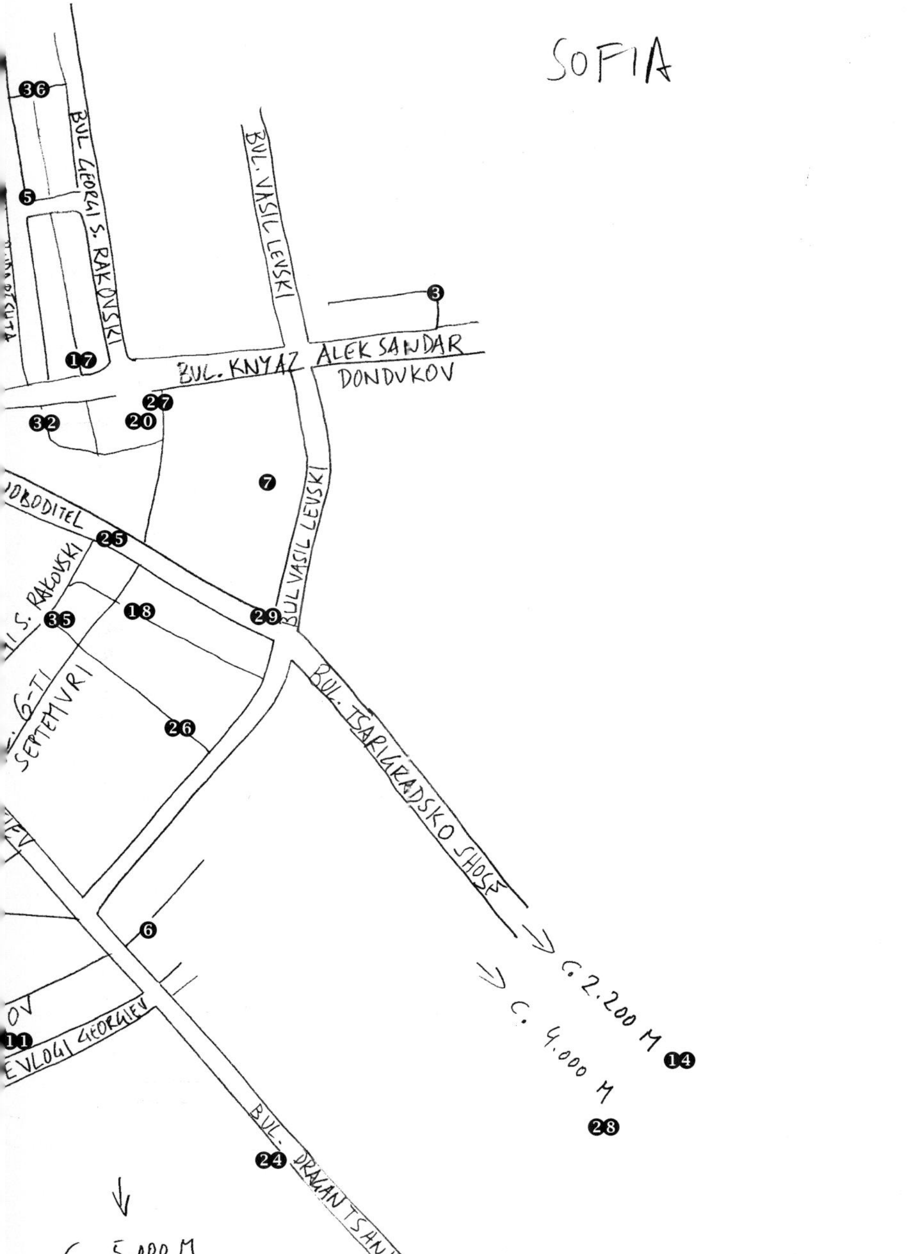
SOFIA
BUL. GEORGI S. RAKOVSKI
BUL. VASIL LEVSKI
BUL. KNYAZ ALEKSANDAR DONDUKOV
BUL. VASIL LEVSKI
BUL. TSARIGRADSKO SHOSE
SEPTEMVRI
EVLOGI GEORGIEV
BUL. DRAGAN TSANKOV
C. 2.200 M
C. 4.000 M
C. 5.000 M
36
5
3
17
27
20
32
7
25
18
35
29
26
6
11
14
28
24
15
200 m

Vienna

Faithful audience at the Bellaria cinema

Vienna is waiting for you

Recycling eternal artistic truths or a creative biotope? In the metropolis on the Danube the mills grind slowly, and that is surprisingly healthy for the city's art production.

By Matthias Dusini

»In London, academy graduates worked for eight hours, and then they made art and organised small galleries«, says Viennese painter Markus Muntean about his work in the English metropolis, then adding: »In Vienna people are accustomed to subsidies and a comfortable life.« With this description, the artist summarises the image of Vienna as a protected workshop. For many artists, a longing for the cool atmosphere of London and the bohemianism of Berlin goes hand-in-hand with the pragmatic decision to live mainly in Vienna. For half the year they jet from one exhibition to another, for the other half they relax in the artist's hideout of the Café Anzengruber.

An immaculate support structure, a gallery scene of international calibre, modern academies and well situated museums and art exhibition spaces provide ideal surroundings for the production of art. To find one's way around this site there is no need for any means of transport. The Vienna art world is less than two kilometres long. At its centre is the MuseumQuartier (MQ). To combat the conservative image of the city surroundings, the cultural administrators and politicians took the Centre Pompidou in Paris as a model for a cultural area for contemporary art, design, new media and dance. In this way the MQ arose alongside the monumental museums of the imperial age as a compromise between the avant-garde and the enemies of progress.The flagship of this popular leisure-time area is the Museum of Modern Art (MUMOK), completed in 2001. Originally the museum, designed by architects Ortner & Ortner, was intended to rise above the Baroque building in front of it, but then it was quietly lowered into the ground. The Kunsthalle Wien, which has undertaken the task to make contemporary art popular, also moved into a building in the MQ. Right next door is the Secession, the building that offers the liveliest exhibition program. A few minutes' walk away are clusters of galleries in the Eschenbachgasse and Schleifmühlgasse.

Muntean/Rosenblum belong to the middle generation of artists who act according to the principles of global contemporary art. Their paintings, representing young people whose body language looks like pathetic formulae emptied of meaning, cannot be assigned to any local idiom in the art-fair cabinets of London or Miami. Suffering from the reactionary climate of the post-war world, a feeling which drove the artists of Viennese Actionism, the only contribution Austria made to art history after 1945, has given way to routine professionalism.

Suffering from the reactionary climate of the post-war world has given way to routine professionalism

»In Austria the artist has no rights«, painter Maria Lassnig said recently for the record. In her words, there are clear echoes of the »Austria-plaint« once heard from the playwright and novelist Thomas Bernhard. The alpine republic has veiled itself in the iden-

Fluc bar and the Riesenrad

Naschmarkt

Viennese pastries

*Metro Station Karlsplatz
by Otto Wagner*

Karlskirche

Outside of Café Korb

Lemurenkopf
by Franz West

Naschmarkt

Cemetery of St. Marx

Flakturm with the permanent installation by Lawrence Weiner

Prater Hauptallee

tity-creating robes of a cultural nation, but in doing so has limited itself to recycling eternal truths. »Modernism was a no-man's-land,« according to Werner Hofmann, the founding director of MUMOK, when looking back at the '60s. Due to powerful galleries in London and New York, Lassnig, at the age of almost 90, has achieved an international breakthrough, not because of, but in spite of, her home in Vienna.

There is a raft of Austrian artists active in the top international level without their origins playing any part. Erwin Wurm's *One Minute Sculptures,* the *Adaptives* by Franz West and the Fluxus pop installations of the gelitin group are displayed in museums all over the world. At home they exhibit regularly in their own galleries. The galleries of Krinzinger, Meyer Kainer and Georg Kargl are among those who play in the international game of art dealership. »Vienna is very lively, but the market tends to be small« comments Thaddaeus Ropac, who operates galleries in Salzburg and Paris.

Vienna is very lively, but the art market tends to be small

For the first time since between the wars, the Viennese art trade enjoyed a boom in the '80s. The young generation of expressive painters profited from the flourishing market of the Yuppie era. At the beginning of the '90s the party was over, the main galleries closed up shop. At a distance from the market, an especially productive combination of art theory and art for readers began to develop. Theory platforms like the Depot or the private art institution Generali Foundation confirmed Vienna's reputation as a discourse metropolis. »Vienna is waiting for you«, was a slogan in Vienna promotion. One might also say: »Don't be in a hurry when you visit Vienna.« The mills of art grind slowly here, but constantly.
—

What do we need Russian artists in Vienna for?

Almost two decades ago *Anna Jermolaewa* fled from St. Petersburg to Vienna for political reasons. She initially worked as a cleaning lady, then she studied at the Academy of Fine Arts in Vienna. Today she is a Professor for Media Art at the ZKM in Karlsruhe and an artist with an international reputation.

—————

By Antje Mayer

Since 1989 Vienna has moved from the absolute perimeter to the centre of a new (old) cultural region in Central Europe. Your life has been influenced by Vienna but Vienna in turn has been formed by your biography and by that of many others from the East Bloc and former Yugoslavia ...

ANNA JERMOLAEWA: I myself started as a cleaning lady in a Polish firm in Vienna. Vienna is the city of Yugoslavian janitors, Polish construction workers and cleaners, Slavic vegetable sellers at the Naschmarkt, Ukrainian prostitutes on the Gürtel, and Russian oligarchs in the first district. But this is not all. After the fall of Communism many young people, like me, emigrated from Eastern Europe to study art in Vienna and a lot of them stayed. With their Slavic temperaments and unusual biographies that often ranged from a childhood under Communism to flight or war, they all shaped the city. Without them the art scene in Vienna wouldn't be what it is. In Vienna, contact with neighbouring and nearby cities such as Bratislava, Prague, Sofia, and Bucharest is extremely intense, at least behind the official scenes. Incidentally this is due to a considerable extent to the good connections (at least by air) between Vienna and Eastern Europe. Budget airlines such as SkyEurope do their bit in this respect. Their advertising slogans play ironically with cliches about the East: To Warsaw: »Why not pay your electrician or plumber a visit?«

But don't you think that Vienna hasn't really yet recognized its potential as a hub in the Central and Eastern Europe region?

When I received the relatively generous T-Mobile Art Award a tax inspector soon came knocking on my door. He asked my tax consultant: »What do we need Russian artists for, haven't we enough of our own?« When I told the story to a colleague she gave me a tip. »Try explaining to him that you do the work that your Austrian artist colleagues don't want to do.«

You were born in St. Petersburg and in 1989 you had to flee for political reasons. You had attracted the attention of the authorities as co-publisher of the legendary samizdat journal Democratic Opposition. *In fact you landed in Vienna more or less by chance. Is life as an artist guest worker in Vienna that pleasant?*

I used to hate Vienna. But now I love the city.

A summons for our arrest had been issued in Russia, so we had to flee practically over night. After our arrival my husband at the time and I lived for a week near the Westbahnhof railway station. All we owned were the clothes on our backs. For fear of being caught by the police we hardly went out at all. We had no money to buy food, we spoke no German, and nobody took an interest in us. This city seemed foreign and unapproachable. I used to hate Vienna.

Anna Jermolaewa (born 1970 in St. Petersburg) graduated in 1998 from the University of Vienna (Faculty of Art History) and in 2002 from the Academy of Fine Arts in Vienna (Painting & Graphic Art/ New Media). Since 2005 she has been a Professor for Media Arts, State School of Design /ZKM Karlsruhe in Germany. She has had several international solo and group exhibitions.

But now I love the city. When I go to buy vegetables at the Naschmarkt I can chat in Russian to the people selling them. Once a man at one of the stands asked what I did for a living. I told him I made videos. He winked at me. It was clear he thought I meant that I made porn videos. This has all become a part of home for me.

But can't this little »metropolis« be incredibly slow moving at times?

I actually see that as something positive, an ideal environment for working in a concentrated way, or for developing yourself culturally. I mean the Filmmuseum alone is a treasure. In Vienna I can build up my energy reserves by swimming in summer on the Donauinsel, or by ice-skating in winter on the Alte Donau. It isn't by chance that a lot of internationally successful artists live in this city: Franz West, gelitin, Elke Krystufek, Valie Export, Hans Schabus, Martin Guttmann, Peter Kogler or Maria Lassnig, just to mention a few.

Everything is within easy reach. You meet people here face to face, not in a chat room. And in comparison to the relatively small size of the city, the range of cultural facilities offered is enormous. Every day quite a number of good (!) cultural events take place, an off-space opens, or a museum or gallery has an opening. Traditionally the amount of music performed is amazing and a lot of things happen at the interface between music, fashion, performing and visual art; a lot takes place in institutions but also through personal initiatives.

Why does art flourish to such an extent in the Viennese biotope?

There are only a few collectors of contemporary art in Vienna; art isn't bought in Vienna but it is communicated here. In Austria, state support of contemporary artists compared, say, to Germany, is exceptional. There are gallery subsidies, studios are financed, grants and scholarships awarded, prizes given and so forth. At times I toyed with the idea of moving to New York, because now my entire family has immigrated to the USA. But how should I make my art there if I have to work three jobs just to pay the rent for my studio? My foreign colleagues envy me for living in this »artist's paradise«.

—

It isn't by chance that a lot of internationally successful artists live in this city

Vienna

By Heinrich Deisl, Matthias Dusini & Susanne Firzinger

Restaurant Anna Sacher, in the famous Hotel Sacher

ART

❶ MQ: MuseumsQuartier — The MuseumsQuartier is the cultural capital of Vienna and one of the ten largest cultural areas in the world. Built on the grounds of the former court stables, MQ includes Baroque architecture as well as contemporary buildings (from architects Ortner & Ortner) and is home to a broad range of cultural institutions, from big art museums like the MUMOK or the Leopold Museum to cultural institutions like the Kunsthalle Wien, Tanzquartier (Dance Centre) and the Architekturzentrum Wien (Viennese Centre for Architecture). There are production studios for new media and for artists in residence. In the summer the MQ has become the preferred hangout for many Viennese citizens. There are cafés, bars and restaurants to relax in and various shops dedicated to contemporary art, music and fashion. Tip: Walther Koenig Books has a wide international selection of titles on art, architecture, design, fashion, film and photography.

Museumsplatz 1, (523 5881 17 31)
U2, U3:Volkstheater, MuseumsQuartier, bus 48A: Volkstheater, bus 2A, tram 49: MuseumsQuartier
Daily noon to 12 pm
www.mqw.at

❷ MUMOK: Museum Moderner Kunst Stiftung Ludwig (Museum of Modern Art Foundation Ludwig) — The MUMOK is the largest Austrian museum for Modern and contemporary art. It presents art history from classic Modern works up to the present day with an emphasis on Pop Art, Photorealism, Fluxus and Nouveau Réalisme. Viennese Actionism, Austria's radical and essential contribution to the international development of post-war art, is excellently documented with works by Günter Brus, Otto Muehl, Hermann Nitsch and Rudolf Schwarzkogler. The museum also shows in-depth retrospectives, including those of Sigmar Polke or Maria Lassnig.

Museumsplatz 1, (525 00)
U2, U3:Volkstheater, MuseumsQuartier, bus 48A: Volkstheater, bus 2A, tram 49: MuseumsQuartier
Tue-Sun 10 am to 6 pm, Thur 10 am to 10pm
Full price admission € 9
www.mumok.at

Kunsthalle Wien and Kunsthalle wien project space — One of the most exciting places when it comes to pop culture and contemporary art. For example, in the recent past there were exhibitions by Raymond Pettibon and Lee Lozano, as well as shows on the history of punk or on the use of pornographic imagery in everyday life and art. The Kunsthalle Wien project space is a glass cube on Karlsplatz, a 10 minute walk from the MQ, across from the Secession and a hot spot for the urban bohéme. Exhibitions there focus on young art, and it is a place often used for lectures, performances and discussions. The Kunsthallen-Café in the same building stands out due to its expansive sundeck right at the heart of Vienna's pulsating urban life. (with DJ-line up).

❸ *Museumsplatz 1, (521 89 33)*
U2, U3: Volkstheater, MuseumsQuartier, bus 48A: Volkstheater, bus 2A, tram 49: MuseumsQuartier
Mon-Sun 10 am to 7 pm,
Thur 10 am to 10 pm
Full admission € 8

❹ *project space*
Treitlstraße 2, (521 89 1201)
U1, U2, U4: Karlsplatz
Tue-Sat 4 pm to 2 am, Sun-Mon 1 am to 7 pm
www.kunsthallewien.at

❺ **Secession** — There are three reasons to visit the Secession: the famous architecture with its golden dome, one of the key works of the Jugendstil period, the famous Beethoven-Frieze by Gustav Klimt in the basement, and the contemporary art exhibitions. This is the oldest white cube in the world and still operates as an artist's association; they take great pains in preparing an overall

ambitious program. Stars like Mike Kelley or Thomas Hirschhorn responded to the Viennese association's invitation. For the local scene, the Secession is a springboard to an international career.

Friedrichstraße 12, (587 53 07)
U1, U2, U4: Karlsplatz, bus 59A: Bärenmühldurchgang
Tue-Sun 10 am to 6 pm, Thur 10 am to 8 pm
Full price admission € 6
www.secession.at

❻ **Bawag Foundation and Generali Foundation** — In 2008, something came together that did not belong together. Out of cost consideration, the exhibition spaces of the Bawag bank and the Gen-

eral Insurance Group united their efforts, and now exhibitions from both groups alternate shows in the Generali Foundation exhibition rooms. The concrete exhibition space, built in 1995 by the Viennese architects Jabornegg & Palffy, has been praised for its pureness and simplicity, and has influenced the style of a whole generation of exhibition architects. The Generali foundation, founded in 1998, can take from its exceptional collection of conceptual and performative art, which has a number of works by Eastern and South-eastern European artists, while the Bawag made its name above all with international artists like Jeremy Deller or Susan Hiller.

Wiedner Hauptstraße 15, (504 98 80)
U1, U2, U4: Karlsplatz, tram 62, 65: Paulanergasse

Tue-Sun 11 am to 6 pm, Thur 11 am to 8 pm
Generali: Full price admission € 6,
Bawag: free admission
www.bawag-foundation.at
www.foundation.generali.at

❼ **MAK: Museum für angewandte Kunst/ Gegenwartskunst (Museum of Applied Arts/ Contemporary Art)** — During the '80s, the MAK's permanent collection was reinstalled. Under the reign of director Peter Noever, established contemporary artists and architects rejuvenated the gallery spaces of the museum. Still impressive: Barbara Blooms Thonet-shadow play and the oriental carpets on floating cement-asbestos panels by Gangart. The highlights of the collection include the *Frankfurter Küche* by Margarete

Schütte Lihotzky and one of a kind pieces from the Wiener Werkstätte. Exhibitions about architecture and art have included Coop Himmelb(l)au, Joep van Lieshout, Franz West, Elke Krystufek etc.

Tip: the MAK-Nite happens each Tuesday. The program features contemporary music, performance art, fashion shows and everything »in-between the arts«. In combination with the MAK-Nite-Ticket, there is free entrance into the MAK museum until midnight. For a nice drink and/or for Austrian cuisine: the restaurant Österreicher im MAK. The MAK design shop is another hot tip.

Stubenring 5, (711 360)
U4: Landstraße, U3, tram 2: Stubentor,
bus 74A, 1 A: Invalidenstraße
Tue 10 am to noon, Wed-Sun 10 am to 6 pm
Full price admission € 7.90, free on Saturday
www.mak.at

❽ **Augarten contemporary** — The contemporary outpost of the Belvedere Museum (which shows Austrian art from the Middle Ages up to Gustav Klimt and Egon Schiele) with solo shows by young artists and thematic group exhibitions. The so-called »Atelier« with an excellent adjoining restaurant is situated in the idyllic Augarten Park not so far from the city centre, which still contains two giant flak-towers from the Second World War. In July and August visitors can enjoy the open-air Augarten Kino unter den Sternen (Cinema under the Stars, www.kinounterdensternen.at). The bobos with children meet on Sunday for brunch at the Café Bunkerei, only a ten-minute walk away (weekends 9 am to 2 pm, weekdays from 11 am) and in the evenings to hear music. (www.bunkerei.at)

Scherzergasse 1a, (216 861 621)
U1: Praterstern, U2: Taborstraße,
tram 2, 5: Am Tabor
Thur-Sun 11 am to 7 pm
www.belvedere.at

❾ **Galerie Andreas Huber** — Andreas Huber belongs to the youngest generation of gallery owners. Since 2005 the gallery behind the MuseumsQuartier has shown Austrian and international viewpoints, mainly in conceptual art. Exhibitions featured, for example, pieces by Leopold Kessler, who intervened in the open space with sabotage influenced gestures, as well as works by American artist Kaucyila Brooke or the feminist artist Carola Dertnig.

Capistrangasse 3, (586 02 37)
U3: Neubaugasse, U2, U3: MuseumsQuartier
Tue-Fri 2 pm to 6 pm, Sat 11 am to 3 pm
www.galerieandreashuber.at

⓾ Knoll Galerie — Hans Knoll evinced a pioneer spirit as early as 1989 when he opened a space as the first gallery owner from the West in Budapest. Knoll has become the primary source for information about contemporary art from this region because of his numerable projects and exhibitions in Eastern Europe. His gallery includes, among others, the Hungarian artist Akos Birkás, as well as the Russian artist collectives AES+F and Blue Noses.

Gumpendorfer Straße 18, (587 50 52)
U2: MuseumsQuartier, U1, U2, U4: Karlsplatz, Bus 59A
Tue-Fri 2 pm to 7 pm, Sat 11 am to 3 pm
www.knollgalerie.at

⓫ Galerie Hubert Winter — This gallery, situated directly behind the MuseumsQuartier, was grounded in 1971 »because I was and am curious and wanted

to become a millionaire on the side« quips Hubert Winter ironically. The gallery represents the minimalist positions of Fred Sandback, Marcia Hafif, Nancy Haynes or of the Austrian artist Ingo Nussbaumer. Birgit Jürgenssen is important artist here as the gallery also manages her estate.

Breite Gasse 17, (524 09 76)
U2, U3, bus 48A: Volkstheater, bus 2A, tram 49: MuseumsQuartier
Tue-Fri 11 am to 6 pm, Sat 11 am to 2 pm
www.galeriewinter.at

GALLERY DISTRICT Eschenbachgasse — Beside the Schleifmühlgasse the Eschenbachgasse in the 1st district is known as »the gallery street« in Vienna. Not far from the MuseumsQuartier and the Secession.

U2: MuseumsQuartier, U1, U2, U4: Karlsplatz, tram 1, 2, D, J: Burgring
All galleries usually open: Thur-Fr 1 pm to 6 pm, Sat 11 am to 3 pm (and by appointment).

⓬ Galerie Meyer Kainer — One of the big names in town. A gallery that exhibits some international highlights of Austrian art from the work of artists such as Franz West, Heimo Zobernig or the infamous art group gelitin. The newest addition is Elke Krystufek. Upstairs is an original bar from the '50s made by architect Erich Boltenstern behind which Christian Meyer likes to serve drinks for his guests at openings. In the so called »Boltenstern.Raum« group exhibitions with predominantly younger artists are shown.

Eschenbachgasse 9, (585 72 77)
www.meyerkainer.at

⓭ Galerie Krobath — After the split from Barbara Wimmer, Helga Krobath now runs this gallery on her own. Here, typical project artists like Austrian Dorit Margreiter or Florian Pumhösl found access to the art market. Artists such as Julian Opie, Jiri Kovanda and Gerold Miller count among the inner circle of artists represented here. Around the corner, in the Nibelungengasse Nr. 11/13, the gallery has been running a second exhibition space in a Viennese apartment since 2008. (Program available on request)

Eschenbachgasse 9, (585 74 70)
www.galeriekrobath.at

⓮ Galerie Martin Janda — Martin Janda founded the »Raum aktueller Kunst« (space for current art) in 1992 where he brought artists like Raoul de Keyser, René Daniels and Liam Gillick to Vienna, and since 1999, he has been running his own gallery. He is interested in making less marketable art marketable, such as film installations by the Romanian artist Roman Ondák. His roster of artists includes Christine & Irene Hohenbüchler, Werner Feiersinger and Jun Yang.

Eschenbachgasse 11, (585 73 71)
www.martinjanda.at

⓯ Galerie Mezzanin — Once an off-space in an old apartment, this gallery has in the meantime developed into a commercial success under the aegis of Karin Handlbauer, time and again unveiling excellent native talent. Mezzanin represents, among others, Austrian artists like Peter Kogler or Christian Mayer, as well as American Elaine Sturtevant.

Getreidemarkt 14, (526 43 56)
www.mezzaningallery.com

GALLERY DISTRICT Schleifmühlgasse — Not only the Eschenbachgasse, but also the Schleifmühlgasse in the 4th district is known as »the gallery street« of Vienna. Not far from the Secession, Kunsthalle project space, Bawag and Generali Foundation and the famous food market Naschmarkt.

U1, U2, U4: Karlsplatz
All galleries usually open:
Thu-Fr 11 am to 6 pm,
Sat 11 am to 3 pm
(and by appointment).

⓰ Christine König Galerie — Founded in 1989/90. Works by international artists like Jannis Kounellis, David Hammons, Rebecca Horn or Nancy Spero had their Austrian premiere at Christine König. The gallery features renowned Austrian artists as well, including Gerhard Rühm, one of the cofounders of the Wiener Gruppe as well as artists from the younger generation including Constantin Luser or the Algerian artist Adel Abdessemed. Open Saturday until 5 pm!

Schleifmühlgasse 1a, (585 74 74)
www.christinekoeniggalerie.com

17 Galerie Senn — Gabriele Senn introduced the work of Cosima von Bonin, Kai Althoff and Georg Herold to Vienna. Early on she showed the Hamburg artist collective Akademie Isotrop, to which belonged the painter André Butzer, now an artist in the gallery. Representatives from the Viennese art scene include Marko Lulic, Barbara Mungenast and Hans Weigand.

Schleifmühlgasse 1a, (585 25 80)
www.galeriesenn.at

18 Engholm Engelhorn Galerie — With lots of neon and concrete, one of the coolest of the galleries from the last decade. The logo art by German artist Daniel Pflumm comes across quite attractively in this ambiance. Austrian artists like Hans Schabus and Mischa Stroj exhibit their installations here, other artists on the roster include Monika Baer, Angela Bulloch and Björn Dahlem.

Schleifmühlgasse 3, (585 73 37)
www.engholmengelhorn.com

19 Galerie Georg Kargl — Georg Kargl combines a passion for art with entrepreneurship. His artist roster spans local matadors like the artist couple Muntean/Rosenblum, to Markus Schinwald, to American artist Mark Dion. Adjacent in the Kargl Box, designed by American artist Richard Artschwager, young artists like Carol Bove or Andreas Fogarasi are presented, or artists are rediscovered, like the 60's Austrian pop-artist Erwin Thorn. Open until 8 pm Thursday!

Schleifmühlgasse 5, (585 41 99)
www.georgkargl.com

GALLERY DISTRICT Seilerstätte and its neighbourhood — A high concentration of galleries can also be found in the very centre, in the 1st district, around the Saint Stefan's Cathedral, not far away from the MAK. The neighbourhood contains lovely Viennese coffee houses like the Prückl, Korb or Engländer (see »cafés«)

U1, U3, bus 1A: Stubentor or Stephansplatz
All galleries usually open Tue-Fri 11 am to 6 pm, Sat 11 am to 4 pm (or by appointment)

20 Charim Galerie Wien — The Charim Galerie lies in the inner courtyard of a typical Viennese Baroque house and is always a place for new discoveries, and is, on this account, always full to capacity at openings. The gallery shows established figures like Valie Export or Christoph Schlingensief as well as promising newcomers, like the Viennese photo-artist Markus Krottendorfer or the Vienna-based artist from St. Petersburg Anna Ceeh. Only open until 2 pm on Saturday!

Dorotheergasse 12/1, (512 09 15)
www.charimgalerie.at

㉑ Galerie Nächst St. Stephan — A gallery with a long tradition. The gallery has been on the same spot since 1920, under this name since Monsignor Otto Mauer opened it in 1954 after the Second World War. The avant-garde from Joseph Beuys to Arnulf Rainer found a place here. Under the direction of artist Oswald Oberhuber, the gallery acquired the role of »information platform« in the '70s in that it informed the scene about classic Modern and contemporary art. In 1978, Rosemarie Schwarzwälder took control and concentrated primarily on minimalism, abstraction and conceptual art, showing works by Helmut Federle, Imi Knoebel and Ernst Caramelle. For the past few years, the gallery has supported successful Polish artists Adam Adach, Agnieska Kalinowska and Aneta Grzeszykowska.

Grünangergasse 1/2, (512 12 66)
www.schwarzwaelder.at

㉒ Galerie Krinzinger — In business since the '70s, today Ursula Krinzinger still attends every important art fair in the world. Originally the gallery was engaged in Vienna Actionism (Brus, Muehl, Schwarzkogler), then focused on international performance and body related art including stars from the American West coast like Chris Burden or Nancy Rubins, and from Austria Erwin Wurm. Krinzinger recognized the value of the German »enfant terrible« Jonathan Meese early on. Recently she shows more work by contemporary artists from China and India like Zhang Ding and Sudarshan Shetty. The gallery space alone is worth a visit because of its dignified, historical ambiance

Seilerstätte 16, (513 30 06)
www.galerie-krinzinger.at

㉓ layr:wuestenhagen contemporary — This gallery was grounded by Emanuel Layr und Thomas Wüstenhagen in 2002; in the meantime it has become successful at international art fairs. They represent only young artists like the painter Tillman Kaiser, Fabain Seiz or the artists' collective mahony, and cre-

ate exciting curatorial projects outside of the gallery. Ateliers and residencies are available for artists and curators. This is one of the meeting place for the young art scene.

An der Hülben 2, (524 54 90)
www.layrwuestenhagen.com

㉔ Galerie Grita Insam — Grita Insam has been running this gallery since 1973, and it is time and again an exciting place for theoretical discussion and experimental positions. She is responsible for innumerable art projects in public spaces, including the legendary project »Kunst Raum Donau« from the late'80s. Some of her artists, among them Candida Höfer or the Slovenian group IRWIN, have become classics. Austrian painter Stefan Sandner is the most important new addition.

An der Hülben 3, (512 53 30)
www.galeriegritainsam.at

ART EVENTS

❷❺ Viennafair – The International Contemporary Art Fair — Around 126 galleries are on show at the small Viennafair (established in 2005) attracting around 15,000 visitors. Its function as a showcase for both national as international galleries focusing on young art with a heavy emphasis on Central and Eastern Europe helped more or less to build up a unique profile amongst international art shows. The side program tries to attract art collectors from all over the world to buy art in Vienna, but they are still waiting for the crowds to arrive.

Messe Wien, Messeplatz 1, hall A, (727 200)
April/May
Daily ticket € 15
www.viennafair.at

festival for fashion & photography — The festival started out in a small cellar in town, today it's one of the cities major society events with a broad program that takes place at the Museums Quartier and other various locations across the city. The festival features national and international designers, artists, photographers and fashion experts. The program includes fashion shows, awards, exhibitions, lectures, shopping venues and of course a lot of »see and to be seen« parties.

Festival office:
Unit f büro für mode
Gumpendorferstraße 56, (219 84 99-0)
May/June
www.9festival.at

viennaartweek — An Art Cluster Vienna event, this is a coming together of all important Viennese museums, exhibition spaces and art institutions. Exhibitions, discussions, tours, and atelier visits pertaining to contemporary art take place in a variety of places all over Vienna. One of the biggest art events in town.

Art Cluster Vienna
Spiegelgasse 16, (402 25 24)
November
www.viennaartweek.com

ALTERNATIVE SIGHTSEEING

❷❻ Sigmund Freud Museum — Museum of one of the world's most important scientists, Sigmund Freud, located in the house where Freud lived and worked from 1891 to 1938. The birthplace of all you wanted to know – or per-

haps not know – about your sub consciousness. Here, Freud developed his revolutionary theory about psychoanalysis. One can see, aside from a few memorabilia and documents about Freud's life, works from the Sigmund Freud Museum Contemporary Art Collection, which consists of donations of art works that cover the topic psychoanalysis in various forms (among others: Pierpaolo Calzolari, Georg Herold, Jenny Holzer, Ilya Kabakov or Franz West).

Berggasse 19, (319 15 96)
Tram 37, 38, 40, 41, 42, bus 40A: Schwarzspanierstraße/Berggasse
Mon-Sun 9 am to 5 pm
Full price admission € 7
www.freud-museum.at

㉗ Schneekugelmuseum (Snow Globe Museum) — The snow globe museum is located in the »Schneekugelmanufaktur«, a family-run company that has existed since 1900. Here one can find all different shapes and fillings of the original snow globe, produced of course by hand. Do you remember the opening scene of the film *Citizen Kane*? The Rosebud-snow globe was manufactured here. In this small museum, handicraft, art and kitsch balance each other out.

Schumanngasse 87, (486 43 41)
Tram 42: Sommarugagasse
Mon-Thu 8 am to noon, 1 pm to 3 pm
www.schneekugel.at

㉘ Narrenturm (Madhouse Tower) — Be aware that the Narrenturm is one of the world's biggest pathological museums, not a freak show. The »tower of fools« was built in 1784 under the reign of Emperor Joseph II as one of the first psychiatric clinics in history. Rumour has it that this haunting tower with its fortress-like architecture was constructed under the principles of freemasonry. The Narrenturm contains scientific examples of diseases, deformations and cripplings, thousands of formaldehyde-exhibits and »moulages« (a special wax-technique for conservation), which give a special insight into the history of medicine. (And sometimes a shivering feeling á la Cronenberg's films.)

Spitalgasse 2, via Van-Swieten-Gasse, (406 86 722)
Tram 43, 44: Alserstraße/Spitalgasse
Wed 3 pm to 6 pm, Thur 8 am to 11 am, every first Sat of the month 10 am to 1 pm
Full price admission € 2
www.narrenturm.at

㉙ Stadionbad (Stadium pool) — An open air swimming area in the green setting of the Prater Park with an exciting history: The Stadionbad was inaugurated in 1931 during the second Workers Olympic Games in the high times of »red« Vienna. It was used as a centre for the then internationally highly acclaimed Jewish sports club »Hakoah« and was totally destroyed after a bombing in 1945. Nowadays, the Stadionbad with its 150.000m^2 swimming facilities is one of the largest public baths in Europe.

Prater-Krieau, (720 21 02)
May/Sept: Mon-Fri 9 am to 7 pm, Sat-Sun 8 am to 7 pm, Jul/Aug: Mo-Sun until 8 pm
Bus 84A: Pierre-de-Coubertin-Platz, 77A: Stadionbad
Full price admission € 4.50

30 Stonborough-Wittgenstein House — One of a kind in Austrian architecture due to its formal radicalness. Not an architect, but rather a philosopher, Ludwig Wittgenstein designed the house together with Paul Engelmann, a student of Loos, in 1925 for his sister Margaret Stonborough-Wittgenstein (Completed 1928). Wittgenstein drew every window, every door, every window sash, and every radiator. Even though the interior of the building is not in its original state, one can still sense the unique workmanship and cleverly designed dimensions. It has been the property of the Bulgarian Cultural Institute since 1975, but is open for visitors.

Kundmanngasse 19, (713 31 64)
U3, bus4A, 74A: Rochusgasse
Mo-Thur 10 am to noon, 3 pm to 4.30 pm
(and by appointment)
www.haus-wittgenstein.at

SHOPPING

31 wieWien (likeVienna) — »Wien, nur du allein...« (»Vienna, only you...«). This verse from a popular waltz seems emblematic for this cosy and fancy shop. Call it a concept store for gadgets, memorabilia and curiosities from and about Vienna: T-Shirts with Viennese motifs

by local artists, books about Viennese lifestyle, architecture and the pop underground, Sissi-cups, etc, etc. Most of these lovingly unnecessary (or can't-live-without) pieces are displayed in suitcases from the '70s. If you are searching for really cool, a bit trashy but always surprisingly funny souvenirs from Vienna, WieWien is the place of choice.

Kettenbrückengasse 5, (961 01 15)
U4: Kettenbrückengasse
Mon-Fri 12 am to 7 pm, Sat 10 am to 5 pm
www.wiewien.at

32 Salon für Kunstbuch — A beautiful small space in the 7th district (near the fashion store Park) run by artist Bernhard Cella. He presents an idiosyncratic selection of artists books and art theory that you wouldn't find anywhere else in Vienna. The aim of the project is to establish a cultural dialogue independent of the big art institutions in town. If you find the shop closed, just phone him, he lives around the corner.

Mondscheingasse 11, (0660 445 71 16)
U3: Neubaugasse, tram 49, bus 13A:
Neubaugasse/Westbahnstraße
Wed-Fri 2 pm to 7 pm, Sat noon to 5 pm
www.salon-fuer-kunstbuch.at

33 Park — Park is a highly prestigious fashion concept store. Its white, open spaces give the impression of a gallery, and that's just how the goods are put on display. Apart from haute couture, Park offers street wear, a jeans section, furniture, jewellery, magazines and the owner's (Markus Strasser und Helmut Ruthner) favourite books. Some brands: Bless, Raf Simons, Ann Demeulemeester, Vibskov or Fred Perry. You can also find fashion from the younger Aus-

trian generation of designers including Pelican Avenue, Edwina Hörl or fabrics interseason.

Mondscheingasse 20, (526 44 14)
U3: Neubaugasse, tram 49, bus 13A: Neubaugasse/Westbahnstraße
Mon-Fri 10 am to 7 pm, Sat 10 am to 6 pm
www.park.co.at

❸❹ Song Fashion Store — Without a doubt one of the best fashion boutiques in Vienna. The shop was designed by Gregor Eichinger. Ambitious in art with an avant-garde touch, the Ms. Saba Song's high end store features on its 500 m² labels like Comme des Garcons, Victor & Rolf or Walter van Beirendonck. Regularly, fashion designers and visual artists like Michael Huey or Jutta Koether are invited to exhibit in the store.

Praterstraße 11-13, (532 28 58)
U1, U4: Schwedenplatz
Tue-Fri 10 am to 7 pm, Sat 10 am to 6 pm
www.song.at

❸❺ Mühlbauer — An Austrian classic for head wear. Since 1903, this family-run company has produced all different kinds of hats, ranging from alpine and creative hunting style to trendy felt cloches, from fur caps to timeless classics like the bowler or the panama-hat. Vis-á-vis the hat shop, Mühlbauer owns a fashion store with an interesting mix of established and new labels like Vivienne Westwood, Schiesser Revival or Citizens of Humanity. Both stores are designed by architects Kuehn Malvezzi.

Hats: Seilergasse 10, (512 22 41),
Fashion: Seilergasse 5, (513 70 70)
U1, U3: Stephansplatz
Mon-Fri 10 am to 6.30 pm,
Sat 10 am to 5 pm
www.muehlbauer.at

❸❻ Unger und Klein — The name Wien (Vienna) comes from wein (wine) but that is not the only reason to take a good bottle of Austrian grape back home, or to try it copiously beforehand. At Unger and Klein one is even seated in the wine rack (designed by Eichinger & Knechtl) and can try 1,200 varieties of wine from around the world. For a solid foundation there are tasty titbits from the kitchen.

Gölsdorfgasse 2, (532 13 23)
Mon-Fri 3 pm to 12 am,
Sa 5 pm to 12 am
www.ungerundklein.at

CAFÉS

❸❼ Café Prückel — Out of the very many cafés that Vienna offers, the Prückel across the street from the MAK can be considered a »must-go«. A preserved '50s interior awaits you there. Wi-Fi for the trendy art lovers, who frequently visit the Prückel, and cheap business menus for all. A popular place, always full, a good way to be alone in the crowd.

Stubenring 24 (Luegerplatz),
(512 61 15)
U3: Stubentor
Mon-Sun 8 am to 10 pm
www.prueckel.at

㊳ Café Korb — The owner of this café is the lovable and exalted Susanne Widl, ex-model and muse of the wild 60's and 70's art epoch. It is not only a meeting point for artists, authors, intellectuals, and actors but also for the neighbourhood shop owners. The legendary waiters don't serve, they administrate, and always have a joke on hand for their guest. Wi-Fi available.

Brandstätte 9, (533 7215)
U1, U3: Stephansplatz,
bus 1A: Brandstätte
Mon-Sun 8 am to 12 am,
Sun 11 am to 11 pm
www.cafekorb.at

㊴ Café Heumarkt — Close to the Konzerthaus, the Heumarkt could be considered a kind of economic miracle. The furniture looks as old as some of its regular costumers. But if you love the patina-charm of a lazy and slow hour long break with a good cup of coffee, a newspaper and especially with some roasted dumplings (»geröstete Knödel«), this café is made for you.

Am Heumarkt 15, (712 65 81)
U3: Stadtpark
Mon-Fri 9 am to 11 pm

RESTAURANTS

㊵ Zum Schwarzen Kameel (At the Black Camel) — The Kameel has practically everything a gourmet could ask for: a top-class restaurant with Austrian and crossover specialities from renowned chef Christian Domschitz, a well-sorted alimentary and wine shop, a bar with a very big selection of take-away dishes. A place where to see and to be seen is a considerable factor, go there early in the morning for breakfast or stop by for a delicious panino, served at the counter. Sandwiches in the bar start at €1, main dishes in the restaurant from €18.

Naglergasse 6, (533 81 25)
U1, U3: Stephansplatz
Mon-Sat 8.30 am to 2 pm,
Restaurant: noon to 3.30 pm, 6 pm to 2 am
(closed on Sun and holidays)
Visa, MasterCard, Amex, Diners
www.kameel.at

㊶ Pfarrwirt — The oldest restaurant in Vienna, located on the village-like outskirts of the town not far away from the Karl-Marx-Hof, a municipal tenement complex and architectural jewel from the '30s. This noble »Beisl« (pub) features a genuine mixture of old and new. Whereas the Prälatensaal is equipped with a stuccoed ceiling and Baroque paintings – it used to be the favourite place of the late Beethoven – at the entrance you'll find a huge art piece by Daniel Spoerri. The top level cuisine offers new interpretations of Austrian classics, the wine card is impressive. Cheap business menus at midday. Main dishes start at €16.

Pfarrplatz 5, (370 73 73)
U4, Heiligenstadt, then bus 38A: Fernmeldeamt – Pfarrplatz
Tue-Sun noon to 12 am
Visa, MasterCard, Amex, Diners
www.pfarrwirt.com

42 Gutruf — It is said that it was here that one of the most glorious pieces in Austrian post-war literature was born. Helmut Qualtinger, the famous cabaret writer, used the Gutruf as one of his living rooms while developing his play *Der Herr Karl.* Basically all the celebrities between 1950 and 1980, like Wotruba, Hundertwasser, Erni Mangold or Hrdlicka, came here. Nowadays the Gutruf is appreciated for its charismatic and slightly trashy atmosphere where you can enjoy some of the best steaks in town and a curious mix of Viennese and Chinese dishes. Main dishes start at €10.

Milchgasse 1, (533 95 62)
U1, U3: Stephansplatz
Mon-Sat 8.30 am to 12 am

43 Engländer — The verb »legendary« seems inflationary when mentioning Viennese cafés. But in this case, it can be used without any doubt. Famous for its resident guests, Martin Kippenberger was once a regular, the Engländer with its solid ambience remains the in-café for the local crowd between culture and politics. Its staff celebrates the cliché of the typical Viennese waiter by being charmingly huffy. Very good restaurant with Viennese cuisine, cheap business menus at midday, often packed. Main dishes start at €9.

Postgasse 2, (966 86 65)
U3: Stubentor
Mon-Sat 8 am to 1 am,
Sun 10 am to 1 am
Visa, Mastercard
www.cafe-englaender.com

44 Skopik & Lohn — One of the things that makes the Skopik & Lohn special is its interesting combination of the original interior and the black and white painting on the ceiling, done by Austrian artist Otto Zitko. The menu contains a nice overview of contemporary Austrian cuisine and international specialities, the wine list is adequate. In summer, the pavement in front of the restaurant is one of the most desirable places around. Main dishes start at €9.

Leopoldsgasse 17, (219 89 77)
U1, U4: Schwedenplatz, bus 5A: Malzgasse
Mon-Sun 6 pm to 1 am
www.skopikundlohn.at

45 Expedit — A trendy, but nevertheless very easy going, restaurant that serves dishes from the northern Italian region of Liguria. Its interior resembles a canteen or a store with an open kitchen and very simple furniture. It is famous for its pasta fresca and a pleasant selection of hams and wines. Those who can't get enough of Ligurian specialities should stop in at Expedit's alimentary shop just next to the restaurant. Also nice for a quick coffee break. Main dishes start at €8.

Wiesingerstraße 6, (512 33 130)
U1, U4: Schwedenplatz
Mon-Fri noon to 11 pm, Sat 6 pm to 12 am
www.expedit.net

46 Kent — A classic in the area of the Brunnenmarkt in Vienna's 16th district. This market zone is dominated by the vibrant flair of a kind of Little Istanbul because of its large Turkish population, but meanwhile it has also become a hotspot for urban bohemians, especially on Saturday morning. The restaurant serves traditional Turkish food adapted to local tastes. It's huge, but somehow always crowed, with a pleasant garden. A good opportunity to start or finish a night out on the Gürtel with its many bars, like rhiz or Chelsea. Main dishes start at €6.

Brunnengasse 67, (405 91 73)
U6: Josefstädterstraße, tram 44: Bergsteiggasse, 2: Neulerchenfelder Straße/ Brunnengasse
Mon-Sun 6 am to 2 am
www.kent-restaurant.at

47 Strandgasthaus Birner — At the Birner, one could get the feeling that Vienna is by the sea. Here, the river Danube shows itself in its full dignity, viewed at best from one of the many places in the Strandgasthaus Birner garden. This traditional, down to earth restaurant specializes in river fish and classic Austrian dishes. In summer, the BBQs are very popular. Main dishes start at €6.

An der Oberen Alten Donau 47, (271 53 36)
U6: Floridsdorf
Winter: Mon-Sun 9 am to 10 pm, Summer: Mon-Sun 9 am to 11.30 pm
www.gasthausbirner.at

48 Mensa Nationalbibliothek — Just because it's near the national library in the heart of Vienna's Ringstraße doesn't mean that you can't find a place to eat for a fair price. The canteen of the library is open to everybody, and the food is way above average. Wait in line at the counter and chose between two daily menus. You'll get things like marbles, little cubes or plastic fruits handed out as vouchers for your meal. Menus start at €5.

Josefsplatz 1, entrance Burggarten,
(534 10 394)
U1, U2, U4: Karlsplatz, tram 2: Burgring
Mon-Fri 9 am to 4 pm, Aug closed

49 Würstelstand Hoher Markt (Sausage stand Hoher Markt) — Typical sausage stand (Würstelstand) in the very centre of Vienna. Open practically around the clock. Here all the different sausages are available: Frankfurter, Debreziner, Käsekrainer Waldviertler, to name a few. Choose between hot or sweet mustard and between a semmel (bun) or schwarzbrot (brown bread). Soft drinks, alcohol and sweets as well. Later, when night flyers are on their way home, a sausage stand like this can present you with an intimate insight into Vienna's soul.

Hoher Markt, (0699 184 62 186)
Mon-Sun 7 am to 4 am

50 Eissalon Tuchlauben — If you have a sweet tooth, this gelateria should be on your to-do list. Just five minutes away from the Stephansdom, this Eissalon invites you to stay with a long list of ice cream creations, coffee specialities and pastries. Try the nougat ice cream.

Tuchlauben 15, (533 25 53)
U1, U3: Stephansplatz
Mon-Sat 10 am to 11.30 pm,
Sun 11 am to 11.30 pm
www.eissalon-tuchlauben.at

51 Heuriger Hirt — The Hirt is nestled right in the middle of the vineyards of the Kahlenberg and offers superior views of Vienna, the Danube, and the Bisamberg from its terrace; on clear days you can even see the Carpathian foothills. Easiest to reach by car.

Eiserne Hand Gasse 165 (318 96 41)
Bus 238, 239, 240: Kahlenbergdorf
By car: Take the road Heilgenstädter Straße in the direction of Klosterneuburg and take a left to Kahlenbergdorf
Apr-Oct: Wed-Fri from 3 pm,
Sat, Sun and holidays from noon
Nov-March: Fri-Sun and holidays from noon
www.zurschildkrot.com/hirt.swf

PARTY

52 Loos Bar — Rumour has it that Adolf Loos constructed this splendid bar in 1908 for his son who liked to drink a glass or two. The bar is only around 25 m2 in size, but with its careful use of mirrors it looks much bigger. The interior is first class with illuminated onyx and deep leather couches and gives the bar an, if not lascivious, at least a lovingly decadent touch. The Loos Bar is hands down one of the best places in Vienna for a cocktail.

Kärntner Durchgang 10, (512 32 83)
U1, U3: Stephansplatz
Thur-Sat noon to 5 am,
Sun-Wed noon to 4 am
www.loosbar.at

53 Café Savoy — A favourite hangout for gays, praised for its opulent décor and frivolous atmosphere. Two of the walls are graced by gigantic mirrors framed in gold, claimed to be the biggest in Europe. They augment and enlighten the room with its old marble tables, scuffed leather sofas and the ceded parquet. A gorgeous lustre, Jugendstil lamps on the walls, fancywork on the ceiling and golden curtains complete the florid ambience. In summer you can sit outside and enjoy the full intensity of the midday sun.

Linke Wienzeile 36, (586 73 48)
U4: Karlsplatz or Kettenbrückengasse
Mon-Fri 5 pm to 2 am,
Sat 9 am to 2 pm

54 Alt Wien — The place is equipped with a lovingly worn-down interior, the walls are plastered with all different kinds of posters and announcements. It's dark, crowded and vibrates with energy. Also famous for its goulash, which is perhaps one of the best in town. Cool mix of cultural and arty people.

Bäckerstraße 9, (512 52 22)
U1, U3: Stephansplatz
Mon-Fri 10 am to 2 am,
Sat-Sun 10 am to 4 am

55 Bonbonniere Bar — Plush and champagne: This bar is definitely not an icon of Minimalism, it is one of those fancy and – with a bit of imagination – frivolous places where red plush becomes a decadent dream. A variety of cocktails are on offer. Live piano music during the week. Way-out, a bit kitschy, tenderly old fashioned.

Spiegelgasse 15, (512 68 86)
U1, U3: Stephansplatz
Mon-Sat 5 pm to 2 am
August closed

56 Tanzcafé Jenseits — This ex-brothel, with its decadent charm of red plush, brings to mind a Parisian vaudeville theatre at the turn of the century. It is one of the favourite meeting and flirting places for the arty jeunesse dorée who dance to funk-, soul- and latin music. Nicely enough, the dress code for this dance café is very down to earth. A true classic in the area of the Mariahilferstraße, and a way to finish the night.

Nelkengasse 3, (587 12 33)
U3: Neubaugasse
Tue-Sat 9 pm to 4 am
www.tanzcafe-jenseits.com

57 Volksgarten Clubdiscothek, Tanzcafé (Dance café) and Pavillion — The music selection of this club discotheque ranges from r'n'b to techno and from funk to lounge sound. Home of the young and beautiful disco lovers. Sometimes long queues at the entrance, es-

pecially on weekends. The Tanzcafé offers music for passionate dancers (latin, salsa, tango etc.) every Sunday (8 pm to 11 pm) with outstanding outdoor dancing. In the Volksgarten Pavillion you can sit outside in a lovely garden at small tables from the '50s, eat, drink, play boules, relax in one of the two porch swings and enjoy the DJ-line up.

Burgring, entrance Volksgarten (532 42 41)
U2, U3, tram 1, bus 48A: Volkstheater
no fixed schedule
Full price admission € 6 to € 13
www.volksgarten.at

pavillon.volksgarten.at
End of April to mid September:
11 am to 2 am

Wurstsalon — Party event organizer, taking it to the road. The series of events has no fixed location and announces its parties only very shortly in advance. Usually, the Wurstsalon does parties that can be considered as much trashy as glamorous. Consult the website for details if you want to be surprised by nearly everything a night can offer.

www.wurstsalon.at

58 Flex — Probably the most prominent club in town when it comes to alternative music. Flex stands out because of it's excellent sound system; its acoustics are praised as one of the best in any club in Europe. Flex has two floors: The Flex Café, a lounge with no admission fee, and the discotheque. The club is pretty fucked up but there's always a crazy party, the prices are cheap and the general audience is presumably between 18 and 35, except for concerts that reach a broader audience. Flex features special DJs from all around the world and it's open every day of the week.

Donaukanal/Augartenbrücke, (533 75 25)
Daily 8 pm - 4 am
U2, U4: Schottenring
Admission € 4 to € 12,
except for concerts or special events.
www.flex.at

59 Fluc — A cultural aggregate and one of the hottest clubs for contemporary pop and electronic avant-garde in front of the Viennese landmark the Riesenrad near the Prater. Fluc consists of two spaces: fluc is a space used for DJ gigs, smaller concerts and art performances, while fluc _Wanne, located in a former pedestrian underpass, hosts larger concerts and events.

Praterstern 5, (218 28 24)
U1, U2, tram 5, O: Praterstern
Daily 6 pm to 2 am, Fri, Sat until 4 am
www.fluc.at

SLEEP

60 Das Triest — A luxury hotel near the Karlsplatz where the interior design was done by Sir Terence Conran. The Triest is used often by artists in show business as a place to stay, not surprisingly, as the hotel fulfils all the needs of high-class lifestyle and architecture. The rooms are very stylish and technically equipped with state of the art facilities,

the restaurant is top class and the extravagant Silverbar is a world of its own. Double rooms start at €280.

Wiedner Hauptstraße 12, (589 18 0)
U1, U2, U4: Karlsplatz,

tram 1, D: Kärntner Ring/Oper
www.dastriest.at

61 Hotel Sacher — The Sacher is perhaps one of the best examples of the aristocratic Vienna of the good old times. It was built by the Sacher family in 1876. This noble 5 star hotel offers

all recreational conveniences you might ask for. Apart from the partly modern, partly end-of-century styled rooms and suites, a high-class spa, and the restaurants and bars provide each guest with international luxury. Home of the world famous Sacher Torte. Double rooms start at € 260.

Philharmonikerstraße 4, (514 56 0)
U1, U2, U4: Karlsplatz, tram 1, D: Oper
www.sacher.com

62 Hollmann Beletage — A cool concept for a hotel: Former Burgtheater-actor Robert Hollmann opened an exquisite and stylish hotel that has no entrance sign, no reception and no

concierge. All you get is a key to your room. Personal service is guaranteed at the Beletage, as it is only comprised of 16 rooms. This ambitious hideaway offers you a good solution if you want to reside in a hidden area right in the centre and want to stay as anonymous and as individual as possible. Spa, children's area and even a cinema are included. Double rooms start at € 150.

Köllnerhofgasse 6, (96 11 96 0)
U1, U4: Schwedenplatz
www.hollmann-beletage.at

63 Hotel Altstadt — In this former patrician residence near the Museums Quartier, not one of its 42 rooms looks like any other. Those who like things a bit frivolous should ask for the new designed rooms by Matteo Thun that were inspired by the fictitious Viennese noble prostitute Josephine Mutzenbacher from the turn of the 20th century. In the

Red Salon, you can relax near an open chimney beside works by Nicki de Saint Phalle, Annie Leibowitz or Andy Warhol. Double rooms start at €140.

Kirchengasse 41, (522 66 66)
U2, U3: Volkstheater,
tram 49: Stiftgasse,
bus 2A: Kirchengasse
www.altstadt.at

64 Hotel Pertschy — This is a classy, lovingly old fashioned four star hotel in the very centre of town where you stay in the Baroque ambience of the Palace Cavriani from the early 17th century. It features a quite typical Biedermeier and Fin de siecle interior with tapestries and lots of red, white and gold. A speciality of the Pertschy is its »Pawlatschengang« (characteristic arcade-like patio from old Vienna). Double rooms start at €115.

Habsburgergasse 5, (534 49 0)
U1, U3: Stephansplatz
www.pertschy.com

65 Hotel Savoy — Elegant hotel near the MuseumsQuartier. Here, the dream of old Biedermeier Vienna comes true. The 42 rooms are spacious, bright, cosy and equipped with Wi-Fi. On the 5th floor, four suites with balcony offer a fantastic panorama view over Vienna. Surprisingly moderate rates: Double rooms start at €85.

Lindengasse 12, (523 46 46)
U3: Neubaugasse, tram 49: Stiftgasse,
bus 2A: Kirchengasse
www.hotelsavoy.at

66 Designapartment — This is a private apartment designed by the Viennese architects plan8, ideal for those who want to stay longer or are travelling with children. The place is fully equipped with everyday and business facilities (from kitchen, flat iron to DVD-player and Wi-Fi). On the beautiful green terrace you can enjoy an overview of Vienna. Per night €100 for two people, plus €15 for a third person, €600/week, €30 for cleaning.

Glockengasse 25/9,
(0650 592 89 41)
U2: Taborstraße, tram N:
Obere Augartenstraße
www.designapartment.at

67 Wombats Lounge Youth Hostel — The place for those who love an international, young atmosphere. You realize instantly that this place was designed by backpack touring professionals. Located just around the corner from the Westbahnhof and at the beginning of Vienna's busy shopping mile Mariahilferstraße, the lounge is way above usual hostel standards. Rooms offer facilities for 2 to 6 people with sanitary facilities for every room. Free internet surfing. From €17/person/night.

Mariahilfer Straße 137, (897 23 36)
U3, U6: Westbahnhof
www.wombats-hostels.com

68 Mitwohnzentrale Odyssee-Reisen (short term dwelling Odyssee-Reisen) — Odyssee is a tourist office and booking agency for rooms. It is a good option if you are in need of private accommodation (room, apartment or even flat) and if you are staying for more than a few days up to a few months. Consult HP for prebooking or visit their office for a personalized recommendation.

Westbahnstraße 19, (402 60 61)
U3, tram 49: Zieglergasse
Office hours: Mon-Fri 10 am to 2 pm, 3 pm to 6 pm
www.odyssee-mwz.at

KIDS

69 ZOOM Kindermuseum (ZOOM Children's Museum) — This children's museum offers a broad range of fun and entertainment with a pedagogic touch. Children can visit exhibitions or be creative with their own hands in the ateliers, which offer workshops for children from three years and up. In the playground Zoom Ocean the youngest can crawl, touch, play, and try. By appointment only.

Museumsplatz 1/Museumsquartier, (524 79 08)
U3, tram 49: Volkstheater,
U2: MuseumsQuartier
Admission for kids € 4 to € 5, one adult free
www.kindermuseum.at

70 Prater — When your child is tired of art and the urban life relax in one of the biggest green areas in town, the Prater, which has plenty of playgrounds, the amusement park Würstelprater nearby and the open air swimming pool Stadionbad (see »alternative sightseeing«). A ride with the Liliputbahn (Lilliputian railway), a little steam train, is big fun for young and old.

U1, U2: Praterstern,
tram 1: Praterallee

71 Strandbar Herrmann (Beachbar Hermann) — Perfect beach feeling in the city centre. Parents know: sand has a hypnotic impact on children. While parents lean back in their deck chairs and enjoy their cocktails, the DJ music, the view on the Danube canal and city skyline, their children can build sand castles. Take away food available.

U1, U4: Schwedenplatz, tram 1: Julius-Raab-Platz
Mid-Apr until end of Sept, daily 10 am to 2 am
www.strandbarherrmann.at

DAYTRIPS

Art Brut Centre Museum Gugging — This museum and gallery displays different kinds of Art Brut from abroad and from its own collection, especially that by the Gugging group. Located in a lovely landscape about 20 km outside of Vienna, in the direction of Klosterneuburg, situated in a former lunatic

asylum. Very famous is the so-called House of Artists. Since 1981 it has been housing the Gugging artists, people who have gained a worldwide reputation due to the high quality of their drawings, paintings, writings and objects. Presently the House provides housing for nine residents with chronic psychiatric illnesses and mental disabilities, 7 of which are artistically active.

Am Campus 2, Maria Gugging,
(0676 841 18 12 00)
U4: Heiligenstadt, then bus 239
(direction Maria Gugging/Lourdesgrotte).
Art Brut Centre Gugging
Museum, gallery, shop: Winter
Tue-Sun 10 am to 5 pm, summer till 6 pm
Atelier: Mon-Fri 10 am to noon,
1 pm to 5 pm;
www.gugging.org

Kirche am Steinhof (Church at Steinhof) — – This trip doesn't need a whole day, but certainly a couple of hours. This impressive church was built between 1904 and 1907 by Otto Wagner, who had been commissioned to construct it as a sacral building for the lunatic asylum at Baumgartner Höhe. That is why there are emergency exits, a doctor's room, hygienic facilities and no sharp edges. It is supposed to be one of the main architectonic achievements of Viennese Jugendstil, resembling the Secession on the Karlsplatz. Distinctive elements of the church are the golden cupola in the Byzantine style, a golden altar in the style of a holy grave and the mosaic glass paintings by Koloman Moser.

Baumgartner Höhe 1
Bus 48A: Psychiatrisches Krankenhaus
Sat 4 pm to 5 pm
Free admission
For guided tours contact: 0664 103 10 50

GOOD TO KNOW

72 Tourist Information
Albertinaplatz/Maysedergasse,
U1, U2, U4: Karlsplatz,
tram 1, D: Kärntner Ring/Oper
Mon-Sun 9 am to 7 pm

INTERNET

Wi-FI — in the MuseumsQuartier and in all bigger cafés

73 Speednet Café
Morzinplatz 4, U1, U3:
Stephansplatz,
U1, U4: Schwedenplatz
Mon-Fri 8 am to 12 am,
Sat-Sun 10 am to 12 am
www.speednet-cafe.com

MEDIA

www.falter.at — Viennese city guide, the best program pages in town. German only.

www.fm4.orf.at — Mostly English speaking alternative radio station.

kalender.esel.at — Openings, concerts, parties. Here you get to know what happens in Vienna's art world.

TRANSPORT

From the airport — A taxi from the airport to the city centre costs about €35. Cheaper is the City Airport Train – CAT. It takes about 16 minutes to the city centre, and a ticket costs €9. Buses to different destinations in town take about 35 minutes, a ticket costs €6. A ticket for the S-Bahn (rapid train) is €3.40.

Taxis — Prices for taxis are quite reasonable. Calling for a taxi is an additional €2. Taxis: 60 160, 31 300 or 40 100

Public transport — You can usually buy tickets at the machines and kiosks in the metro and railway stations, at the tobacco stores (newsagents) and in the trams and buses. Normal price for a ticket is €1.70 (€2.20 when purchased inside a bus or tram). Changes are allowed. A ticket for a week is €14, for three days not much cheaper: €13.60, 48hours: €10 and 24hours: €5.70. Ask for the so-called Vienna Card for three days (€18.50) that offers discounts for some museums, restaurants and shops. Night buses run every half hour along the main routes, make sure that your ticket is valid for them. Check out more discounts, routes and special offers at: www.wienerlinien.at

Car — In town, the main speed is usually 50 km/h, unless otherwise indicated. On highways, the limit is 130 km/h. Alcohol tolerance is 0.5. Viennese driving mood can be considered moderate and easy going. Many areas of the first district are pedestrian zones. You can buy parking tickets at tobacco stores (tabak), gas stations and some groceries. Times to pay for parking are usually 9 am to 10 pm during the week. In some areas, like around the Stadthalle, payment is until 11 pm. Regular parking time is 2 hours, a ticket costs €2.50.

Bike — A fine alternative for mobility in Vienna is a bike, but mind the daily business traffic. At 60 stations in town you can rent and return a »city bike«, no matter where your point of origin. You have to register with Visa, JBC or Mastercard at one of the bike kiosks before you can rent. 1 hour is free, the 2nd: €1, 3rd: €2, 4th: €4, max. 120 hours.

www.citybikewien.at

Important Numbers

Telephone country and city code	*+43 1*
Telephone information	*11 88 77*
Police	*122*
Fire Brigade	*133*
Ambulance	*144*
24h-Pharmacy	*Check out any pharmacy nearby, an info screens at the door informs you if there is night service or about the nearest pharmacy which has off-hour service.*

City in Numbers

Inhabitants	*1.7 million*
Average income	*€ 1,480*
Cup of coffee	*€ 2.50*
Bottle of beer	*€ 3.70*
Cigarettes	*€ 3.50*

Most talked about contemporary artists	*gelitin, Franz West, Erwin Wurm*
Collectors of contemporary art	*50*
Biggest art scandal	*»Uni Ferkelei« 1968 by the Viennese Actionists (who urinated, masturbated and shitted in the auditorium of Vienna University while singing the national anthem)*

Short Art History
VIENNA

1947 Foundation of the Art Club, whose centre, the »Strohkoffer«, becomes the meeting place for bohemians. Its first president is Albert Paris Gütersloh, who as President of the Secession also has considerable influence on the younger generation of artists.

1954 The Catholic clergyman Monsignor Otto Mauer opens the Gallery Near St. Stephan's, which becomes the meeting point of the art scene in Vienna.

1962 Foundation of the Museum of the 20th Century, a kind of restitution for the Modern movements suppressed by the Nazis.

7.6.1968 In the University of Vienna *Art and Revolution* takes place, the best known action by Viennese Actionism. Günter Brus, Otto Muehl, Peter Weibel and Co. masturbate, defecate and have themselves whipped, while the Austrian national anthem is being sung. Some of the main performers of the so-called »Uniferkelei« (uni-swinishness) received prison sentences.

1975 The exhibition *Magna. Feminismus: Kunst und Kreativität* takes place in the Gallery Near St. Stephan's, curated by Valie Export, and is the first women's exhibition in Vienna.

1981 Peter Pakesch opens his gallery in Vienna. He presents artists like Martin Kippenberger, Heimo Zobernig or Franz West to a wider public for the first time.

1994 Opening of the Depot – Kunst und Diskussion. It becomes an important place for an art scene interested in theory.

2003 The exhibition *Blood & Honey. Future in the Balkans* in the Sammlung Essl in Klosterneuburg, curated by Harald Szeemann, makes artists from the Balkans known to a wider public in the West. The show is strongly criticised for its geographic labelling of »Balkans«. Even so, it is a springboard for many artists into an international career.

Flakturm in the Augarten

C. 1.000 m
27
41
51
46
Friedmanng.
LERCHENFELDER GÜRTEL
WIENER GÜRTEL BUNDESSTR.
NEUSTIFTGASSE
SCHOTTENFELDG.
NEUBAUGASSE
63
WESTBAHNSTR.
68
75
LINDENG.
EUROPAPL.
67

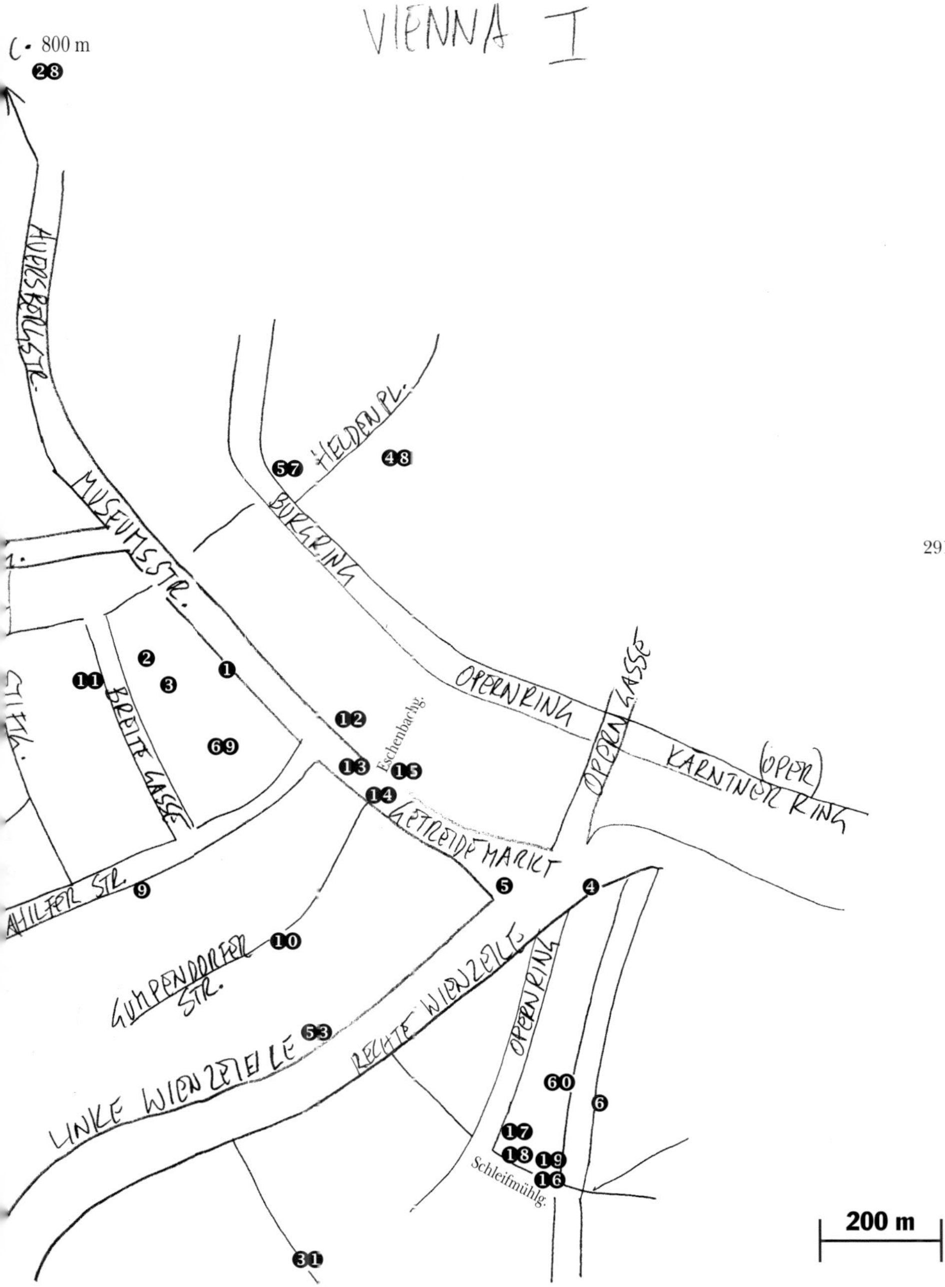
VIENNA I
c. 800 m
AUERSPERGSTR.
MUSEUMSSTR.
HELDENPL.
BURGRING
OPERNRING
OPERNGASSE
KARNTNER RING
(OPER)
Eschenbachg.
GETREIDEMARKT
BREITE GASSE
HILFER STR.
GUMPENDORFER STR.
LINKE WIENZEILE
RECHTE WIENZEILE
OPERNRING
Schleifmühlg.
200 m

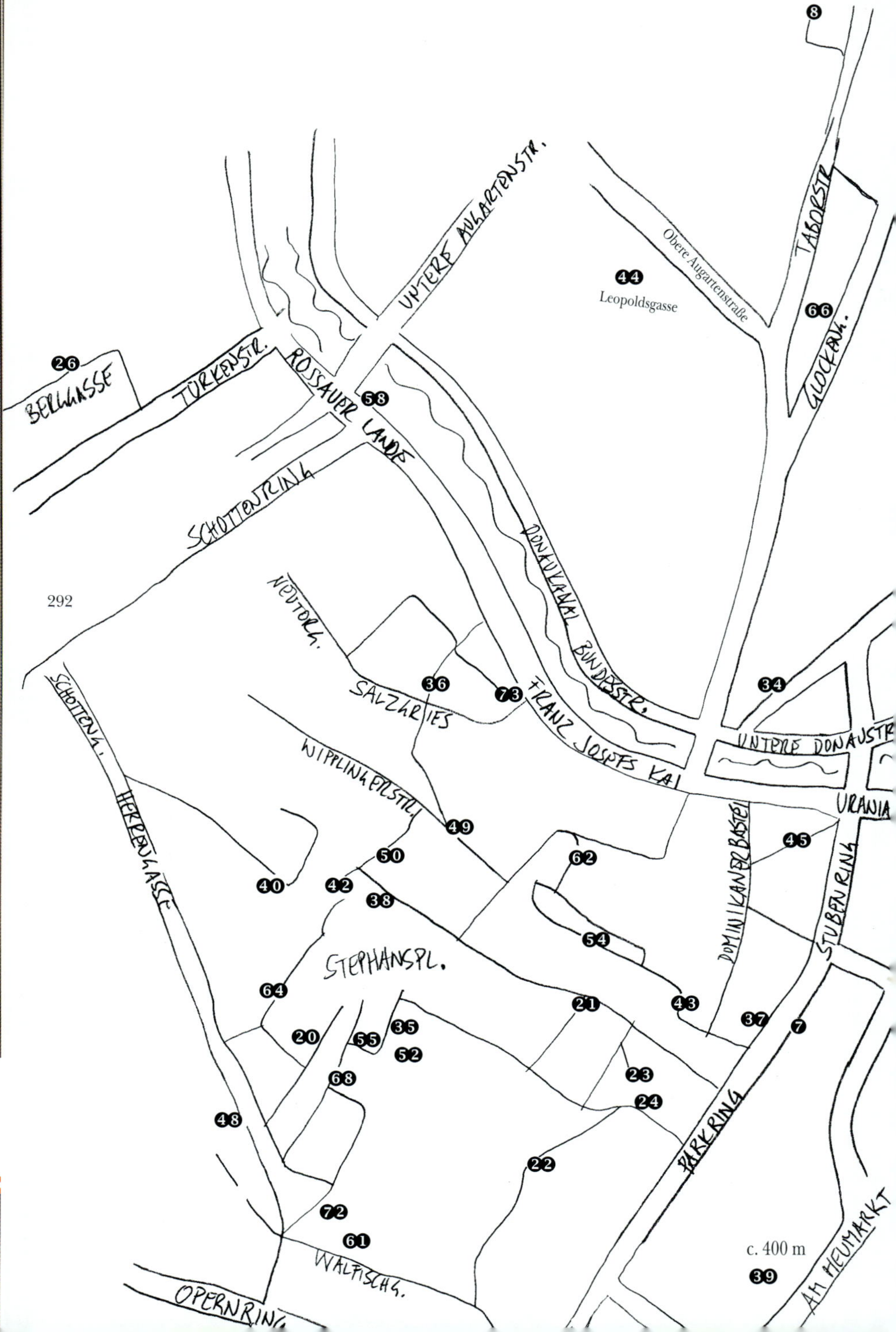
8
UNTERE AUGARTENSTR.
Obere Augartenstraße
TABORSTR.
44
Leopoldsgasse
66
GLOCKENG.
26
BERGGASSE
TÜRKENSTR.
ROSSAUER LÄNDE
58
SCHOTTENRING
DONAUKANAL
BUNDESSTR.
NEUTORG.
36
73
SALZGRIES
FRANZ JOSEFS KAI
34
UNTERE DONAUSTR
URANIA
WIPPLINGERSTR.
SCHOTTENG.
HERRENGASSE
49
45
DOMINIKANERBASTEI
STUBENRING
62
50
40
42
38
54
STEPHANSPL.
64
21
43
37
7
20
55
35
52
68
23
24
48
PARKRING
22
72
61
c. 400 m
39
AM HEUMARKT
WALFISCHG.
OPERNRING

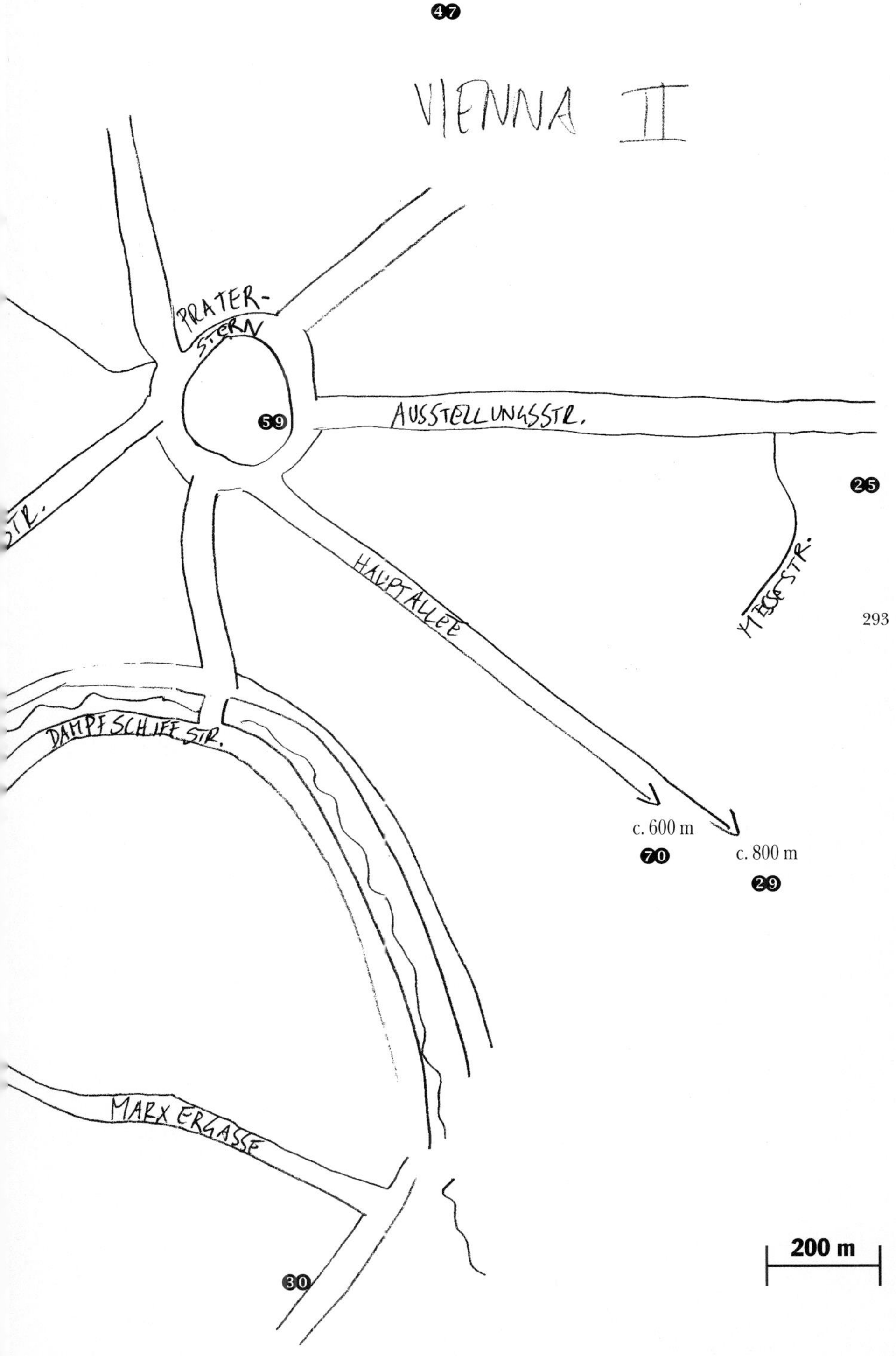
47
VIENNA II
PRATER-
STERN
59
AUSSTELLUNGSSTR.
25
HAUPTALLEE
MESSESTR.
DAMPFSCHIFFSTR.
c. 600 m
70
c. 800 m
29
MARXERGASSE
30
200 m

The River Sava

Ilica, Zagreb's main street

Zagreb

A relaxed attitude

Nothing spectacular, but each week there is something happening in Zagreb's art scene.

296

By Marko Rajković

Culture doesn't poke you in the eye while you stroll around Zagreb. Visually the city doesn't inspire. The usual Eastern European transitional craving for Westernized goods, and the aesthetics that accompany that trend, can be seen on every corner. People are obsessed with following global trends; no wonder Croatia was so hard hit by the financial crisis. Fifteen years ago everybody was dreaming about the EU. Today Croatia is sulking because of the fact that, in many ways, under-developed Balkan countries like Romania, and Bulgaria hitched onto the EU before Croatia, which was omitted primarily because of the unsolved legacy of the civil war that followed the political demise of ex-Yugoslavia. This hurts even more when you consider how Croats hysterically claim to have nothing to do with the Balkans. Currently, EU sceptics are becoming more common in every perspective, and yet everybody is taking for granted that in a couple of years Zagreb will become another EU capital. On the surface, art is invisible, both in media and on the street. Only high profile international exhibitions and a handful of artists get any proper media coverage. But in reality, the scene is very much alive.

»For a person whose life evolves around art, Zagreb is a place that can satisfy your needs«, says Jasna Jakšić, a 31 year curator that works for the state run Museum Suvremene Umjetnosti (Museum of Contemporary Art). Nothing spectacular, but each week there is something happening. There are a lot of small galleries, independent galleries, street art, festivals and interesting artists. Contemporary art has a long tradition in Zagreb; conceptual, socially engaged artists like Sanja Iveković, Braco Dimitrijević and Mladen Stilinović got Zagreb natives accustomed to living with contemporary art and learning from it. Sadly, those days are gone with the wind, or, more precisely, with the bombs. The civil war after the demise of Yugoslavia caused a plague of cultural dumbness and insensitivity. This sparked the founding of many NGOs that aimed at fighting this virus and, in the end, gave birth to Clubture, a platform that unites independent cultural initiatives. Today we have a great network of intellectuals and artists working together and making a difference. Still, the reality in Zagreb is that culture survives as long as it doesn't stand in the way of commerce or transportation, and finds its way into the headlines only before election time, when politicians somewhat absurdly try to polish their redneck images by backing some initiatives that they then usually discard with a ready made split-second »I'm sorry« apologetic smile. So far in 2009, the new Museum of Contemporary Art has opened, and next the Centre for Independent Culture is going to receive a grant to use abandoned spaces in Zagreb. Even the smelly squatters from the anarchic organization Attack have received the right to use

Today we have a great network of intellectuals and artists

The Uspinjača funicular

Dolac Market

The Capuchin Stairs

At Marko Marulić Square

Medika, an abandoned pharmacy factory close to the city centre. Here, it's good to have elections.

The organizing virus also hit contemporary art. Two great examples are the curator collectives WHW (What? How? For Whom) and Kontejner. WHW is a socially engaged collective run by four young women who lit up the scene after a successful debut commemorating 152 years of the Communist Manifesto. They were instantly recognized by the European art community but are not so popular with senior state cultural workers, who felt offended that some »little girls« were criticizing their mistakes. Kontejner, on the other hand, is not so political and focuses on creative projects that connect art with science, technology and the human body. Their contributions to Zagreb's calendar of events are the Touch me festival, Device_art and the Extravagant bodies festival. The cultural scene is well organized, but the artists?

»The artists work quietly. There's a very intimate relationship between most artists in Zagreb«, says Davorka Perić, an art journalist and part time curator. »Artists are very supportive of each other; they often collaborate, as individual artists have greater difficulty in receiving state funds, a legacy of the Socialist dislike for the individual. But there is no large programmatic movement. The common thing about most contemporary visual artists is their everyday routine. They usually survive by doing commercial jobs such as camera work, web design, scenography, illustrations, photo shoots, and still they produce a lot of great work.«

The state funds usually cover costs, but then work is seldom bought as the market for contemporary art resembles a desert with only three or four »oases«. If you're not loved by the »oasis« curator, you must spend a lot of energy doing the ephemeral jobs that buy food in the end. Or you can do what some Croatian artists do: leave the country. Yet very few leave for good. The great thing about artists in Zagreb is that they are usually very open, they don't mystify their work and they really do art because they love it. Otherwise they'd be filming commercials for the mobile company billboards that dominate the visual world of everyday Croats.

There's something really good about the art scene in Zagreb. It exists as an almost separate entity, as an outcast on the fringes of everyday life, but it has a very faithful following and a relaxed attitude. A great place to experience this is when an exhibition takes place in the atelier complex Zhitnjak on the outskirts of Zagreb. Politics is seldom the topic; usually people discuss projects, have fun and hold fine and impressive theoretical discussions about the quality of the barbecue. —

The great thing about artists in Zagreb is that they do art because they love it

The Zagreb art scene is pretty vibrant

Emina Višnich is a well-known figure in Zagreb. For a number of years she's been the »Big Mama« of the cultural scene, running various cultural NGOs. Appropriately, Marko Rajković speaks to her in MaMa, the multimedia centre that spawned a flourish of cultural activities in the independent scene of the last decade.

By Marko Rajković

Share your intimate view of Zagreb with us. What do you like about it?

EMINA VIŠNICH: Well, I don't think I have a meaningful answer, maybe the size of the city, the people I hang around with. I like the area around Britanski trg and westward the most. Maybe it's the least representative part of the city centre but it suits me well. When I don't work, which is not very often, I visit the SC or Student Centre and its gallery, a great space for exhibitions. They have a fantastic cultural program. Besides that, my favourite art galleries in Zagreb are the Galerija Nova and Galerija Miroslav Kraljević. My preferred stops for coffee are somewhere on the Cvjetni trg, the pedestrian part of the Preradoviceva street, especially when the sun brings the outdoor terraces to life. At night you can sometimes find me in the Sedmica bar. As far as going out, it's the electro scene I'm after, like in the newly opened club Sirup.

The local contemporary art scene: how do you see it compared to other places?

The Zagreb art scene is pretty vibrant, but I believe today's world has reached the point where it's pointless to speak about locally specific contemporary art. It doesn't really exist anymore. If I had to single out something specific about Zagreb, it's the network of contemporary cultural organizations and individuals, some of them connecting what is, at first glance, not connectable. For example, organizations like Shadow Casters that unite urbanites, architects, artists and theoreticians in examining urban spaces from an art perspective.

But then there's the public. Are people in Zagreb interested in contemporary art?

Well, the contents will produce the public. If a continuous, easily accessible production is served to the average person, the change will come. The SC Student Centre is an example of how to do things. After coming under new management it has become a space open for artists and now it's far too crowded for all the programs wanting to use the space and all the visitors.

A big problem in Zagreb is the »festivalization« of culture

What about the multitude of festivals in Zagreb?

Indeed, a big problem in Zagreb is the »festivalization« of culture. From February until October there's hardly any week that doesn't have a festival of some kind. This is an overload of representative art, which often takes up most of the media attention and, what's much worse, a huge chunk of the cultural funds handed out by the ministries. This is just a reflection of the general trend of entertaining show business spectacles dominating our lives. On the other hand, inclusive permanent programs that incite social dynamics and have a far greater impact on the actual scene tend to be put aside because they're not attractive to the media.

What is the main problem facing contemporary culture in Zagreb?

A lack of open, non-institutional cultural facilities in town. There are a lot of individuals and organizations doing interesting stuff but there is not enough room in the city itself to showcase these productions. This, in turn, has the effect that you get the feeling that nothing's going on. And then, of course, there's the under financing of local independent initiatives. A lot of money is flooded into culture in Zagreb and Croatia, but the funding goes to conservative institutions that prefer showing traditional shows, be it the Vienna Philharmonic or a piece of classical theatre. The people in these institutions are often paranoid about anything new and different.

So you get, for instance, the situation with WHW, the curators collective, who are responsible for great contemporary art projects both locally and internationally, but have yet to receive any recognition, let alone funds, from the institutions that should be backing them. Even worse, some people from the ruling institutions say that what the girls are doing is rubbish, and yet you see them being applauded for their work all over the world. —

Emina Višnich was born in 1977. She was managing director of the cultural network Clubture, member of the executive board of Culture Action Europe, one of the founders of Urban Festival, an interdisciplinary multimedia street festival, and an active participant in numerous other NGOs. Currently she is the initiative behind the newly formed Centre for Independent Culture.

Zagreb

By Marko Rajković

The funicular Uspinjaca

ART

❶ **MSU: Museum suvremene umjetnosti (Museum of Contemporary Art)** — The controversial (a never ending construction story, architecturally uninspiring, controversial naming of the managing staff) new building, will open it's doors in 2009 on the southern bank of the river Sava in the part of town known as Novi Zagreb, a residential area of large blocks of mid-sized skyscrapers from the time between 1950 and 1980. Most of the art public is disappointed with the conservative, modernistic look of the museum, designed by Croatian architect Ivan Franić. The director is Snježana Pintarić. In 14,500m², 4,800m² is used as an exhibition space for exhibiting a large chunk of the museum's collection of approximately 9,000 artworks. The artworks are divided into five »alternating collections« determined by associating artists using the similarities of their ideas, thus giving a »curated« vision of Croatian and world contemporary art. In addition there's a multimedia hall, a children's workshop, a library with a reading hall, a restaurant and three cafes.

Katarinin trg 2, (485 18 08)
Tram 6, 14: Siget, bus 219, 220, 221, 234: Av. Dubrovnik - Av. V. Holjevca
Tue-Sat 11 am to 7 pm, Sun 10 am to 1 pm
Full price admission 15 HRK
free on Tuesday
www.msu.hr

❷ **Moderna Galerija (Gallery of Modern Art)** — A nice exhibition space located on the busiest road in the centre of town and on the edge of the Zrinjevac, one of the parks of the »Green Horseshoe«, a complex of parks in the centre of town. The permanent exhibits of this state run gallery are somewhat confusing, a chronological mumbo jumbo with a great collection of Modern Croatian work up to the '60s. The contemporary collection is rather lacklustre and underprivileged, but then that's why we have the Museum of Contemporary Art. The benches of nearby parks are a nice place to spend a sunny day eating chocolate. And if your cultural needs aren't satisfied, you can visit the nearby Art Pavilion.

Andrije Hebranga 1, (481 25 99)
Tram 6, 13: Zrinjevac
Tue-Fri 10 am to 6 pm,
Sat-Sun 10 am to 1 pm

❸ **Umjetnički Paviljon (Art Pavilion)** — The Art Pavilion is Zagreb's oldest exhibition space. It is a formidable building whose iron structure hails from the 1896 millennium exhibition in Bu-

dapest, a reminder of somewhat forgotten ties with Hungarian imperialism. Occasionally it hosts some special exhibitions by guest curators.

Trg kralja Tomislava 22,
(487 64 87 or 484 10 70)
Tram 6, 13: Zrinjevac
Mon-Sat 11 am to 7 pm,
Sun 10 am to 1 pm
Full price admission 20 HRK,
free on Monday
www.umjetnicki-paviljon.hr

❹ **Galerija Klovićevi dvori** — Top of the pops, the top celebrity of Zagreb's art world. If there is one gallery space in Zagreb where you can see the usual household names then this is the place. Rembrandt, Mondrian, Chagall to name a few, but then there was also the biggest international contemporary art exhibition in Croatia to date here, *Enigma*. There are also some less pompous contemporary exhibitions. Three separate spaces located close by in Gornji grad are run buy this heavily financed state institution. On Saturdays parents can also leave their children to learn art tips at the hands of artists and art students. Afterwards, visit the heavenly Pig for a bite, or if you haven't made a reservation, get a drink in the pub Pod Starim Krovovima.

Jezuitski trg 4, (485 19 26)
Funicular from Radićeva, or a five minute uphill walk from the main city square
Tue-Sun 11 am to 7 pm
www.galerijaklovic.hr

❺ **HDLU: Hrvatsko Društvo Likovnih Umjetnika (Croatian Association of Visual Artists)** — The House of the Association, designed by Croatian sculptor and architect Ivan Meštrović and built in 1938, has undergone severe transformations during its existence depending on state policies and changing ideologies. It was inaugurated as an artists' house, then became a mosque during World War II, only to turn into a Museum of Revolution during the Communist regime, and now it has finally returned to its original function as an art venue. The round building is still known as »the mosque-đamija« in Zagreb. Under its dome thrive four galleries that give interesting possibilities for presenting contemporary art exhibits: Meštrović Pavilion, Galerija Bačva, Galerija Prsten and the most famous in contemporary art circles, Galerija PM-Expanded Media Gallery, which made a name for itself in the '80s when new and radical upcoming artists found it a place where they could present their works in the way they wanted to under the influence of curator Želimir Koščević.

Trg žrtava fašizma bb, (461 18 18)
Tram 1, 17: Trg žrtava fašizma
Tue-Fri 11 am to 7 pm,
Sat-Sun 10 am to 2 pm
Full price admission 15 HRK
www.hdlu.hr

❻ **Galerija Nova** — Zagreb's pride and joy. A vibrant contemporary art gallery run by four young women that form the curators collective WHW: Nataša Ilić, Sabina Sabolović, Ana Dević and Ivet Ćurlin. The signature of this gallery is that it addresses and examines relevant social and political issues through art. A lot of clever stuff is interestingly presented here, and some even gets printed, as the gallery has its own newspaper. Read it next door in BP, the clas-

sic Zagreb jazz club and take a bite from the Penguin, Zagreb's favourite night-time fast food.

Teslina 7, (487 25 82)
Tram 1, 6, 11, 12, 14:
Trg Bana Jelachicha
Tue-Fri 11 am to 8 pm,
Sat-Sun 11 am to 2 pm
www.agm.hr/dgalerija.php

❼ **Galerija Nano** — A little artist run gallery that artist Martina Mezak transformed from an apartment into a gallery. New contemporary artists, a lot of conceptual video and unexpected authors can be met here. If nobody answers your relentless banging on the door try the sushi bar next door run by Martina's brother, also an artist. Maybe the sushi man will let you in.

Gajeva 26, (098 515 323)
A five minute walk from the main square
Trg Bana Jelačića
Tue-Thu 2 pm to 6 pm
www.artenativa.hr

❽ **Galerija Miroslav Kraljević** — This is a gallery that has special meaning for contemporary art of the region. Run by Antonia Majača and Ivana Bago, the gallery is located in the basement of a building owned by the Croatian oil company Ina. Apart from the interesting marriage of art and oil, the basement of this building is where the Croatian parliament, while sheltering itself from air raids, proclaimed independence from the former Yugoslavia. As well as creative interactive exhibitions and an inspiring residency program novel to Zagreb, it occasionally hosts lectures by top notch theoreticians. If you get hungry cross the street and indulge in the second biggest food market in Zagreb, Kvatrić where you can taste some freshly hand picked fruits and vegetables.

Šubićeva 29,
(459 26 96)
Tram 1, 5, 9, 17: Šubićeva
Tue-Fri noon to 7 pm,
Sat 11 am to 2 pm
www.g-mk.hr

❾ **Atelje Žitnjak – Galerija Žitnjak** — In 2003 a large abandoned school on the industrial outskirts of Zagreb was handed to a group of artists. The building now hosts nearly twenty ateliers where artists of several generations do their work in harmony. Every now and then the artists organize an exhibition which is always accompanied by some nice barbecued food and drinks served in the old schoolyard. The only problem is the remoteness of the location and that the artists forget to tell the art press when something is happening. Often the only way to know that there is an exhibition is to receive a text message from the artist. Then again, if you just knock on the door during visitor's day you will surely be invited to see something interesting in the making.

If you use public transport it's an adventure getting there. The bus passes through an old industrial part of town where you sense the decay of industrialization. Then you reach the houses where some of Zagreb's poorest inhabitants live. An ominous sign is the fact that the bus stops on this line have no names and that the buses are the oldest and smelliest in Zagreb, and the drivers are also sometimes drunk. A god-forsaken place.

Žitnjak 53,
Bus 217 to Struge,
get off at the »no name stop«
308 *after bypassing the roundabout by*
Domovinski most (ask the driver)
Saturday is open door day,
otherwise open when an exhibition is announced
www.a-z.hr

❿ Galerija SC — The Studentski centar (Student centre) complex recently changed its managing board and received a strong influx of people with strong intentions. The glory days of the '70s, when this was the playground for emerging conceptualist socially engaged artists who first turned galleries into exhibits, are back. The gallery is run by Ksenija Baronica, who invites interesting artists such as Nicole Hewitt, a Croatian video artist and professor of new media at the Akademija likovnih umjetnosti (Academy of Fine Arts), her very successful pupil Ana Hušman (recently acclaimed for her experimental movie *Ručak*) and Silva Kalčić, a young and very inquisitive curator. They swarm the place with young artists of all shapes and sizes. The exhibitions also take place in the hall of the SC Cinema, which hosts a large number of popular festivals and concerts.

Savska cesta 25,
(459 35 67)
Tram 4, 9, 12, 13, 14, 17:
Studentski centar or Tehnički muzej
Mon-Fri noon to 8 pm,
Sat 10 am to 1 pm
www.sczg.hr

⓫ Filip trade building — Not a gallery, obviously. This blue building is the headquarters of an eclectic importer and distributor of condoms, children's goods and, above all, dental care products. The inner walls of the building are peppered with exhibits from Croatian contemporary artists courtesy of Tomislav Kličko, the owner of the company and avid collector of Croatian contemporary art. He and Marinko Sudac are practically the biggest collectors of contemporary art in the country due to the negligence of institutional buyers such as the Museum of Contemporary Art. They are in possession of collections worthy of a little museum. So you can act as if you're interested in buying a lot of toothbrushes or just ask nicely to see the exhibits that adorn the building.

Križna 18, (630 21 11)
Tram 6, 7, 8: Slavonska,
bus 218: Lastovska-Križna
Call before visiting

ART EVENTS

25 FPS: Internacionalni festival kratkog eksperimentalnog filma i videa (International Experimental Film and Video Festival) — This festival for Experimental Film and Video takes place in autumn (mostly in September). The festival's enthusiastic management keeps this

strange boat loaded with odd non-commercial artefacts afloat. If you're one of those freaks crazy about strange visual experiences this will be a feast for your senses. The Studentski centar (Student centre) hosts this event.

Festival office:
Vlaška 70, (457 22 03)
September
www.25fps.hr

Animafest: Svjetski festival animiranog filma (The World Festival of Animated Film) — A festival that has its foundations rooted in the golden days of the Zagreb School of Animation. Now scheduled for the first week of June, the festival has given up the fight against Annency, which by and large attracts more commercial films, whereas Zagreb insists more on the artistic side. The festival used to be biannual but has recently transformed into an annual event by alternating short and feature animation film editions each year.

Festival office:
Nova Ves 18/3, (390 70 74)
June
www.animafest.hr

UrbanFestival/C'est is the Best/Operacija: Grad (Operation: City) — These three festivals interact with the urban landscape in such a way that they bring culture to the people whether they like it or not:

The Urban Festival idea was to offer Zagreb a multimedia street festival with a message. Each year there's a different theme that addresses current urbanistic, artistic and social problems in Zagreb and the world.

C'est is the Best is a street performer festival that focuses more on merry and playful performing arts and in bringing a lot of music to the streets.

Last to be recommended is Operacija Grad, a periodical multimedia, multidisciplinary happening organized by the independent scene that speaks loudly of what's troubling artists, architects, urbanists and intellectuals in the city. You never know when it's going to occur, but as long as there are problems, the happening will take place. That means there's material for a long future.

www.urbanfestival.hr (May)
www.kraljeviulice.com (June)
www.operacijagrad.org

Festival novog cirkusa (New Circus Festival) — This festival in late autumn (November) brings a breath of fresh air into the performing arts scene and usually brings along a lot of street artists that liven up the streets of Zagreb. The charismatic organizer (enfant terrible journalist star) Ivan Kralj made Zagreb realize that the circus is not just people making animals dress up and jump around.

Festival office:
Sv. Mateja 68, (485 43 04)
November
fnc.s3.novenaweb.info

ALTERNATIVE SIGHTSEEING

⓬ Antique fair Britanski trg — On Sundays this part of town has a French charm about it. The antique fair attracts many visitors that just like to spend time on this square with its intimate ambiance, and there's the odd few looking for old cameras, LPs, ashtrays, postcards, chandeliers, etc. It's one of the rare places where Zagreb natives feel comfortable being slow. There must be some strange cosmic force in the square that keeps everybody around it happy.

Tram 6, 11: Britanski trg
Sun 8 am to 2 pm

⓭ Sajam Jakuševac (Hrelić) — A legendary place on the outskirts of civilization, very attractively located close to the garbage pyramids of Zagreb's biggest city dump. But don't let this put you off; this is a place not to miss. Apart from the second hand car fair and a part with stalls where cheap Chinese stuff is sold, there's a humungous wild flea market that offers everything from a pack of cigarettes from the '70s, Communist memorabilia, Elvis Presley LP's, guns, stolen bicycles and an occasional masterpiece of art. The sellers are mostly Roma and retired people who are trying to survive by adding a few kunas to their meagre pensions by selling their belongings. Artists often dress themselves here, collectors roam around looking for valuables and the poor of Zagreb scavenge the grounds looking for cheap things. When you get tired, eat a greasy sweet flatbread with a sausage while watching the sea gulls and river gulls fighting over tasty chunks of garbage.

Sajmišna cesta 8, Jakuševec
(660 99 00)
Bus 295: Jakuševac
Sun 7 am to 3 pm

⓮ Rokov perivoj (Rokov Park) — Just a few hundred steps from the city centre (the steps start going up just before you reach the Cinema Tuškanac from Dezhmanov prolaz) an oasis of green and quiet. The park lies on the ancient graveyard of the inhabitants of Grich (medieval town, today old, upper town). If you get lucky there is also the possibility that you will see the small chapel at a time when it is open. Macedonian Orthodox church services are held here. An art school is located nearby as well as some beautiful moss covered Modernist villas.

Tram 6, 11: Frankopanska or Britanski trg

⓯ Villa Richter — The house of constructivist artist and architect Vjenceslav Richter, member of the Exat 51 movement, hosts a collection of his pieces. The collection is run by the Museum suvremene umjetnosti (Museum of Contemporary Art). Although there is a nice collection of artworks the nicest thing about the house is the garden where Richter's sculptures enrich the view of the city.

Vrhovec 38a, (485 18 08)
Bus 129b: Vrhovec-Zatišje
Wed, Sat 11 am to 4 pm
www.richter.com.hr

⓰ Kino Tuškanac — After practically all cinemas by the state run Kinematografi shut down at the turn of the millennium, there was a void that scared Croatian cineastes. In the whole country there wasn't a single cinema showing classic films let alone non-Hollywood movies. Here is a cinema that filled this ghastly void. Films are subtitled, which is thankfully still customary in Croatia. There are also regular experimental film screenings. If you don't like the movie visit the nearby Studio 13, one of the rare places that managed to keep the atmosphere of good old Socialist Zagreb.

Tuškanac 1, (484 87 71)
Tram 1, 6, 11: Frankopanska
Admission 10 HRK
www.filmski-programi.hr

SHOPPING

⓱ Dolac — This main food market in Zagreb has an everyday influx of natural pieces of art. The market is a living piece of art, there are both performing arts from the vendors and customers as well as pieces of art being sold. And they taste good. See Ana Hušmans film: *Plac/The Market* as an appetizer: *www.egoboobits.net/AnaHusman_Plac*

Dolac 2
Tram 1, 6, 11, 12, 14:
Trg Bana Jelačića, a short walk
from the main city square
Mon-Sat 7 am to 2 pm,
Sun 7 am to noon

⓲ Prostor »multiracionalnakompanija« (Space »multirationalcompany«) — After having earned some money working on a tourist ship, passionate devotee of special clothes and music decided to give it a shot at giving Zagreb something special. This shop offers clothing and accessories from independent designers and manufacturers, both local and foreign. The prices are also reasonable. And yes, Prostor also frequently hosts exhibitions of young contemporary artists. The place is really a positive hotspot in Zagreb.

Mesnička 5 (in the courtyard), (484 60 16)
Tram 6, 11, 12, 14: Frankopanska
Mon-Fri noon to 8 pm, Sat 10 am to 3 pm
www.multiracionalnakompanija.com

⓳ Libellus — Fans of comic books in Croatia have a strikingly similar resemblance to people addicted to contemporary art. You are part of a tiny percentage of people that find meaning in something that the general public doesn't even perceive as existent. The shop has some originals in English and French.

Gajeva 17, (481 96 36)
Tram 6, 13: Zrinjevac or Trg Bana Jelačića
Mon-Fri 11 am to 7 pm, Sat 10 am to 2 pm
www.sklibellus.com

20 Saša Šekoranja Flower Gallery — Not your average florist. Sasha is a painter who has a love for creating weird and wonderful bouquets. Spending a good meal's worth of kunas on flowers is not your idea of an ideal day? Well then just have look around the flower shop. There is always something special.

Ilica 82, (484 70 70)
Tram 6, 11: Britanski trg
Mon-Fri 9 am to noon, 5 pm to 7 pm,
Sat 9 am to noon

21 Zrn — A place for all of you obsessed with eating healthy, locally produced food. All around town you can find the Bio-Bio chain that capitalised on the recent hysterical trend of buying healthy food. Unlike this chain, Zrno is definitely not a supermarket. A large part of the food on offer is produced on the owner's farm, an old aunty with a passion for using forgotten ingredients to come up with tasty stuff. Well, some take-away stuff is predictably bland (did I mention there is nothing for carnivores?) but there are some tasty cakes, pottages and stews. The tastiest part of the season is when the fresh vegetables and fruit comes around. Oh, and yes it's incredibly expensive compared to the supermarket world.

Lička 27
Tram 3, 5, 13: Miramarska
Mon-Fri 10 am to 7 pm, Sat 10 am to 2 pm
www.bio-zrno.hr

DAYTRIPS

Galerija Galženica in the town of Velika Gorica — Technically Galženica is not in Zagreb, but the city of Velika Gorica is just a half hour bus ride away from the Zagreb city centre. Another socially engaged gallery that tries to examine contemporary phenomena and often exhibits works by up and coming artists. If you really want to have a memento from visiting Velika Gorica try the nearby marketplace. In spring and autumn there's a good offer of wild mushrooms.

Velika Gorica: Trg Stjepana
Radića 5, (622 11 22), Bus 268, 330:
VG-Matice hrvatske-Galženica
Tue-Fri 10 am to 7 pm,
Sat-Sun 10 am to 1 pm

The town of Grožnjan — Take the A6 by car from Zagreb to Rijeka, and then proceed in the direction of Buje (3 hours). This little medieval Istrian town was practically abandoned until 1965, when it was picked as a platform for a cultural experiment. Music festivals and workshops were introduced, houses given over to artists as ateliers, and slowly the town sprung back to life. A bit old fashioned but the wine (called Teran) is delicious and at night it's one of those places where you can enjoy the silence.

www.tz-groznjan.hr

The hill of Sljeme — Sljeme is the name of the little 1,000 meter hill just above Zagreb, which Zagreb natives insist on calling a mountain. Skiing in the winter, hiking and mushroom picking during the summer. Beware of weekends when hoards of motorized vehicles bring an unbelievable amount of people for their fresh air fix. Go at night and get lost. It's easy to find your way back. Just turn to the lights of Zagreb.

At the bus terminal Mihaljevac (tram 8, 14), take the bus with the sign »Sljeme« and exit at the Hotel Tomislav just below the peak.

Town of Samobor and the region of Žumberak — A half hour drive away from Zagreb, Samobor, historically a centre of artisanship, is a favourite excursion place for Zagreb dwellers. If you keep going toward Slovenia and then follow the border southward you'll be warped back in time. Žumberak is a region where some houses in villages look like they could be puffed away by the big bad wolf, or a puff of wind. People survive from agriculture and live the old fashioned way. They go to sleep after nightfall and rise before dawn. The best period to visit Žumberak is in the summer when the rivers and little canyons keep the temperature bearable, which cannot be said for Zagreb during summer.

www.phy.hr/~dpaar/samobor/enindex.html

KIDS

❷❷ Muzej Grada Zagreba (Zagreb City Museum) — This museum, located in the 17th century Convent of the Clares, has a display that shows you how Zagreb evolved from a temporary Iron Age settlement into a modern day shopping centre. From the settlement of Slavic tribes in the 8th century the story evolves into the usual Balkan bloodbath of attacks by Huns, Hungarians, the Habsburgs, Ottomans, etcetera, etcetera. There's a nice theme section offering a reconstruction of 19th century shops

and then a room which exhibits some artefacts from the Oscar winning Zagreb school of animated movies. There are some interactive exhibits, English explanations of most exhibits, and it's definitely not worth a second visit, but is a nice way to find a few facts if you've never been to Zagreb before. After this historical experience relax in Runa, the nearby heavy metal joint, to chase the medieval spirits out of your head.

Opatička ulica 20, (485 13 61)
Bus 105: Ilirski trg, or a ten minute walk from Trg bana Jelačića
Tue-Fri 10 am to 6 pm, Thur 10 am to 10pm, Sat-Sun 10 am to 2 pm
Full price admission 20 HRK
www.mgz.hr

㉓ Park Maksimir — This green refuge a quarter of an hour away from the city centre is a nice place to take a stroll if you're the type who can't live without singing birds and screaming children. Well, on weekdays during working hours it's really nice and quiet, but on a sunny weekend day you get the feeling that every Croatian has a lot of kids. This screaming cacophony of children on 800 acres of land is accompanied by the innocent cries of the only permanent inhabitants of Maksimir, the animals in the Zoo garden. The Zoo is modest by all means, but the animals are kept in good shape, just like the footballers from the biggest football stadium in Zagreb, located across the street. In the winter you can even try to ice skate on Maksimirs' frozen lakes, but global warming seems lately to endanger this suicidal tendency.

Tram 4, 5, 7, 11, 12:
Maksimir
Park open all day and night,
Zoo 9 am to 6 pm
www.park-maksimir.hr

㉔ Kazalište Trešnja (Trešnja Theatre) — Trešnja is a merry little place where not only kids come to see the plays for children. The plays by director Rene Medvešek are arguably the best that Croatian theatre in general has to offer. Special, quirky and yet warm, these plays are a must see for everyone who loves theatre. The acting ensemble is young and steadily produces plays for children from the age of two and up.

Moščenička 1, (363 85 56)
Tram 3, 9, 12: Selska,
bus 109: Selska-Zagrebačka
www.kazaliste-tresnja.hr

㉕ Rekreacijsko-športski centar Jarun (Sports and Recreation Centre Jarun) — After it was designed specially for the 1986 World Youth Games, sports addicts cherished this complex, situated around an artificial lake, as a sanctuary at the edge of town. Today sport is under heavy attack from commercial enterprises. Rowers, runners, roller bladders, cyclists, tri-athletes, swimmers, kayakers, all have their clubs and events by the artificial lake. But so do clubbers in Aquarius, folk music fans in Lake City, and trendsetters in Piranha. But as most sports are practiced during the daytime, the biggest enemies are those who pay to enter the complex in their favourite cars. These guys cruise around for a while, bring down a few cyclists, and then have a barbecue to celebrate. There's also a children's playground on the southern part and of course a café next to it. In summer, the unlucky hoard that doesn't manage to leave Zagreb for the holidays makes Jarun overcrowded, apparently looking for a cool down, which is a bit strange as the water heats up easily and you often feel like a boiled egg while swimming.

Jarun bb, (303 18 88),
Tram 5, 17, bus 113: Jarun
www.jarun.hr

CAFÉS

㉖ Cafés in the pedestrian zone of Zagreb — This is of course not one café but in reality a big closely knit platform of numberless cafés that operate from springtime till autumn in Zagreb's little pedestrian zone by spreading their terrace web when the weather permits. A few notable places with a good reputation are Cica in Tkalčićeva (a good selection of brandies to accompany your morning coffee and keep you drunk), Princess, the patisserie in Gajeva (a great offering of traditional Zagreb cakes), Golf, and PIF in Preradovićeva. People who sit in these places like to see and be seen, which is especially specific for Bogovićeva, a favourite terrace for Zagreb's jet setters. The rest look elsewhere for more intimate places. In the winter most of these relatively small cafés are a bit too crowded, but the hot chocolate in the café Golf is usually a nice thing to have when it's minus something outside.

Tkalčićeva/Cvjetni trg/
Preradovičeva/Bogovičeva/Gajeva
All a minute or two from Trg Bana Jelačića
Tram 1, 6, 11, 12, 13, 14, 17:
Trg B. Jelačića

Cica 1
Tkalčićeva 18
Mon-Sun 8.30 am to 12 am

Princess 2
Ksaver 14, (481 10 37)
Mon-Sun 8 am to 10 pm

Golf 3
Preradovičeva 2, (481 47 46)
Mon-Sun 8 am to 1 am,
Sun 9 am to 1 am

PIF 4
Preradovičeva 4, (487 29 59)
Mon-Sat 8 am to 1 am,
Sun 11 am to 1 am

27 Klub Purgeraj — During the day, this is a cosy place to take a nice cup of coffee and read what's new in the papers, or on the web, as it's a free Wi-Fi Hot

spot. It's located in the middle of a park situated only five minutes away from the centre of town (by foot, of course). The main problem is to beware of dog droppings when approaching it. Then relax under the sun if the weather permits and the summer terrace to open, and spend the whole day in the park waiting for the evening when the café transforms itself into a crowded club with a harangue of people. Hungry? Well, you can order a pizza delivered from a nearby restaurant and share it with the waitress.

Park Ribnjak 1, (482 92 53)
Tram 1, 4, 6, 11, 12, 14, 17:
Trg Bana Jelačića or Draškovićeva
Mon-Sun 9 am to 4 am
www.purgeraj.hr

28 Karamel and Piece of Cake — Lately Zagreb's cakes have started deteriorating under the influence of cheap ready made cake production techniques coming from Italy. In Karamel the cakes are made with real ingredients, the coffee and tea is posh and expensive, and the taste is really good. The strange L-shaped interior is a bit claustrophobic and the service a bit pompous, but the cherry cake compensates nicely for the bad feelings.

If the house is full of cake addicts, try Piece of Cake next door. This patisserie is owned by the mother of a well known Croatian contemporary artist, Ivana Franke, so you can say you're helping the contemporary art economy by eating their cakes. I prefer the nutty and dryish Karamel ones; Piece of Cake is more for the cream addicts. If you hear a lot of babies crying nearby, don't worry, this little cake heaven square is close to Petrova hospital, the place where most of Zagreb's babies are born.

Jakova Gotovca bb, (466 44 87)
Tram 4, 5, 7, 11, 12, 13:
Kvaternikov trg
Mon-Sat 8 am to 10 pm,
Sun 11 am to 2 pm

RESTAURANTS

316

㉙ Marcellino — The best and most expensive restaurant in Zagreb for some time, according to food critics. If you're willing and able to pay the price of a 740 HRK lunch, well suit yourself, any dish will do and if you're into international haute cuisine you'll know better! Nobody is disappointed after Marcellino, but most keep it for a special occasion. Or once in a lifetime. Main dishes from 100 HRK. Make a reservation in advance!

Jurjevska 71, (467 71 11)
Bus 109: Ksaver 3
Mon-Fri noon to 11 pm,
Sat 1 pm to 11 pm
American Express, Visa, Diners, Mastercard
www.marcellino.hr/en/index.php

㉚ Dva Goluba 2 — Way back, 70 years ago, this restaurant opened its doors. This is a place to try classical Zagreb cuisine like roasted turkey with mlinci, a traditional north-Croatian pasta or maybe traditional pit roasted veal. The dishes are savoury, but neither the cheapest in Zagreb, nor the most expensive. The dishes are still served on oval metal trays the way it used to be served in every decent restaurant in Yugoslavia. Main dishes from 80 HRK.

Maksimirska 7, (232 89 50)
Tram 4, 7, 11, 12, 13: Kvaternikov trg
Mon-Sat 8 am to 11 pm, Sun 8 am to 9 pm

㉛ Prasac (The Pig) — This is a place for gourmets. The meals served here are something special. Dino Galavanja, the young owner and main chef (himself a fusion of Sicilian and east Croatian blood), is hopelessly in love with Dolac, Zagreb's main food market. Every morning he picks out the best of the freshest and then cooks it to everybody's delight. His speciality is using neglected animal parts, such as the heart or cow intestines, and delighting his customers with surprising results. The prices bite your wallet, but they don't devour it. Main dishes from 60 HRK. Reserving a table is a must.

Vranicanijeva 6, (485 14 11)
Funicular from Tomićeva street, a couple

minutes walk from trg Bana Jelačića
Mon 7 pm to 2 am,
Tue-Sat noon to 3 pm, 7 pm to 11 pm
American Express, Diners, Mastercard
www.prasac.hr

32 Gostionica Tip-Top (a.k.a. Blato) — A simple fish oriented restaurant that everyone in Zagreb knows as Blato, the name it held for ages. It is boasted as the favourite place of Croatian poet par excellence, Tin Ujević. Pasticada is the dish to try out. A traditional Dalmatian dish washed down with some Dalmatian wine will make you think: »Why on earth didn't I go to the seaside?« To soothe your pain try amareta for desert, a strange sweet made from eggs and almonds. Main dishes from 50 HRK.

Gundulićeva 18, (483 03 49)
Tram 12, 14, 17: Trg Maršala Tita
Mon-Sat 7 am to 10 pm
Visa

33 Sofra — Bosnia is close to Zagreb. Jokes about Bosnians are a common staple. But hey! This is the place to appreciate Bosnians, not make fun of them. Start with ushtipci (fritters) sa kajmakom, proceed with sogan dolma, onions filled with meat and rice floating in a delicious tomato gravy, and finish it off with baklava, a classic walnut filled pastry bomb designed to fill the stomach of even the most gluttonous subject. Digest with black coffee and traditional Bosnian music. Main dishes from 15 HRK.

1. gardijske brigade Tigrovi 27, (613 10 26)
Bus 218: Ulica grada Chicaga /
Gardijske brigade Tigrovi
Mon-Sun 9 am to 12 am
American Express, Visa, Diners, Mastercard

34 City Club Grill — Yes, this is a place that is almost always open. People usually eat ćevapi, spiced ground meat formed into short rolls and barbecued, then eaten in sweet bread with kajmak, curdled cream. Simple and nutritious. The nickname of the place is »At the Poison Man«. Don't worry. If you're used to meat, you'll digest it. Somehow. Oh and it's cheap of course, 30 HRK will stuff you.

Ilica 125, (3704 585)
Tram 1, 2, 6, 11, 12: Austrijska
Mon-Sun 8 am to 5 am

35 Daily Fresh — The yuppie fast food restaurant of choice. The usual fusion mumbo jumbo of light and presumably healthy food combined with a mix of local and exotic dishes make these places a favourite with your average 30 year old »I hate to cook« Zagreb dweller. Try the cranberry tart. Seven of the places are around the city centre, Masarykova 23 close to the Croatian National Theatre is maybe the nicest. Main dishes from 20 HRK.

Masarykova 23, (639 66 50)
Mon-Sun 8 am to 11 pm
www.dailyfreshgroup.com

36 Mali Phoenix — A no nonsense fish grill with smelly and oily fish ready to grease your favourite shirt. It's cheap and it's tiny, if there's no room check out Ribice kod Mimice next door.

Jurišićeva 19,
(481 44 11)
Tram 1, 4, 8, 11, 12, 14, 17:
Draškovićeva or Trg hrvatskih velikana
Mon-Sat 9 am to 11 pm,
Sun 11 am to 11 pm

❸❼ Studio 13 — This is what it used to look like in Yugoslavia. The waitresses were middle aged and wore drab clothes, the air was stale with smoke, the chairs wooden, the alcohol cheap, and of course there was always someone drunk enough to make the whole bar aware of it. But nobody minded. A great place for theoreticians analyzing authors of the '70s and '80s. The place provides real insight. If nothing else, the decorative photos on the walls are of that age, and they serve Velebitsko beer, which sometimes can inspire.

Dežmanov prolaz 13,
(484 74 95)
Tram 6, 11, 12, 14: Frankopanska
Mon-Sat 8 am to 11 pm, Sun 10 am to 10 pm

❸❽ Sedmica — This bar has seen generations of artists and intellectuals pass through it, and it's not only because the academies (art and architecture) are nearby. The dark interior and loud but not necessarily commercial music attract people to keep coming. But at night it is often overcrowded, perfect for a cup of coffee in the afternoon.

Kačićeva 7a, (484 66 89)
Tram 1, 6, 11: Britanski trg
Mon-Sat 8 am to 12 am,
Sun 5 pm to 12 am

❸❾ Pod Starim Krovovima — An ancient place in the most ancient part of town, Gornji grad, and in case you're guessing, yes, also a lot of ancient people, but there's loads more. Under the old rooftops is one of the rare places where the lively senior intellectual and cultural scene mingles with the young. Photo exhibitions, jazz concerts, poet's nights, and on top of that you can eat some traditional Zagreb dishes like fresh cottage cheese and cream, or pork sausages with garlic, češnjovke. Gornji grad has turned into a strange location due to the fact that the Croatian government resides there. This means police and government officials moving around in black Audis subconsciously discourage people to venture into this historic and beautiful part of town.

Basarichekova 9, (485 13 42)
Funicular from Tomićeva street,
a couple minutes walk from trg Bana Jelačića
podstarimkrovovima.blog.hr

❹⓿ Bacchus jazz bar — Once the first gay friendly place in town, this bar was closed for some time. Soon after reopening the summer terrace, laidback waitresses and frequent jazz concerts spiced up with the sporadic poetry night put the club high up on the scene. The coffee is sometimes awful, the crappy little toilet bogged down during concerts, but that's not what you come looking for. A lot of fun decorative details keep your eyes busy. Don't be confused when you receive a book with your order: the bill is inside. In the summertime the terrace really feels like the right place to be. Slow, breezy and you're sitting next to an old green tin car with a cypress growing out of it, or some other wonderful artefact that the owner brought from the Hrelić flea market. And sometimes the coffee is even good. One of the rare cafés and bars in Zagreb where the TV set plague doesn't infect the ambiance.

Trg Kralja Tomislava 16, (322 804)
Tram 4, 6 13:

Glavni Kolodvor or Zrinjevac
Mon-Sun 9 am to 12 am
www.bacchusjazzbar.net

41 Sakata neman — As close as Zagreb gets to an underground club. You have to make an effort to find this joint. Take a walk from the main bus terminal along Radnička street until you see a factory sign with a black and yellow raven. Pass the gate and enter the warehouse complex then just keep on going until you reach a painted building. That's the bar with pinball, darts, classic rock and elaborately decorated walls. The atmosphere is reminiscent of an empty saloon in the Wild West.

Radnička 27
Tram 2, 5, 6, 7, 8: Držićeva
4 pm to after midnight

42 Krivi put — A filthy place that manages to offer the filth as its charm, it's cheap, noisy and alternative, full of students and shady faces. There's a fight at least once a week, the music can be anything, disco, ethno, house, hard rock, punk, reggae, rock, techno, you name it. Some low key concerts. The best thing about it is the fact that it's one of the only places that's always going after midnight. Come to think about it, is that good at all? A nice sausage bar is right next to the place where a gallery once stood. Try the spicy sausage and hang around with Zagreb's underworld.

Runjaninova 3, (4843 453)
Tram 2, 4, 9, 13: Vodnikova
Mon-Sun noon to 2 am

43 Sirup— A modern clubbing place built with a lot of care and a lot of cyber materials. Looks like the restaurant on the USS Enterprise. The Syrup has started flowing recently so that not much can be said about its agenda: electronic, house, progressive.

Donje Svetice 40, (091 945 0037)
Tram 2: Donje Svetice
Thur-Sun 10 pm to 5 am
www.sirupclub.com

44 KSET — This electro-technical student club is a place with a mission: to introduce great and independent bands. Mate Škugor is the man behind

everything, and although Mate keeps telling everyone he's calling it a day he keeps at it. Žedno uho (the thirsty ear) festival is his labour of love with 400 people thirsty for special bands. However, KSET is not only a place for audiophile music snobs. Techno parties, disco, yu-rock, punk, jazz, you name it. There is even the occasional film evening and exhibition.

Unska 3, (612 97 58)
Tram 5, 13:
Sveučilišna Aleja
Mon-Fri 8 pm to 12 pm,
Sat 9 pm to 3 am
www.kset.org

45 Gjuro 2 — The classic disco of the '90s, Gjuro has an eclectic program of house, r'n'b, '80s and rock concerts. It's a place to go out dancing and a popular mating ground.

Medveščak 2, (468 33 67)
Tram 8, 14: Grškovićeva
Tue-Sat 10 pm to 4 am
www.gjuro2.hr

SLEEP

46 Hotel Regent Esplanade — This is a vintage five star accommodation. The hotel was built in 1925; its target group were travellers on the Orient express (Paris-Istanbul) that passed through Zagreb. Everything is the way you'd expect it to be. An Art Deco style lobby, a great restaurant, Zinfandel, qualified and helpful staff and it's located very close to the city centre. Miroslav Krleža, the famous Croatian 20th century writer, loved this place. He used to say that this was Europe's border, south of the hotel the Balkans reign supreme. Double rooms from € 180.

Mihanovičeva 1, (456 60 21)
Tram 2, 4, 6, 9, 13:
Glavni Kolodvor
www.regenthotels.com

47 Hotel Arcotel Allegra — Has the modern look and is modern, simple, and the closest Zagreb gets to a designer hotel. It's far from spectacular, but satisfies everyone's needs: sauna, sunbed, wireless, the lot. There are usually free apples in each room, or at the reception desk. If you're a shopaholic just step out of the hotel and enter Branimir cenatar shopping centre, or take a five second

walk and pick a movie in Zagreb's most popular cinema, Cinestar multiplex. Double rooms from € 90.

Branimirova 29, (469 60 00)
Tram 2, 4, 8, 9: Branimirova
www.arcotel.at/allegra

48 Hotel Fala — Zagreb has a chronic shortage of simple, yet comfortable, budget hotels. Either you find yourself in an unpleasantly squalid dump, or throwing up loads of money when checking out. Well, Fala is a nice alternative. It's a family run hotel that serves only breakfast and is located a fair bit from the city centre. On the other hand it is conveniently placed on the route from the airport to the centre, and if you're visiting Zagreb craving art and knowledge the location is great. It's just a five minute walk from the new MSU (Museum of Contemporary Art) and if you take the other direction you reach the National Library. Close by you can walk on the embankment sheltering Zagreb from the river Sava where you can observe the sculpture alley envisioned by renegade sculptor Ratko Perich. Look at nine works by contemporary Croatian sculptors while dodging the occasional runners and cyclists trying to appease their yearning for health. After all this activity you can visit the nearby healthy food shop Zrno. Double rooms from € 65.

II Trnjanske ledine 18, (611 10 62)
Bus 166, 218, 219, 220, 221, 268:
Nacionalna i sveučilišna knjižnica
www.hotel-fala-zg.hr

49 Carpe Diem Hostel — Nice and cosy hostel in the residential area of town. Free Wi-Fi, a nice garden, lively coloured rooms, hookahs in the common room, young idealistic owners that chose to proclaim the place as gay friendly. Maybe not the cleanest hostel in town, but definitely the friendliest. Fifteen minutes away from the city centre. € 20 in a double room, € 16 in a six bed dorm, € 10 for camping in the garden.

Milana Shufflaya 3, (468 01 99)
Bus 106, 201, 226, 238:
Grškovićeva-Bijenička
www.hostel.com.hr

50 Hostel Ravnice — One of the hostels that emerged recently after people realized that there were a lot of budget travellers having major trouble finding accommodation in Zagreb. Vera Pesjak, an architect returning from Australia, turned her house into a cosy hostel with a garden and a winter terrace. Classic hostel accommodation. It's all a hostel needs to be: safe, friendly, clean and simple. The only drawback is that some find it too far from the city centre. Anyway you can rent a bike, that's the best way to get to know Zagreb. € 20 in a double room, € 17 in a 4 bed room, € 15 in 6&8 bed rooms.

1. Ravnice 38d, (233 23 25)
Tram 12, 4, 11, 9: Ravnice
www.ravnice-youth-hostel.hr

GOOD TO KNOW

51 Tourist Information

Trg bana Jelačića 11, (481 40 51)
Tram 1, 6, 11, 12, 13, 14, 17:
Trg B. Jelačića
Mon-Fri 8.30 am to 8 pm,
Sat 9 am to 5 pm, Sun 10 am to 2 pm
www.zagreb-touristinfo.hr

INTERNET

52 Booksa — A book club that offers literary people a nice getaway. Excellent choice of contemporary literature. It sometimes hosts some interesting contemporary art exhibitions. For 50 HRK a year, or 30 HRK for six months, you can use the premises, which offers good wireless connection. While checking your mail take a sip of coffee and have your breakfast. A few steps away from the club take the opportunity to have a look at the youngest building to become a monument of culture in Zagreb, the Modernist 1958 skyscraper by the colour-loving architect Ivo Vitić, Laginnjina 9.

Martićeva 14d, (4616124)
Tram 4, 12: Petrova
Tue-Sun 9 am to 11 pm
www.booksa.hr

53 Net kulturni klub mama — This is much more than an internet café, it's a multimedia club that for a number of years has hosted progressive socially active urban intellectuals searching for better solutions and discussing various clever things. There are film nights as well.

Preradovićeva 18 (courtyard)
A short walk from the main square,
tram 1, 6, 11, 12, 13, 14, 17:
Trg Bana Jelačića,
Mon-Sun 1 pm to 9 pm
www.mi2.hr

Preradovićeva — The pedestrian part of Preradovićeva is also a hotspot which functions nicely in the summertime when the cafés take their place on the street.

MEDIA

www.culturenet.hr — Calls itself »Web center hrvatski culture« (Web portal to Croatian culture) with a long list of cultural institutions in Croatia, like festivals, art galleries, design, literature, media art and architecture venues and so forth. Also in English.

TRANSPORT

From the airport — Pleso- Zagreb's airport is situated in Velika Gorica, a satellite of Zagreb that has city status. Bus shuttle to Zagreb will cost you 30 HRK, the airport's bus shuttle is the simplest and cheapest way to get to Zagreb. The bus drops you off at the Zagreb bus terminal from which you can take a tram to any part of town.

Taxis — The cab fares in Zagreb are relatively high. A ride from the airport to the city centre should cost you around 150 HKN. Beware of fraud, Sundays, night time and holidays, then the fares are even higher.

Public transport — Special tourist discounts for public transport are only available if you purchase a Zagreb Card sold in tourist info centres and in some hotels. A 90 HRK Zagreb card will offer you three days of free transport and also discounts for most museums and some hotels and restaurants. There is also a one-day 60 HRK Zagreb card that's not exactly a value for the money.

Car — For drivers 50 km/h is the speed limit if not otherwise marked, but you will seldom find people obeying these limits, as the only way that Croatian drivers obey these limits is when they are stuck in traffic jams. As of late there is a 0.5 % tolerance for drinking and driving for drivers with more than five years driving experience, or older than 23 years. Parking in the city centre is expensive, 14 HRK per hour, yet there's always a problem with finding a spot. The garages in the city centre are crowded and full of nervous people.

#

Important	Numbers
Telephone country and city code	*+385 1*
Telephone information	*988*
Emergency	*112*
Police	*92*
Fire brigade	*93*
Ambulance	*94*
24h-Pharmacy	*Trg bana Jelačića 2, (481 61 59), tram 1, 6, 11, 12, 13, 14, 17: Trg B. Jelačića*

City in	Numbers
1 Euro	*ca. 7.40 HRK (Croation kunar)*
Inhabitants	*772,000*
Average income	*€ 1,044*
Cup of coffee	*7 – 14 HRK (ca. € 1 – 2)*
Bottle of beer	*10 HRK (ca. € 1.50)*
Cigarettes	*10 HRK (ca. € 1.50) for Opatija, disgusting but special*
Most talked about contemporary artists	*Sanja Iveković, Mladen Stilinović*
Collectors of contemporary art	*3*
Biggest art scandal	*The architecture and personal politics of the new MSU (Museum of Contemporary Art)*

Short Art History ZAGREB

1954 The Galerija Suvremene Umjetnosti (Gallery of Contemporary Art) is founded in Zagreb. It surfaces in time to witness and showcase the works of the 50's movement Exat 51, Croatia's first major contribution to the world of contemporary art. Reacting to the dull practice of Socialist Realism, the movement fights for the rights of Abstract art.

1959 – 1966 Grupa Gorgona (Gorgona Group), which consists of artists and art historians, operates along the lines of »anti-art« in Zagreb. Besides individual works linked to traditional techniques, the members propose different concepts and forms of artistic communication, run a gallery and publish the anti-magazine *Gorgona.* They are interested not only in Existentialism and Neo-Dadaism, but also in Reductionism and Zen philosophy.

1978 The exhibition *New Art Practice* in the Gallery of Contemporary Art in Zagreb, curated by Marijan Susovski, looks back on a decade when names like Sanja Iveković, Dalibor Martinis, Goran Trbuljak, Tomislav Gotovac, Mladen Stilinović and Ivan Kozharic started a wave of conceptual and socially engaged art. This period was made exciting by impromptu exhibitions that were organized in alleyways, and performances that started pestering the public eye.

2004 *Enigma objects,* curated by Želimir Koščević, is the most expensive contemporary art exhibition to date, exhibiting works on loan from the Georges Pompidou collection in the galleries Klovićevi dvori and Miroslav Kraljević. The exhibition proves that with the help of media hype even contemporary art can attract an audience.

2009 The opening of the Muzej Suvremene Umjetnosti (Museum of Contemporary Art or MSU) in Zagreb, a new building born of hard labour. Contemporary art finally gets a proper home.

Part of Student Centre courtyard,
Cibona Tower in the background

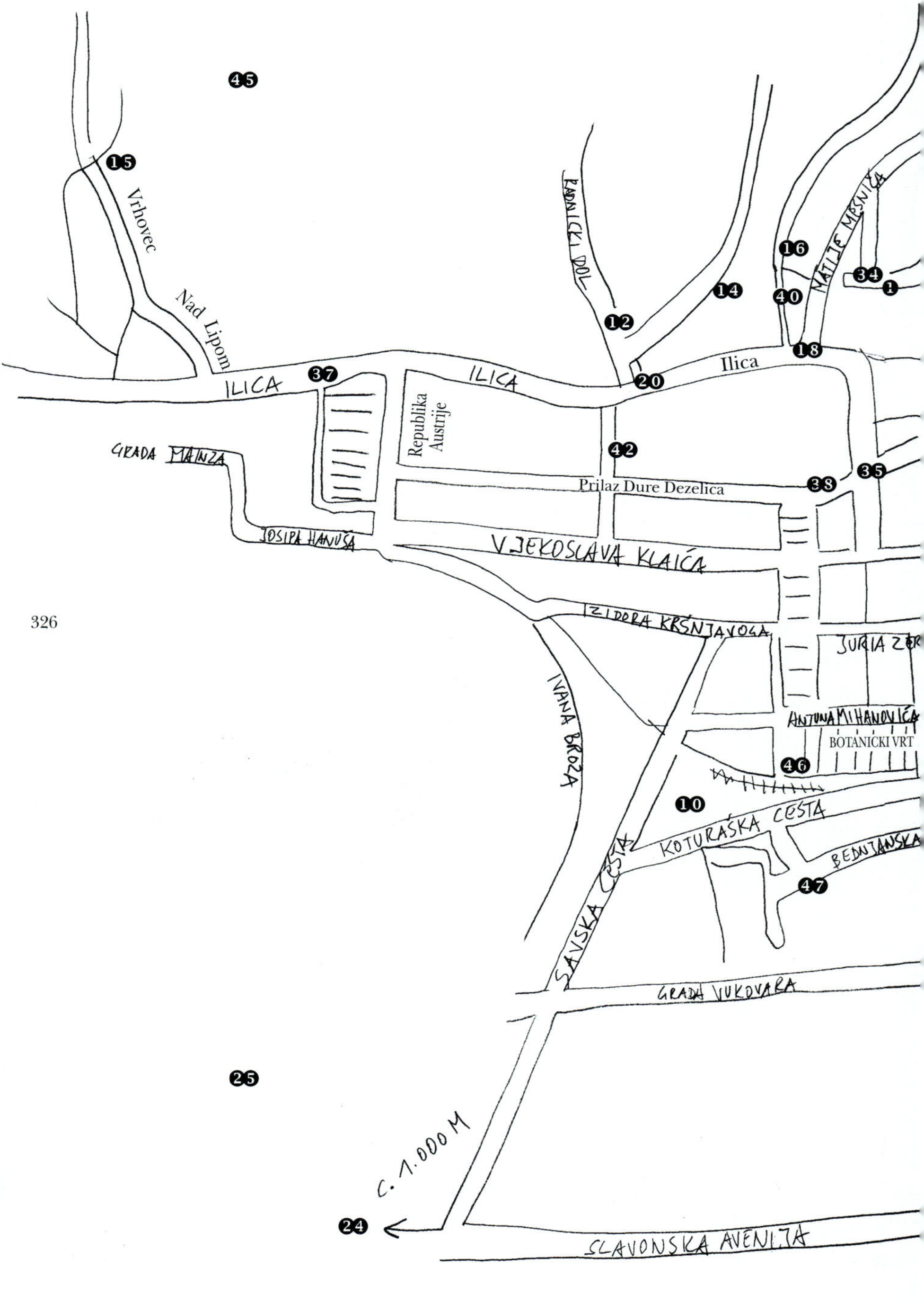
45
15
Vrhovec
Nad Lipom
RADNIČKI DOL
16
MATIJE MESNIĆA
34
1
14
40
12
18
Ilica
20
ILICA
37
ILICA
Republika Austrije
GRADA MAINZA
42
35
Prilaz Dure Dezelica
38
JOSIPA HANUŠA
VJEKOSLAVA KLAIĆA
IZIDORA KRŠNJAVOGA
JURJA ŽER
IVANA BROŽA
ANTUNA MIHANOVIĆA
BOTANICKI VRT
46
10
KOTURAŠKA CESTA
BEDNJANSKA
SAVSKA CESTA
47
GRADA VUKOVARA
25
C. 1.000 M
24
SLAVONSKA AVENIJA

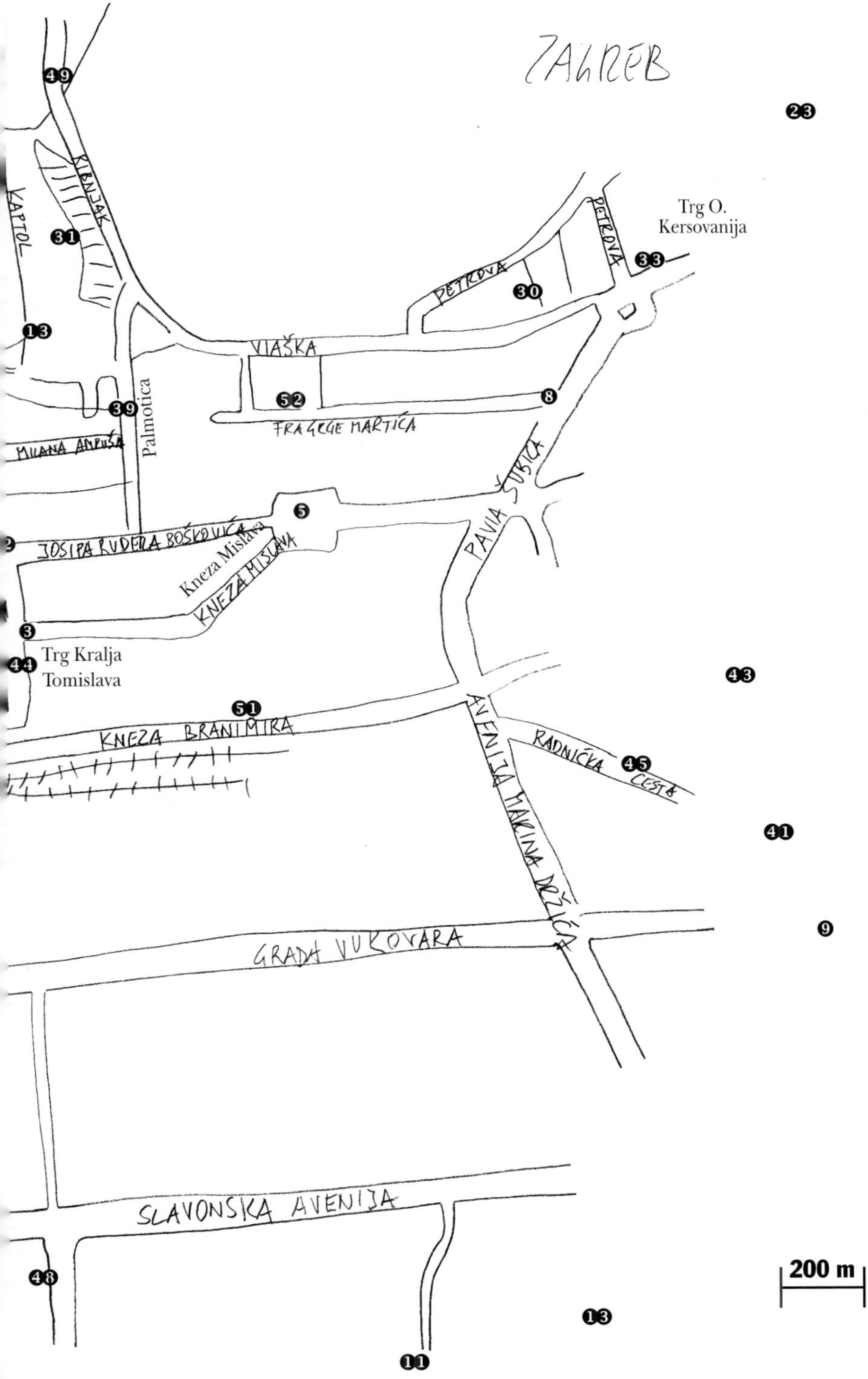
ZAGREB
49
23
KAPTOL
RIBNJAK
31
Trg O.
Kersovanija
PETROVA
PETROVA
33
30
13
VLAŠKA
Palmotica
39
52
8
FRAGEGE MARTIĆA
MILANA AMRUŠA
PAVLA ŠUBIĆA
5
JOSIPA RUĐERA BOŠKOVIĆA
Kneza Mislava
KNEZA MISLAVA
3
44
Trg Kralja
Tomislava
43
51
KNEZA BRANIMIRA
RADNIČKA CESTA
45
AVENIJA MARINA DRŽIĆA
41
GRADA VUKOVARA
9
SLAVONSKA AVENIJA
48
200 m
13
11

EXHIBITIONS
Tue to Sun 11 a.m. to 6 p.m., Thurs to 8 p.m.
REFERENCE ROOM
Library | Media Library | Archive
Tue to Fri 11 a.m. to 6 p.m., Thurs to 8 p.m.
COLLECTION
http://foundation.generali.at
GENERALI FOUNDATION
Generali Foundation
Wiedner Hauptstraße 15
Foundationsquartier
1040 Vienna
Installationsansicht, UN COUP DE DÉS, Generali Foundation, Wien, 2009
Dominik Steiger, Ian Wallace, Joëlle Tuerlinckx, Marcel Broodthaers
Foto © Stefan Olah

M A K
Design Shop
Select Design
The most exceptional gifts in town
Tuesdays open till midnight
Tue MAK NITE© 10 a.m.–12 midnight
Wed–Sun 10 a.m.–6 p.m.
MAK Stubenring 5, 1010 Vienna
www.MAKdesignshop.at

hollmann
BELETAGE
www.hollmann-beletage.at
Surrounded by centuries of history and a great past, Hollmann Beletage features an unique living-experience in the very heart of Vienna's city centre.
THE ART OF HOSPITALITY
Two unique boutique hotels - in two beautiful parts of Vienna
Art – combined with old fashioned charm and uniqueness – the secret of success of the Altstadt Vienna, located in Vienna's artists quarter, the "Spittelberg".
ALTSTADT
VIENNA
www.altstadt.at

HEINRICH DEISL (*1972 in Salzburg, A) is a music critic, researcher and theorist in the field of popular culture, a part-time musician and DJ. In recent years he has also specialised in travel and tourism. He holds a degree in communications, history and film and is co-editor of the Viennese magazine *skug – Journal für Musik*. He lives in Vienna.

MATTHIAS DUSINI (*1967 Meran, I), is a cultural journalist and writes for a number of magazines and periodicals, primarily as an art critic for the Viennese weekly paper *Falter*.

MARIA FARCAS (*1977 Tirgu Mures, RO) studied languages and literature in Bucharest. She works as a freelance writer for various magazines and for the new Romanian fashion brand Rozalb de Mura. She is also part of Liste Noire, an interior design group in Bucharest.

SUSANNE FIRZINGER (*1981 in Linz, A) is a singer, music critic and freelance journalist. She lives in Vienna.

HERWIG G. HÖLLER (*1974 in Rottenmann, A) studied Slavonic languages and physics in Graz and Moscow. Since 1998 he has been working as an art critic (with a focus on the former Soviet Union and Ex-Yugoslavia) for *springerin* (A), *Camera Austria* (A) and *Falter* (A). Curator for the Forum Stadtpark in Graz.

MANUELA HÖTZL (*1972 in Graz, A) has been working as a journalist for international magazines and publications since 1994. In 2000 she founded the journalistic collective Redakionsbuero in Vienna. 2002 – 2007: Teaching position at the Institute for Visual Design at the Technical University in Vienna. 2004 – 2009: Editor in Chief for *REPORT. Magazine for Arts and Civil Society in Central and Eastern Europe* (with Antje Mayer). 2007: Founding of OFROOM, a forum for experts and an architecture gallery. Numerous publications with a focus on architecture and culture in Eastern Europe. She lives in Vienna.

SILVIJA DERVIŠEFENDIĆ (*1983 in Sarajevo, BiH) is a curator and art critic and studied art history and comparative literature. She worked within the teams of the Ars Aevi Museum/Centre for Contemporary Art Sarajevo and Sarajevo Centre for Contemporary Art on exhibition-related projects. She lives in Sarajevo.

JÓZSEF KÉSZMAN (*1968 in Budapest, H) studied art history and is curator, art critic and production manager at the Műcsarnok (Kunsthalle) in Budapest.

ASJA MANDIC (*1975 in Sarajevo, BiH) is a curator and art critic. She studied art history and museum studies in Jersey City and Boston (US). From 2000 – 2007 she was curator for the Ars Aevi Museum/Centre for Contemporary Art in Sarajevo. Most important exhibitions: Retrospective of Michelangelo Pistoletto, Pavilion of Bosnia and Herzegovina at the Venice Biennale showing Joseph Kosuth and Maja Bajevic. She currently works as a senior teaching assistant for Modern and contemporary art at the University of Sarajevo). She lives in Sarajevo.

ANTJE MAYER (*1971 in Stuttgart, D) studied philosophy and art history in Berlin, Prague and Vienna. Since 1998 she has been working as a journalist, editor and publisher for several international publications with a focus on culture in Eastern Europe in Berlin,

Prague, Kiev and Vienna, among others for *Kunstzeitung* (D), *spike art quarterly* (A) and *Der Standard* (A) etc. In 2000 she founded the journalistic collective Redaktionsbuero in Vienna. 2004 – 2009: co-founder and editor-in-chief for *REPORT. Magazine for Arts and Civil Society in Central and Eastern Europe* (with Manuela Hötzl). She lives in Vienna.

LÝDIA PRIBIŠOVÁ (*1980 in Bratislava, SK) lives and works in Bratislava and Rome. She is editor of *Flash Art Czech and Slovak Edition* and other publications. She is curator of the Studio Trisorio Gallery in Rome and a collaborator at the Slovak Institute in Rome and the SPACE Gallery in Bratislava. She was curator of various exhibitions in Rome, Prague, Bratislava and Novi Sad.

MARKO RAJKOVIĆ (*1977 in Zagreb, CR) is a freelance journalist for art, popular culture and sport. In addition, he is the author of several books for children. He lives in Zagreb.

MIMI FRONCZAK ROGERS (*1963 in Chicago, US) studied art history and photography in Iowa and New York. Since 1994 she has been based in the Czech Republic and is the long-time editor of the arts section of the English-language weekly newspaper *The Prague Post* as well as writing about art and culture for other publications.

KATARÍNA SLANINOVÁ (*1978 in Banská Bystrica, SK) is a curator and art critic working for SPACE Gallery in Bratislava. She regularly contributes to *Flash Art Czech and Slovak Edition*. She has curated shows in Slovakia and the Czech Republic.

TINA SMEKAR (*1978 in Ljubljana, SV) studied design in Ljubljana and photography in Leipzig. She works in photography, video, installation and research projects as well as performance. Her works have been exhibited in several European countries. She lives in Ljubljana.

MARIA VASSILEVA (*1961 in Sofia, BG) studied art history in Sofia and furthered her studies through work in Budapest, Rochester (US) and at the MoMA in New York; she obtained a PhD in Sofia. She is an art critic and curator as well as chief curator of the Sofia City Art Gallery a founding member of the Institute of Contemporary Art-Sofia and curator of the Bulgarian women's artist group The 8th of March. She has curated many exhibitions and published a number of essays and articles in catalogues, magazines and newspapers. She lives and works in Sofia.

RITA VITORELLI (*1972 in Eisenstadt, A) studied graphic arts and painting at the Academy of Fine Arts in Vienna. In 2004 she founded the art magazine *spike art quarterly*. From 1999 to 2005 she was the co-organiser of the Viennese art club Futuregarden, 2006 she founded New Art Club in Vienna. 2007: guest professor for painting and graphic arts at the Art University in Linz. Numerous international exhibitions. She lives in Vienna.

RALUCA VOINEA (*1978 in Bucharest, RO) is an art critic and curator. She studied art history, theory and contemporary art curating. She is co-founder of the E-cart.ro Association. Since 2008 she has worked as an editor for *IDEA. Arts + Society magazine*. She lives in Campina.

winner **2002**

winner **2003**

winner **2004**

winner **2005**

Henkel Art.Award. 2009: Art Prize for Central Eastern Europe

Henkel Central Eastern Europe (Henkel CEE) with its headquarters in Vienna coordinates the company's business operations in 32 countries throughout Central and Eastern Europe as well as in Central Asia. Since 2002, Henkel CEE announces the Henkel Art.Award. in cooperation with KulturKontakt Austria. On the basis of the expanded cooperation concluded with the modern art museum „Museum Moderner Kunst Stiftung Ludwig (MUMOK)" this year, Henkel not only offers the winner an exhibition in his or her homeland, but an individual exhibition at MUMOK in Vienna in the following year. At the same time, Henkel is also granting the Henkel Art.Award. Promotional Prize for Talented Young Austrian Artists, which includes a monetary grant of EUR 2,000. In cooperation with its longstanding partner KulturKontakt Austria, Henkel CEE is also bestowing a third prize, namely the Henkel Art.Award. for Young CEE Artists, featuring a monetary award of EUR 2,000. The prize winner is selected from among the participants in the Artists-in-Residence Program of KulturKontakt Austria.

Information about the Henkel Art.Award. under http://artaward.henkel.at

year	*category*	*winner*
2002	*contemporary drawing*	***Dan Perjovschi, RO***
2003	*photography*	***Vidmantas Ilciukas, LT***
2004	*experimental design*	***Ines Vlahovic, HR***
2005	*contemporary drawing*	***Petar Mirkovic, SRB***
2006	*photography*	***Sona Goldova, CZ***
2007	*industrial design*	***Rajmund Doman, H***
2008	*contemporary drawing*	***Miha Strukelj, SLO***
2009	*Different fields – painting, drawing, photography, video and installation*	

winner **2006**

winner **2007**

winner **2008**